Complete

Book

of / **GYMNASTICS**

NEWTON C. LOKEN

Gymnastic Coach and Supervisor of Physical Education
University of Michigan

ROBERT J. WILLOUGHBY

Associate Professor and Chairman
Men's Division of Health, Physical Education, and Recreation
Eastern Michigan University

Complete

Book

of

GYMNASTICS

SECOND EDITION

PRENTICE-HALL, INC., *Englewood Cliffs, New Jersey*

COMPLETE BOOK OF GYMNASTICS, SECOND EDITION
NEWTON C. LOKEN AND ROBERT J. WILLOUGHBY

LIBRARY OF CONGRESS CATALOG CARD NO. 67—18281

Current printing (last digit):
10   9   8   7   6   5   4   3

PRINTED IN THE UNITED STATES OF AMERICA

PRENTICE-HALL INTERNATIONAL, INC., *London*
PRENTICE-HALL OF AUSTRALIA, PTY. LTD., *Sydney*
PRENTICE-HALL OF CANADA, LTD., *Toronto*
PRENTICE-HALL OF INDIA (PRIVATE) LTD., *New Delhi*
PRENTICE-HALL OF JAPAN, INC., *Tokyo*

Dedicated

TO THE ENTHUSIASTIC AND LOYAL
GYMNASTIC PARTICIPANTS, COACHES, TEACHERS AND FANS WHO
HAVE SUPPORTED THE REVIVAL OF THE SPORT OF GYMNASTICS
TO ITS RIGHTFUL PLACE ALONGSIDE THE OTHER FINE SPORTS
OF OUR SCHOOLS, CLUBS AND COLLEGES
THROUGHOUT THE COUNTRY.

Foreword

During the past eighteen years I have had the pleasure of observing the teaching of the authors. Both have demonstrated that they are genuine students and master teachers of gymnastics. Newt Loken and Robert Willoughby have learned their gymnastics as performers, teachers and coaches. The former was honored by his colleagues in the coaching field by being elected President of The National Gymnastic Coaches Association and Coach of the Year in 1963. Their experiences and writings attest to their qualifications. It is only logical that their combined talents could be channelled into writing a useful compendium in the field of gymnastics. I take pleasure and pride in commending to teachers and coaches this work, Complete Book of Gymnastics, by Newt Loken and Robert Willoughby.

Paul Hunsicker

Chairman, Department of Physical Education
University of Michigan

Preface

With the recent nationwide surge of interest in physical fitness, there has been a campaign for the inclusion of more
gymnastics in our physical education curricula. It has been
found that development of the upper body has been inade-
quate and that gymnastics makes a unique contribution
toward overcoming this lack. With this in mind, many
schools throughout the country are dusting off apparatus
that has stood in storage rooms, seldom used. But now that
this equipment is on the floor once again, we find that many
instructors are not qualified to teach this activity.

Nearly everyone has seen acrobats perform in circuses or
in films. Many have witnessed competitive gymnastics as
performed by accomplished gymnasts. Few, however, realize
all that has transpired to produce this high level of performance. All of these expert performers had to start at the
elementary level and be taught solid fundamentals by an
instructor, either in an organized class or informally in small
groups. Certainly every physical education instructor is not
expected to be a gymnastic coach and produce experts, but
he should know how to teach the beginning and intermediate levels of this activity. This then is a challenge to
all teacher-training institutions to provide basic instruction
in gymnastics.

Several books have been written covering one or two
specific areas within the total gymnastic field. These books
usually cover their subject matter thoroughly from the elementary stunts through the advanced levels. There are very
few books, however, that include the whole field of gymnas-

tics under one cover. Therefore, it is the purpose of this book to:

1. Cover adequately gymnastic instruction for both men and women at the beginning, intermediate, and even advanced levels of gymnastic skills.

2. Include in one book the complete range of gymnastics, plus such allied activities as rope skipping, rope climbing, and exhibitions.

To do this, we have not exhausted all of the stunts that could be performed in each event, but instead have selected the ones which we feel adequately cover the various skill levels. In doing this we have tried to present the material in a manner suitable for class instruction.

Good luck, good spotting, and good performances!

N.C.L.
R.J.W.

ACKNOWLEDGMENTS

We are indebted to many individuals who have contributed greatly to the development of this book. Those who contributed specific material used in some of the chapters are: Dr. James Baley, Herb Loken, Gordon Hathaway, Jess Meyers, Bob Sullivan, and Erna Wachtel.

Sincere appreciation is expressed to Colonel Ted Bank of the Athletic Institute for the use of many fine pictures throughout the book. These pictures came from four gymnastic films produced by his company. Thanks also to Dallas Jones and his staff for the fine work on the pictures and parts of the description. The *Athletic Journal, Scholastic Coach* and the *Journal of Health, Physical Education and Recreation* very graciously allowed us to use pictures from their files.

Our deepest thanks to Dr. Elmer D. Mitchell for his constant encouragement and support throughout this lengthy project. Appreciation is extended to Ray Chinn, Ed Gagnier, Marv Johnson and Connie Riopelle for their thoughts and opinions regarding descriptions and selections of stunts.

A special note of thanks to the many fine performers who are pictured throughout the book. These include: Ed Cole (Big Ten and NCAA Trampoline Champion), Dick Kimball (Midwest Trampoline Champion), Nino Marion (NCAA Still Rings Runner-up Champion), Richard Montpetit (Big Ten Champion on High Bar, Parallel Bars, Still Rings and All-Around), Jim Brown and Bill Skinner (Tumbling Champions), Tom Francis and Tony Turner (outstanding divers and tumblers), and Carolyn Osborn (Champion Women Gymnast). In the revised edition thanks are given to many of the fine Michigan Gymnasts pictured throughout the text and especially to Mike Henderson (NCAA Floor Exercise Champion), and to Gil Larose, former Michigan great, who won the NCAA titles in All-Around, Vaulting, and High Bar and who just recently has won the Canadian National All-Around title. Also to Dave Jacobs and Wayne Miller, both United States Trampoline Champions, Members of the USA Trampoline Team in the World Trampoline meet, and Gary Erwin, World Trampoline and twice NCAA Champion.

Contents

ONE / history and values of gymnastics   1

HISTORY, 1. GENERAL VALUES, 4.

TWO / tumbling   5

VALUES, 5. ORGANIZATION, AREA AND EQUIP-MENT, 6. SAFETY, 7. PROGRAM OF INSTRUC-TION, 8. TWISTING TUMBLING, ROUTINES, 20. DOUBLES TUMBLING, 21.

THREE / balancing   28

VALUES, 28. ORGANIZATION, PROGRAM OF INSTRUCTION, SINGLES BALANCING, 29. DOUBLES BALANCING, 34. PYRAMIDS, 43.

FOUR / floor exercise   45

VALUES, 45. ORGANIZATION, PROGRAM OF INSTRUCTION, 46. BALANCING STUNTS, 47. STRENGTH BALANCE MOVES, 50. AGILITY STUNTS, 52. FLEXIBILITY STUNTS, 59. ROU-TINES, 60.

FIVE / trampolining   62

VALUES, ORGANIZATION, AREA AND EQUIP-MENT, TEACHING METHODS, 63. PROGRAM OF INSTRUCTION, SAFETY, 65. ROUTINES, 86.

SIX / side and long horse 87

VALUES, 87. ORGANIZATION, AREA AND
EQUIPMENT, TEACHING METHODS, 88. SAFE-
TY, PROGRAM OF INSTRUCTION, 89. VAULT-
ING WORK ON THE SIDE HORSE, 90. LONG
HORSE VAULTING, 94. SUPPORT WORK ON
THE SIDE HORSE, 104. ROUTINES, 114.

SEVEN / horizontal bar 116

VALUES, 116. ORGANIZATION, AREA AND
EQUIPMENT, TEACHING METHODS, SAFETY,
117. PROGRAM OF INSTRUCTION, 118. LOW
BAR, 119. HIGH BAR STUNTS, 123. ROUTINES
139.

EIGHT / parallel bars 140

VALUES, ORGANIZATION, AREA AND EQUIP-
MENT, 140. TEACHING METHODS, SAFETY,
PROGRAM OF INSTRUCTION, 141. ROUTINES,
164.

NINE / rings 166

VALUES, 166. ORGANIZATION, AREA AND
EQUIPMENT, TEACHING METHODS, SAFETY,
PROGRAM OF INSTRUCTION, 167. ROUTINES,
180.

TEN / women's floor exercise 182

VALUES, ORGANIZATION 182. PROGRAM OF
INSTRUCTION, BALLET MOVEMENTS, 183.
FLEXIBILITY STUNTS, 185. BALANCE MOVE-
MENTS, 186. AGILITY STUNTS, 188.

ELEVEN / women's vaulting 190

VALUES, ORGANIZATION, PROGRAM OF IN-
STRUCTION, 191. COMPETITIVE VAULTING,
193.

TWELVE / women's balance beam 196

VALUES, 196. ORGANIZATION, AREA AND
EQUIPMENT, TEACHING METHODS, SAFETY,
PROGRAM OF INSTRUCTION, 197. MOUNTS,
198. MOVEMENTS ON BEAM, 200. STUNTS ON
BEAM, 203. DISMOUNTS, 208. ROUTINES, 211.

THIRTEEN / women's even and uneven parallel bars   **212**

VALUES, 212. ORGANIZATION, PROGRAM OF INSTRUCTION, EVEN PARALLEL BARS, 213. UNEVEN PARALLEL BARS, MOUNTS, 217. DISMOUNTS, 222. STUNTS OR COMBINATIONS, 225. ROUTINES, 234.

FOURTEEN / rope activities   **235**

VALUES, 235. ORGANIZATION, PROGRAM OF INSTRUCTION, ROPE SKIPPING, 236. ROPE JUMPING, 238. ROPE CLIMBING, 239. COMPETITIVE ROPE CLIMBING, 241. TUG OF WAR, 242.

FIFTEEN / springboard trampoline   **243**

VALUES, ORGANIZATION, 243. PROGRAM OF INSTRUCTION, 244. TUMBLING, 247. CHEERLEADING, DIVING, TRAMPOLINE MOUNTING, STUNTS FOR TWO PERFORMERS, 248. VAULTING, 249.

SIXTEEN / gymnastic exhibitions   **250**

VALUES, 250. PLANNING, COMMITTEE ASSIGNMENTS, THEME, 251. LENGTH OF SHOW, PUBLICITY, TICKETS, COSTUMES, 252. DECORATIONS, PROPERTY, CONCESSIONS, PRINTED PROGRAM, PROGRAM SCHEDULE, 253. PROGRAM OF INSTRUCTIONS, TIGER LEAPING, 254. TUMBLING AND BALANCING STUNTS, 255. HORIZONTAL BAR STUNTS, PARALLEL BAR STUNTS, 257. TRAMPOLINE STUNTS, 258.

selected list of reference materials and visual aids   **261**

BOOKS, 261. PERIODICALS, 263. GYMNASTICS RULE BOOKS, TEACHING AIDS FOR GYMNASTICS, 264. AUDIOVISUAL AIDS FOR GYMNASTICS, 266.

index   **268**

CHAPTER ONE / *history and values of gymnastics*

history

Gymnastics and tumbling, comprising some of our most basic motor skills, also include some of the oldest skills. Their beginnings are somewhat obscure, but can be placed at about 2600 B.C., when the Chinese developed a few activities that resembled gymnastics, particularly of the medical type. However, the actual development of gymnastics began in the Grecian and Roman periods of history. The Greeks first gave great emphasis to gymnastics; in fact, the word itself is derived from the Greek. Systematic exercise was endorsed by the most eminent educators of ancient times, and it became prominent in state regulations for education. In fact, the time spent on gymnastics was equal to that spent on art and music combined. The Spartans were most rigid in providing gymnastic training for their youth. Girls also were ex-

pected to be good gymnasts. The exercises consisted of various tumbling, dancing, running, leaping, rope-climbing, and balance movements.

The early Romans copied the physical-training program from the Greeks but adapted it to their military training program. With the fall of the Greek and Roman civilizations, gymnastics declined; in fact, all forms of physical activity were discouraged. This was true throughout the Middle Ages and in the Renaissance, when a renewed surge of interest in systematic physical activity swept the European countries. Perhaps the earliest contributor to this renewed interest was Johann Basedow (1723–1790) of Germany, who in 1776 added gymnastic exercises to the program of instruction in his school. Johann Guts Muths (1759–1839), who is known as the "great-grandfather of gymnastics," introduced gymnastics into the Prussian schools. He wrote several works on the subject, in-

1

cluding *Gymnastics for Youth*, considered the first book on gymnastics. The actual "father of gymnastics" was Friedrich Jahn (1778–1852). Jahn, who is regarded as the founder of the *Turnverein*, conceived the idea of combining gymnastic training with patriotic demonstrations. This was well received by the government, and thus the program grew rapidly, involving huge playgrounds and whole families participating. Jahn invented several pieces of equipment, among them the horizontal bar, parallel bars, side horse, and vaulting buck. Later, when threat of war subsided, Jahn's motives were misunderstood, and the authorities had him jailed for planning to overthrow the government. The *Turnverein* societies then moved into closed buildings for protection where they still function in Europe and in the United States.

Adolf Spiess (1810–1858) is responsible for introducing gymnastics into the schools of Switzerland.

Pehr Ling (1776–1839), of Sweden, was the first to appreciate the corrective value of gymnastics. He simplified exercises for the individual. Ling invented the equipment known today as Swedish apparatus, including the stall bars and the vaulting box.

Franz Nachtegall (1777–1847) started the first school for training gymnastics teachers at Copenhagen.

The development of gymnastics in America began with physical education programs patterned after European programs. This European influence was felt greatly through the Turnverein movement. When the Turners organization needed training instructors for its numerous clubs, it established in 1865 the Normal College of American Gymnastics in Indianapolis, Indiana. For years this college produced superb instructors in gymnastics and related activities.

One of the first American contributors to gymnastics was Dr. Dudley Sargent. While still a student, he became a teacher of gymnastics at Bowdoin College. Within two years he had developed the activity as an official part of the regular college curriculum. He later served

A GYMNASTICS ROOM

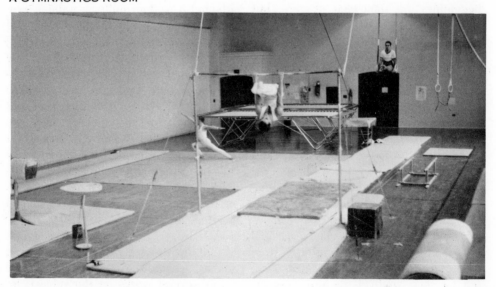

at Yale before moving to Harvard, where he became Director of the Hemenway Gymnasium. During his life Dr. Sargent invented many pieces of apparatus, including pulley weights and leg and finger machines. He also developed a system of anthropometric measurements for determining the physical condition of the student.

The YMCA's also made a notable contribution to the gymnastic program in the United States with their encouragement and inclusion of the activity in their programs. They installed apparatus in their gymnasiums and provided instruction in gymnastics at their training school at Springfield, Massachusetts. One of their early leaders who became prominent in the movement of physical training along educational lines was Dr. Luther Gulick.

Renewed emphasis on gymnastics and tumbling in World War II physical training programs resulted in increased growth of that activity in our schools after the war. Within the last decade, there has been a phenomenal surge of interest in the sport. Old gymnastic centers like Philadelphia, Minneapolis, and Los Angeles are still active, and many new areas produce an energetic flow of top-notch gymnastic coaches, teams, and fans. This is especially true of the Chicago suburban area. The National Collegiate Gymnastic Meet is now a large affair attracting many top-flight teams, whereas a short time ago there were only a few schools entered. Clinics have sprung up throughout the country, highlighted by the annual Sarasota (Florida) Clinic, which began in 1951. Larger clinics now being held annually are: Western National Clinic at Tucson, Arizona; Eastern National Clinic at Ft. Lauderdale, Florida; National Summer Clinic at East Lansing, Michigan; North-

western Clinic at Seattle, Washington; and Northern California clinics.

The active and functional National Association of College Gymnastic Coaches was formed in 1950 by a small group of gymnastic coaches led by Chet Phillips. Past presidents of the Association are: Phillips, Charles Pond, Lyle Welser, Tom Maloney, Charles Keeney, George Szypula, Newt Loken, Hal Frey, Gene Wettstone, Bill Meade, and Jake Geier. In 1955, the NACGC adopted a policy of honoring one person each year who has made an outstanding contribution to gymnastics over a period of twenty-five years or more. The ones so honored have been: Max Younger, Hartley Price, Roy E. Moore, Leslie Judd, Leopold Zwarg, Gustav Heineman, Charles Graves, Louis H. Mang, Ralph Piper, Erwin Volze, Henry Smidl, and Gus Kern.

In 1959 a committee headed by George Szypula completed plans to have gymnastics represented in the nationally famous Helms Hall of Fame. Since that time, forty-five gymnasts, coaches, and contributors have been cited.

In the past few years a tremendous growth has taken place in the sport of gymnastics on all levels: instructional as well as competitive. A corollary of this renewed interest is the adaptation of apparatus to younger children in the elementary and junior high schools. The innovation of portable riggings for rings, high bar, and so on, have increased the use of this equipment. Also, much of the equipment has been redesigned to provide easier handling, moving, and storage. Competition throughout the United States has become more standardized in events and in scoring because of the influence of the FIG (International Federation of Gymnastics).

Obviously, a great deal is happening

in gymnastics. It is being rediscovered that with proper supervision and instruction gymnastics can be one of the most popular and exciting activities in the school program.

general values

What are some of the contributions that gymnastics makes to the development of the individual? Recent studies involving physical fitness indicate that gymnastics should be a vital activity in physical fitness training. The movements in this activity are fundamentally big muscle-movements and will develop greatly the muscle groups in the arms, shoulders, chest, and abdomen. These areas of the body are often neglected in other sports. Tumbling and trampolining also develop the musculature of the legs. Besides building strength and power, gymnastics also contributes to other factors of physical fitness, such as agility, flexibility, coordination, and balance. A general improvement in posture also can result from this type of activity.

Gymnastics has special meaning as a sport. Emphasis is on coordination and skill. Students whose capabilities and size may not fit them for contact sports can find in gymnastics the satisfaction of competition and the thrill of accomplishment in skillful physical activity.

In addition to these physical factors, gymnastics also develops such mental qualities as alertness, daring, and precision. Split-second timing is necessary in many of the stunts that call for quick thinking. Because gymnastics is an individual sport, the gymnast is the only person who can make himself overcome his fears in learning new stunts. By repeating stunts, the gymnast develops habits of definite decisions and actions that must be correct for the successful completion of the stunt.

Such character traits as self-confidence, perseverance, and self-discipline are developed from gymnastic activities. If the gymnast works to make progress, he quickly learns that he must develop perseverance to the highest degree. He must apply self-discipline and force himself to try the same stunt repeatedly until mastery is finally accomplished. Because gymnastics is a self-testing activity, each individual may progress at his own speed. A gymnast who is challenged by a particular advanced stunt or routine is not prevented from trying it by the lack of progress of his fellow gymnast.

Creative ability has unlimited opportunity in the sport of gymnastics. Great pleasure is derived from working out possible combinations and routines. This develops in the gymnast an understanding of symmetry, continuity, coordination, balance, and timing. It also develops an understanding of the need for strength and endurance in order to complete some of the routines created by the gymnast.

Another value is the fun and enjoyment received from participating in the activity. The joy of successfully completing a stunt is outstanding. The elation of learning a handspring, kip, or giant swing is indescribable. To see children laughing and shouting with joy and pride as they successfully complete a stunt is indeed rewarding to the gymnastic instructor.

CHAPTER TWO / *tumbling*

Tumbling is a basic motor skill that covers extensively the mechanics of rolling, turning, springing, and twisting. From watching children at play, one can see that it is a natural activity to include in a physical-education program. Besides the fun aspect, it serves as a fine background for apparatus work and also as a carry-over activity for other sports. It is challenging and exciting to develop tumbling skills, whether they are elementary or advanced.

Tumbling is generally done on tumbling mats in a gymnasium, but there is no reason to avoid performing stunts outdoors on a suitable area of grass or beach.

Several different sizes of mats are available. The more common sizes are 4' x 8', 5' x 10', and 6' x 12' and range in thickness from one to three inches depending on the type of material used. Many instructors prefer the 6' width be-

cause it provides more space for working across the mats. Longer mats or a series of mats offer the opportunity to perform combinations of stunts, which increases the variety and difficulty of a tumbling program.

values

The specific values of tumbling activities are:

1. Tumbling develops coordination and timing.

2. Tumbling develops agility and flexibility because of the nature of the movements involved. Much bending, tucking, and twisting is required to perform the stunts well.

3. Because of the running and springing necessary in tumbling activities, strength is developed in the legs. This

is somewhat unique in that most other gymnastic activities tend to neglect the legs.

4. Courage and determination are developed in some of the more daring and difficult tumbling stunts. More advanced stunts involve movements performed with the body completely in the air.

5. Learning to control the body in basic tumbling skills has great carry-over to the other sports.

6. The art of falling correctly, as learned in tumbling, is of great importance in many sports as well as in normal daily activities. A relaxed rolling fall often prevents or reduces injury and enables a person to regain his feet quickly after a fall.

7. Because tumbling is a natural activity, it is self-motivating and provides a great deal of fun and enjoyment for its participants.

organization

AREA AND EQUIPMENT

Beginning tumbling can be taught in a small area. However, when more advanced stunts are taught or combinations of stunts are put into routines, a run is helpful to build up momentum.

Tumbling is taught best with the use of mats. The mats can be put in a small area if used by a squad only or they can be put end to end in a row for mass instruction. For a large class, more than one row of mats may be required. In order for the instructor to see all of the pupils and for the pupils to see the demonstration, a horseshoe pattern would be advantageous. A circle formation is also possible, but it doesn't enable the instructor to view the whole class as well.

TEACHING METHODS

Perhaps one of the major pitfalls in teaching a tumbling program is to let one pupil work and the remainder of the class stand in line and observe. Too many instructors line up the entire class at one end of the gymnasium and have them perform individually. This type of class organization leads to discontent and will kill the fun element, with consequent discipline problems.

Beginning tumbling lends itself well to the mass method of teaching. Have the class line up along the length of the mats and work across the mats on the command of the instructor. After the class executes one stunt, have them do an about-face and return in the opposite direction while performing the same or another stunt. You will find that the students will not only get more activity out of this type of teaching, but they will also have more fun. It is not uncommon to see the students trying to outdo each other, consequently creating a healthy atmosphere of competition. For most beginning stunts, a maximum of three people can work on a 5' x 10' mat, although two is preferable. More can be accommodated by using shifts of pupils lined up one behind the other.

If the number of mats is insufficient for the whole class, tumbling can also be taught by the squad method. In this method some other activity, or activities, is combined with tumbling, and the squads are rotated during the period. Keep in mind that other gymnastic activities probably will require mats also. As the students become more advanced, they will require more space for tumbling and will need more rest between turns. Thus the squad method may be more advantageous for advanced work than the mass method.

Balancing activities can be combined well with tumbling instruction. Both require the same equipment and are organized and conducted in much the same manner. There is some advantage in changing periodically the type of movements; balancing and tumbling provide a good combination for this. After performing two or three rolling movements such as found in tumbling, it could be restful to execute two or three of the stationary movements found in balancing, and so on. Also, the two activities complement one another. For example, it is helpful to be able to do a forward roll before learning the roll-out ending of a head balance. Similarly, being able to perform a head balance is helpful in learning a headspring.

Evaluation of tumbling probably is best done by use of a stunt chart; this serves to motivate the students as well. For more advanced classes, evaluation could be based on competitive routines.

SAFETY

Tumbling is a relatively safe activity. However, certain safety procedures should be practiced to minimize the risk of injury:

1. Always use mats for tumbling wherever possible. A grassy area or beach could be used for selected stunts.

2. When using more than one mat in a row, one is well advised to secure them together. This will prevent the mats from slipping and leaving "holes" in the tumbling area. Similarly, guard against overlapping of mats, which will cause ridges on which one may turn an ankle.

3. When placing mats, be sure to maintain adequate clearance from walls and obstructions.

4. For purposes of comfort and cleanliness, always keep the tied or button side down.

5. Inspect the mats to see that there are no ripped places in them where a performer could catch his toe.

6. To make the mats last longer always carry them instead of dragging them.

7. No student should be allowed to perform a new or intricate skill without a spotter until he is capable of doing so without danger. Encourage the students to learn the spotting techniques so that they can help each other.

8. It is very important that the necessary progression be used in learning tumbling skills. No one learns to run before he can walk. By the same token, somersaults cannot be learned before

SPOTTING

the basic fundamentals can be successfully performed. Too many instructors try to push the class too rapidly. This could result in the development of bad habits as well as injury. Fundamentals cannot be stressed too heavily.

9. Students should be encouraged to perform stunts with good form inasmuch as this teaches and indicates control of a stunt as well as adding to the beauty of it.

There are two main methods of spotting: with the hand and with a safety belt. For hand spotting, one man gets close to the performer to assist in doing the stunt if necessary and to act in preventing injury if the situation arises. For some stunts two spotters are desirable. A common mistake of spotters is to stay too far away. A person falls quickly, and unless they can step in and catch him the spotting is useless. However, the spotter should also be cautioned about standing so close that he hampers the performer. The performer should be watched closely while going through the stunt so that conditions leading to a fall can be seen as early as possible. Spotters are simply to break a fall and ease the person to the mat, not necessarily holding him clear of the mat. The best position for the spotter varies with the stunt. In general, try to figure in which part of

the stunt the fall is most likely to occur or where the most help is vital and then station the spotter accordingly. When spotting is particularly important, special directions should be given along with the description of the stunt.

For advanced stunts, spotting is done best with a safety belt. Generally, two people are required to assist by lifting up on the belt. For stunts involving a twist of the body, the ropes must be crossed around the performer in the opposite direction of the way in which the twist is executed unless a twisting belt is used.

program of instruction

The following stunts are recommended for learning in the approximate order in which they appear:

1. *Forward Roll.* From a squatting position place the hands on the mat about shoulder width apart. Place the chin on the chest and lean forward, pushing with the feet and bending the arms. Allow the back of the shoulders to touch the mat first as the roll is executed and continue rolling on over the back. When the shoulders touch the mat, take the hands from the mat and grasp the shins, pulling the body into a tight tuck.

FORWARD ROLL

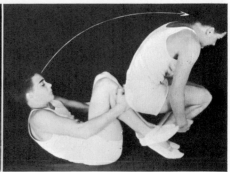

Roll forward in this small ball up to the feet and then straighten to a standing position. The forward roll can also be done with the knees on the outside of the arms. For some pupils, this technique facilitates learning.

After learning the technique of doing a roll from a squat, try it from a standing position. More of a forward lean will be evident when going to the mat from a stand. Be sure that the weight of the body is caught by the hands and arms rather than the head or back of the shoulders.

2. *Backward Roll.* Start from a squatting position with the hands on the mat and the knees between the arms. Lean forward slightly and then backward into the roll. Push with the hands, sit down, and start to roll onto the back. Place the hands above the shoulders with the fingers pointed back and the palms up. Keep the chin on the chest throughout the roll. Roll over the top of the head and onto the hands, keeping the knees tucked into the chest. Push with the hands and continue the roll to the feet. Finish in a squat position.

A preliminary move for this stunt is the rocker, which consists of rocking back and forth on the back with the knees in a tuck position and the chin on the chest. Keep the hands over the shoulders, with thumbs toward the head, and rock partially on them during the rocker. Repeat this rocking motion until you have the feeling of rolling smoothly across the back, and then on one backward roll simply continue on over to the feet. This constitutes a modified backward roll.

After learning the technique of doing a roll from a squat position try it from a standing position.

3. *Side Roll.* Start from a hands-and-knees position and then place the fore-

BACKWARD ROLL

SHOULDER ROLL

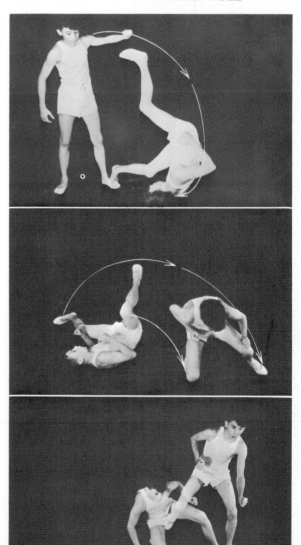

arms flat on the mats, assuming a "doggie" position. Roll sideward across the back, holding the knees in toward the chest and continue on over to the hands, forearms, and knees position.

4. *Shoulder Roll.* Stand at the end of the mat with the feet spread slightly. Lean forward and throw the left arm toward the mat, looking between the legs as the arm is thrown. Strike the mat at the elbow first and roll up the arm, across the shoulders and back, and end up on the feet facing sideward. The right arm can be used to push the performer to his feet. After doing this several times, the stunt may be done from a run, simulating the fall that occurs in some games, but in a relaxed and non-injurious way.

5. *Roly Poly.* Start by sitting in a straddle position with the legs flat on the mats. Grasp the ankles with each hand. Keeping the arms and legs straight, roll sideward across the back to a sitting position again.

6. *Back Extension.* This is a variation of the backward roll, in which the performer momentarily passes through a handstand position and snaps the legs down to the floor. As the performer pushes with the hands, he fully extends the arms and shoots the feet upward to a momentary handstand. When in the handstand position, bend the knees slightly and snap the legs down from the waist. As the legs are snapped down, push with the hands so that the whole body will be completely off the mat. Finish in a standing position.

To practice the snap-down, kick up to a momentary handstand and repeat the last part of the back extension.

7. *Cartwheel.* The cartwheel may be performed either to the left or to the right. It is here described to the left, but may be done to the right by reversing the instructions.

Start with the left side facing down the mat with the legs and arms outstretched and apart as in the spokes of a wheel. Rock to the right side by placing the body weight on the right leg and lift the left foot off the ground. Then rock back to the left by placing the body weight on the left leg. With the momentum established by this rocking motion, bend to the left side at the waist and place the left hand on the mat about 2 feet to the side of the left foot. Force the right leg overhead and simultaneously push off the mat with the left leg. As the feet approach the handstand, place the right hand on the mat about shoulder width from the left hand. It is important here that the arms be kept straight and the head craned back so that the eyes are trained on a spot about

BACK EXTENSION

CARTWHEEL

12 inches in front of, and between, the hands. At this point, the body is in a handstand with the legs held straight and apart and the back arched slightly.

As the body passes through the handstand from the side, bring the right foot down on the line established by the left foot and hand, by bending to the right at the waist. The left foot will follow to the mat, and one finishes facing the same direction as at the start.

In the event of difficulty in learning the cartwheel, several corrective measures can be taken. First, practice kicking up to a partial handstand, landing on the opposite foot from the one that was last to leave the mat. This simulates the proper hands-and-feet coordination. The handstand may be increased in height, and also a turning technique may be added as proficiency is increased. Next, mark spots on the mat with chalk to show correct placement of each hand and foot. Next, try the cartwheel in the other direction; many times this will correct the difficulty. If this does not work, start the cartwheel from a squatting tuck position. From there place the left hand on the mat about 1 foot from the left foot. Simply jump and execute a cartwheel, keeping the feet close to the mat and placing the hands on the mat as described above. Land facing the same direction as at start. Progress by carrying the feet higher overhead until the trick is done with the body held straight.

If there is trouble when landing, practice the back end of the cartwheel separately. Kick up to a handstand and bring the right foot down close to the right hand. After the right foot strikes the ground, execute a quarter turn counterclockwise and land with the feet about shoulder width apart. When this can be accomplished successfully, try the cartwheel from the beginning.

ONE ARM CARTWHEEL

8. *One Arm Cartwheel.* In executing the one arm cartwheel lean in the direction of the stunt and place the inside hand down and do a cartwheel without using the other arm. At first the stunt may have to be done on a small arc basis just as in learning the two arm cartwheel. As skill progresses it may be done correctly with the legs extended straight overhead and the body straight.

9. *Cartwheel with a Quarter Turn.* Execute a regular cartwheel and as the first foot strikes the mat, turn the body a quarter twist, bringing the other foot to the mat with the toes pointing in the direction of the momentum. This stunt is an excellent lead-up for a front handspring.

10. *Roundoff.* The roundoff is considered an important key to tumbling because it is used to start the majority of the backward tumbling exercises. The purpose of the roundoff is to change the forward motion established by running into backward motion so that backward tumbling stunts may be performed. This stunt may be executed either to the left or to the right, but in this chapter it will be explained to the left.

Take a good run, skip on the right

ROUNDOFF

foot, and bring the left foot forward. Place the left foot on the ground, bend forward at the waist, and place the left hand on the mat about 2 feet in front of the left foot. Kick the right foot overhead followed by the left and place the right hand on the mat in front and slightly to the left of the left hand. As the stunt progresses the hands and arms pivot in the same direction and the body turns. The fingers of both hands are pointing toward the edge of the mat. When the feet pass overhead, execute a half turn. Snap the feet down from the waist and simultaneously push off the mat by extending the shoulders and flexing the wrists. Land on both feet, facing in the direction opposite from that of starting. When the feet strike the ground, bound off the balls of the feet. It is important that the eyes be trained on a spot about 6 inches in front of the hands during the entire trick. Placing chin on chest will mean loss of relative position and inability to complete the roundoff.

The roundoff should be learned from the cartwheel. The two skills are essentially the same, with the exception of the landing. Perform the cartwheel, and

instead of facing sideways on the landing, execute a quarter turn more and land on both feet simultaneously.

11. *Neckspring* (Snap-Up, Kip, Nip-Up). From a straight sitting position roll backward, bringing the legs overhead to a pike position, and place the hands on the mats behind the shoulders with the fingers pointing toward the shoulders and the thumbs by the ears. From this position on the shoulders roll forward and at the same time: (a) whip the legs forward at about a 60° angle and arch the back; and (b) push off the mat with the hands and back of the head. Continue the whip of the legs until the body lands in a squat position on the feet.

Before trying the kip in its entirety, first try a bridge position on the shoulders and feet. This will give the feeling of lifting the hips. Then go to the bridge from the kip position on back of the shoulders using the kipping action. When this can be accomplished successfully, try the neckspring as described above. A technique using a partner to learn this stunt is as follows: Have one person sit on the mats with the knees flexed, the hands behind the hips, and the feet flat on the mats. The person trying the neckspring lies on the mat with his head between the spotter's legs and his shoulders resting on the lifting partner's feet, grasping the partner's ankles on the inside of the ankles with the thumbs. The performer rolls backward, lifting his hips with his legs coming near his partner's head. From this position he should then execute the neckspring technique of whipping his legs upward and forward while the assisting partner lifts his legs, thus pushing the performer's shoulders upward, which helps the completion of the neckspring. See illustration.

12. *Headspring.* Take a slight run, hurdle, and land on mat with both feet at the same time. Place both hands on the mat with the top of the head about 6 inches in front of the hands as though doing a headstand. Push off the feet, keeping the body in a deep piked position with the legs straight. The hips are carried over the head until the body weight falls off balance down the mat. Whip the legs overhead from the waist and on toward the mat in one continuous arc, simultaneously pushing with the hands. Land on the feet with the

HEADSPRING

knees bent slightly, depending on how high the headspring is executed. This skill is not done by kicking or pushing the feet from the knees but rather by snapping or whipping the legs out of the piked position from the waist.

The headspring should first be learned from a rolled mat and with the use of a spotter. First try the headspring from a standing position. Place the hands on the near side on top of the rolled mat, with the head on the far side as though going to a headstand. Move the feet close to the mat roll, keeping the body in a deep pike position until the body weight is off balance down the mat. At this point whip the feet overhead from the waist and then down to the mat in one continuous arch, simultaneously pushing with the hands. Land on the feet. Once mastered from a mat roll, the stunt can be performed on a level mat as described above. The same bridging technique used in learning the neckspring is suggested in learning the headspring.

The spotter sits on the mat roll. As the performer places his hands on the rolled-up mat, the spotter grasps the performer's upper arm with one hand, places

PARTNER ASSISTING THE
NECKSPRING

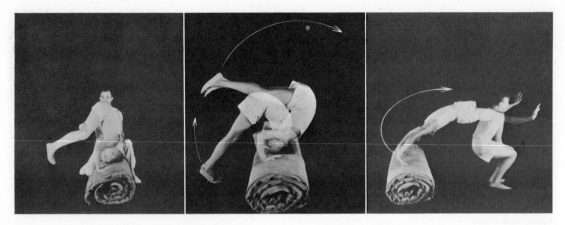

HEADSPRING WITH SPOTTER AND ROLLED MAT

the other hand under the upper back, and assists him through the stunt.

13. *Front Handspring*. Take a good run, skip on the right foot, and bring the left foot forward. Place left foot on the mat, bend forward at the waist, and place both hands about 2 feet ahead of the left foot. Kick the right foot overhead, followed by the left. As the feet are being carried overhead, the arms should be held straight and the eyes trained on a spot about 6 inches in front of the hands. As the body passes through the handstand position, push off the mat with the shoulders and wrists without bending the arms. Continue on over to the feet and land with the knees flexed.

Like the headspring, the handspring should be learned with a mat roll and with the use of spotters. Start from a standing position. Place the hands on the mat in front of the rolled mat, and with the aid of spotters kick up to a handstand. Arch over the rolled mat. Two spotters should assist the performer throughout this arch. Do this arch over the mat several times to establish the feeling of turning over, with the arms straight, back arched, and so on. Then try the stunt with a small run and execute a front handspring over the rolled mat. The position of the spotter is to sit straddling on the rolled mat or kneeling in front of it. As the performer places

FRONT HANDSPRING

his hands on the mat, grasp his upper arm with one hand and place the other hand behind his shoulders. As he over-balances, assist him to a landing position on his feet.

Some students may learn the front handspring more easily by using the following technique with a partner:

Have one person stand on the mat facing the performer. The performer kicks into a handstand with the partner catching his legs at the calves. This is repeated several times with a stronger kick each time, with the partner catching the legs surely with each kick. After this has been done several times, the partner then grasps the performer by his hips and allows the performer's back to ride slightly over his shoulders. With confidence the partner will eventually lift the performer slightly from the mats but always place him back to his hands in the direction from which he came. This develops the feeling of kicking the legs upward with the arms straight and the back slightly arched, which are essential parts of a good front handspring. After the above has been done several times, the performer attempts the handspring with the spotter (or spotters) stepping to one side and simply lifting him over as he executes the stunt.

FRONT HANDSPRING WALKOUT

TINSICA

Variation: A variation of this handspring is to finish on one leg with the other following. This makes for easy access into stunts in sequence.

14. *Tinsica.* Start by taking a good run, skip on the right foot and bring the left foot forward. Place the left foot on the mat and by bending forward from the waist, place the left hand about 2 feet in front of the left foot, simultaneously kicking the right leg overhead followed by the left and place the right hand on the mat about 6 inches in front of, and about shoulder width from, the left hand. The arms should be held straight, and the eyes should be trained on a spot about 18 inches ahead of the hands. The legs pass overhead and the right foot lands about two feet ahead of the right hand, with the left foot following and landing about 18 inches ahead of the right foot. This trick should be completed facing in the same direction as starting.

The tinsica may be easily learned by using the cartwheel as a lead-up stunt. At the completion of the cartwheel as the left foot nears the mat, execute a quarter turn and come to a standing position facing down the mats. Repeat this until the quarter twist comes easily.

FORWARD SOMERSAULT

15. *Forward Somersault*. Take a good run, skip on the left foot, bring the right foot forward, simultaneously raise both arms overhead, and land on the mat with both feet at the same time (hurdle). It is important here that the hurdle be short and fast so that the forward motion established by running may be directed upward. Throw the arms upward, forward, and downward and place the chin on the chest. Continue the circular motion with the hands, by grasping and pulling at the shins, into a tuck position. The chest should be close to the knees and the heels close to the buttocks. After completing the somersault, shoot out of the tuck and land in a standing position on the mat.

The forward somersault can be easily learned by stacking mats on top of each other to a height of about three feet. Take a good run, hurdle, and execute a forward roll onto the stack of mats. Continue this action until the roll becomes easy. Progress by taking the weight off the hands until the roll can be completed without touching the hands to the mat. From here try the front somersault to a sitting position on the stack of mats. When this is com-

pleted successfully, take the mats away one at a time and try to finish standing on the feet after completing the somersault. Another method of teaching a front somersault is to provide a rolled up mat over which the performer executes a front somersault with the spotter sitting on the mat assisting throughout the stunt. The trampoline can also be used effectively to teach the fundamentals of a good forward somersault.

Still another method of learning a front somersault is with the use of a tumbling belt and two spotters. The spotters simply run alongside the performer and help him through the stunt by lifting up on the belt as the somersault is executed. A springboard trampoline can also assist the performer if spotted by this method.

When spotting this stunt without the use of a safety belt, the spotter stands at the take-off point, placing one hand beneath the performer's head or shoulders to insure a good tuck and to lift him if needed. The other hand should grab the upper arm to prevent an overspin. Variation: *Forward somersault—Russian technique*

FORWARD SOMERSAULT—
RUSSIAN TECHNIQUE

Prior to taking off from the mats, swing the straight arms downward and backward past the hips, keeping the body erect with the chest up. After the arms have swung past the hips, duck the head toward the chest and begin the somersault. Grasp the underside of the thighs, pulling the knees tightly into the body. Continue the somersault to the feet.

16. *Tigna.* A tigna is a type of front somersault following a tinsica in that the take-off is from one foot. The body somersaults in a semituck position.

17. *Back Handspring.* This is one of the more advanced tumbling stunts and should not be attempted without a spotter.

Start from a standing position with the feet about shoulder width apart and with the arms held straight out in front of the body. Swing the arms downward, simultaneously bend the knees, and sit back as though sitting in a chair. As the body falls off balance backward, swing the arms upward overhead, simultaneously forcing the head backward. Straighten the legs and push off the mat with the toes. As you push off with the toes, force the hips upward and make a big circle with the hands. As the hands land on the mat, the body is approaching a handstand position. From this position, snap the legs down from the waist as in the snap-down and land in a standing position on the feet. It is important that you continue to force the arms over in the arc until they finally reach the mat.

When spotting by the hand method, the two spotters should take a position on the knees or simply standing on the mat at the side of the performer. Have the performer do a back bend and assist by supporting his body weight. When he is in the back bend position, have him keep his arms straight and force his head

BACK HANDSPRING

back so that he is looking at a spot about 12 inches in front of his hands. Carry his feet overhead so that he passes through the handstand position. Have the performer then come to a stand on the mat by bending down from the waist. Repeat this several times until he gets the idea of turning over. Progress by having him try the back handspring in its entirety.

To hand spot the back handspring in its entirety, place the right hand in the small of the performer's back and use the left hand to assist him in turning over. This may be accomplished by lifting him behind the thighs with the left hand as he starts the back handspring and flipping his feet overhead. When using this method of spotting, it is important to stand close to the performer because it may be impossible to support his body weight at arm's length.

A tumbling safety belt may also be used for spotting purposes in first learning this stunt. Two spotters may then assist the performer through the back bend action as mentioned previously.

After learning the handspring from a standing position, try it from a snap-down. This involves kicking into a momentary handstand and snapping the feet down vigorously while pushing off from the fingers. This brings the performer back into a standing position

BACK HANDSPRING FROM
SNAP-DOWN

with the momentum already started for a back handspring.

A good technique of teaching a back handspring that follows in line with a roundoff back handspring is as follows: Have the performer stand on the mats with knees slightly bent and back straight, with the arms overhead. Two spotters, one standing on each side, grasp hands behind the performer's back, with the free hands prepared to lift the legs. The performer then slowly leans backward, placing his hands on the mat, and the spotters hold the performer off the mat and at the same time lift the performer's legs through the back handspring movement. The performer, after passing through the handstand, snaps the feet downward to the mat to finish in a standing position. In succeeding attempts, the performer should obtain more spring from the legs and throw his head and arms backward more vigorously, which in turn will make the completion of the back handspring easier. After successfully completing one back handspring, the performer should try two or more in sequence.

18. *Back Somersault.* The standing back somersault should not be attempted without a spotter. Start from a standing position with the feet about shoulder width apart and the arms hanging in a natural position at the sides. Bend the knees, swing the arms downward, and jump up, swinging the arms overhead as though catching a horizontal bar. Throw the head and arms backward hard, simultaneously bringing the knees up to the chest. Circle the arms sideways to grasp the shins, pulling the body into a tight tuck. It is important to pull the knees to the chest hard, continually forcing the head backward. Land on the feet in a standing position.

Before trying the back somersault in its entirety, first attempt the jump tuck. From a standing position, jump into the air and bring the knees up to the chest. As the knees strike the chest grasp the shins and hold the tuck position. It is important here to bring the knees up to the chest rather than the chest down to the knees. Shoot out of the tuck and land on the feet. Do not throw the head and arms backward when practicing this lead-up stunt as it can cause partial turn-

BACK SOMERSAULT

over and possible injury. A spotter may assist here by standing behind the performer and simply placing a hand on his back to prevent overspring. After this jump tuck has been tried several times, try the back somersault with the use of a spotter or two.

In spotting this stunt, it is suggested that two spotters be utilized, one on each side of the performer. As the performer and simply placing a hand on his assist by supporting the performer in the small of the back, aiding the somersault.

19. *Roundoff–Back Handspring.* Take a good run and execute the roundoff as described earlier. It is important here to push off the hands on the roundoff so that the entire body is in the air at one point. As the feet are snapped downward, they should be pulled well under the body to impart back motion. Before the feet land on the roundoff, the back handspring should be started. The hands should come off the floor during the roundoff and be carried as though making a big circle. Keep the arms straight and continue the circle so that the hands will be forward of the center of gravity of the body when they reach the mat. Snap the legs down from the waist, as in doing a snap-down, and come to a stand on the mat.

Do not attempt this trick without a spotter. The method used in spotting may again be determined by the size of the performer. A small boy or girl may be successfully hand spotted. Larger individuals should be spotted with the use of a safety belt and two spotters. It is important that the spotters be experienced; otherwise injury may result.

20. *Roundoff–Back Somersault.* Take a good run and execute a roundoff as described earlier. It is important that the feet *are not* pulled through on the

roundoff but instead are kicked out backward so that the backward motion established by the roundoff can be directed upward. The arms should move off the mat directly from the roundoff and be carried upward and overhead. As the feet leave the mat, bring the knees up to the chest (tuck) and simultaneously throw the head backward. As the knees are forced up to the chest, the arms complete a small circle and grasp the shins. When one revolution is complete, shoot out of the tuck and land. The back somersault should be taken high and spun fast to give more time for the landing. In order to increase the rate of spin, think about kicking the chin with the knees as the tuck is made. While in the tuck, pull the knees up tight to the chest and force the toes overhead.

The roundoff–back somersault should not be attempted without spotters. It is suggested here that the safety belt and two spotters be used for this stunt.

21. *Roundoff–Back Handspring–Back Somersault.* Take a good run and execute a roundoff and back handspring as previously described. Snap off the hands on the roundoff and pull the feet under the body for the back handspring. The landing on the handspring is very important because it will determine the height of the back somersault. Kick back on the handspring, simultaneously reaching upward with the arms so that the back motion established by the roundoff and handspring will be directed upward. As the feet leave the floor, bring the knees up to the chest into a tight tuck and simultaneously throw the head backward. Complete one somersault and shoot out of the tuck for the landing.

The roundoff-back handspring-back somersault should not be attempted without a spotter. The hand belt, with two spotters running along side the performer, should be used when attempting this skill.

TWISTING TUMBLING

For the purpose of continuity, all twisting moves will be explained from the roundoff and handspring, and to the right. These moves should not be attempted until the roundoff–handspring– and back somersault can be completed successfully and should be attempted only with a spotter. The twisting belt should be used in learning all twisting moves.

1. *Half Twisting Backward Somersault.* Start by taking a good run and execute a roundoff–back handspring. It is important here that you kick out on the back handspring so that the half twister is carried high. As the feet land on the back handspring, carry the arms overhead and force the hips high as though doing a layout back somersault– with the body completely straight. Carry the head backward and then to the right side, simultaneously dropping the right shoulder and arm and bringing the left arm across the chest. Complete the back somersault with one half twist and land on the feet. It is important that the head and shoulders are forced over the body on landing. Failure to do this will result in underturning the somersault, causing a sit-down landing.

2. *Full Twisting Backward Somersault.* As the feet land on the back handspring carry the left arm upward and over the right shoulder, simultaneously carrying the right shoulder and elbow backward and downward. The head moves backward and to the right, looking over the right shoulder. For best results the mat should be seen over the

right shoulder as the twist starts and remain visible throughout the twist. The body is in a layout position with the head remaining in one spot and acting as an axis around which the body rotates. After the initial throw, bring the arms into the chest to increase the rate of spin. On completing one revolution, force the arms away from the chest to stop the spin and land on the feet.

routines

Innumerable combinations are possible and there is much value in allowing the performers to put together their own combinations into a longer routine. Some suggestions are:

1. Alternating diving rolls with low tight rolls.
2. Forward roll—cross legs into backward roll.
3. Alternate two arm cartwheel with one arm cartwheel.
4. Series of cartwheels.
5. Cartwheel into a roundoff into a back extension.
6. Handspring to headspring into a forward roll.
7. Series of headsprings.
8. Series of cartwheels with a one-quarter turn.
9. Series of tinsicas.
10. Front somersault—forward roll—headspring.
11. Roundoff—two or three back handsprings.
12. Tinsica—roundoff—back handspring—back flip.
13. Roundoff — back handspring — back somersault — back handspring — back somersault.
14. Roundoff into bounding back somersaults.

doubles tumbling

Doubles tumbling consists simply of two persons executing tumbling feats together. This activity can be a great deal of fun and extremely rewarding. It does require close cooperation between the two performers, however, and it is also suggested that at least one and possibly two spotters should assist the performers. Some of the doubles tumbling stunts include:

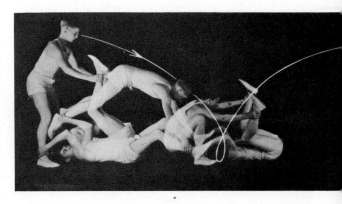

DOUBLES FORWARD ROLL

1. *Doubles Forward Roll.* Start with one partner lying on the mat with his feet in the air while the other stands at his head in a straddle position. They grasp each other's ankles. Then the top man dives forward into a forward roll taking the bottom man's feet down toward the mat with him. The roll brings the bottom man up onto his feet and he in turn dives forward. Then the other man is on top again so they continue in a steady roll down the mat.

2. *Doubles Backward Roll.* Start in the same position as the doubles forward roll. The top man sits down pulling the bottom man's feet back with him. The bottom man executes a backward roll, pushing up vigorously with his hands. Thus, the positions of both men are now reversed, and the stunt may be continued in a steady roll backward down the mat.

3. *Log Rolls.* Start with three persons kneeling on the mat parallel with one another. The middle performer rolls sideways to the left and at the same time the left outside person jumps sideways over the rolling body to the center position. On landing he immediately rolls sideways to the right, and at the same time the outside right man jumps sideways over the rolling body into the center and then proceeds to roll sideways to the

left. At this time the ouside left person will then jump sideways to the right and then roll. This log roll action is repeated as long as desired.

4. *Triple Rolls (Monkey Shines).* Start with three persons standing on the mat with the outer persons facing the middle and the middle man facing the left outside man. The middle man performs a tight forward roll toward the outside person, who in turn straddle-leaps over the rolling body to the center position; on landing on his feet he immediately squats into a tight forward roll in the direction of the right outside performer. At this moment the right outside performer straddle-leaps over the rolling body, landing on his feet in the center position, and then proceeds to do a forward roll to the outside, whereupon the outside man straddle-leaps over the rolling body into the center position. This action is repeated as long as desired.

5. *Knee and Shoulder Spring.* The bottom man lies on his back with his knees raised and slightly spread. The top man approaches toward the feet and with a short run places his hands on the bottom man's knees. As the top man performs a headspring motion the bottom man assists him by placing his hands on

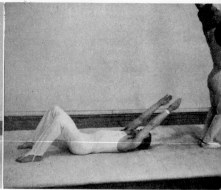

KNEE AND SHOULDER SPRING

BACK TO BACK TOSS

the shoulder blades of the top man. The top man continues over and lands on his feet just beyond the head of the bottom man.

6. *Back to Back Toss.* In this stunt one person tosses the other person over his back. Start standing back to back with the hands clasped over the shoulders. One person bends his knees, then leans forward, and proceeds to lift the other person over his back The thrower or bottom man should be sure to dip slightly with his knees so that the top

person's buttocks rests against the lower back of the bottom man. The thrower should stop his forward lean and raise up as he feels the top man rolling off his back. The top man should continue to pike the body until ready to land. Be sure to have a spotter available throughout the early learning phases of this stunt.

7. *Front Flip Pitch.* Start with both performers standing, facing the same direction. The flyer bends one knee and places his shin and instep into the

FRONT FLIP PITCH

SIDE LEG BACK FLIP PITCH

thrower's hands. Both performers then take a small dip in their knees and then the flyer proceeds to lift for a forward somersault, with the thrower lifting hard under the top person's shin and instep. The flyer, with the aid of the lift, should then execute a forward somersault.

8. *Side Leg Back Flip Pitch*. The flyer places his straight leg into the thrower's hand and places his right hand on the thrower's shoulders. The thrower lifts the leg up into the air and with the aid of the other hand on the flyer's back throws him into a back flip. The flyer should keep the lifted leg taut so that the thrower will have a solid means of lifting him into the air.

9. *Back Flip Toe Pitch*. This is done by the flyer placing his hands on the thrower's shoulders and setting one foot in the thrower's hands. The flyer then straightens upward and backward into a

BACK FLIP TOE PITCH

back somersault pitch. The thrower lifts upward into the air and throws the flyer into the somersault. Be sure to use a spotter in learning this stunt.

10. *Doubles Cartwheel*. This consists of two persons executing a double cart-

DOUBLES CARTWHEEL

wheel with one pair of legs on the ground while the other pair are in the air. One person stands with his legs slightly bent in straddle position with the arms to the side and front of the body. The other performer approaches from the side of the standing person and thrusts his head between the person's legs with the shoulders resting on the top side of the thighs. The hands grab the back side of the standing person's legs. At the same time the standing person circles the top person's waist in preparing to execute the double cartwheel. The top person should swing the forward foot around to the ground as quickly as possible in order to lift the standing person over into the second cartwheel. The two should hold tightly to each other, which will insure the completion of the double cartwheel. The spotter should stand behind and assist by lifting the performer's waist.

11. *Assisted Back Flip Over Arm*. The thrower should place one arm across the waist of the performer and the other

hand under the back side of the knees. The performer grasps the top arm of the thrower and prepares for the back flip. The performer kicks both legs and knees upward and around the arm of the thrower, similar to kicking over a bar in the playground. The thrower lifts and turns the performer around his arm as pictured.

12. *Back Flip Off Partner's Feet.* One person is in a supine position with the legs elevated. The other person stands in a straddle position over the bottom person's legs and hips, facing away from the bottom man. The bottom man places his feet in the small of the back of the performer as the performer leans backward into an arch position. The bottom person grasps the performer's shoulders as he leans backward, and when the shoulders are over the bottom person's face and the weight is well over the bottom man's feet, the top person then continues over in a flip action to a stand on

the other side of the bottom man's head. Do slowly at first like a slow arch back bend (handspring technique) until the timing is learned, and then a more flipping action is incorporated into the stunt. A good push with the bottom man's legs gives height and excitement to the stunt.

13. *Wheelbarrow Pitch to Forward Somersault.* The performer assumes a push-up position with the body elevated from the mat by straight arms and with the legs extended backward into the thrower's hands. With a beat consisting of an extension of the performer's waist and a slight dip in the throwers hands, the flyer then whips his hips upward and over and then ducks his head and commences the forward somersault. The thrower lifts vigorously with his arms (hands under the performer's feet) and thus assists the performer in the forward somersault to his feet. Be sure to wait before beginning the forward somersault

ASSISTED BACK FLIP OVER ARM

WHEELBARROW PITCH

ANKLE PICK UP

tends them upward; at the same time the thrower lifts forcefully upward and then activates a throw of the feet over beyond the flyer's head. The performer continues this back extension action on over to his feet. With proper timing, a good lift by the thrower, and a good push by the performer, the ankle pick-up can be executed at a fascinating height, particularly if the thrower is taller than the performer. This stunt can be done from a handstand position, with the thrower standing behind the performer grasping the uplifted ankles. From here the performer simply ducks his head and lowers his shoulders, downward into a partial forward roll. When the performer reaches his back, he bends his knees slightly and then proceeds back upward into the back extension action with the thrower lifting him upward and over to his feet.

15. *Sitting Assisted Back Flip.* The thrower sits on the mat with his legs in

SITTING ASSISTED BACK FLIP

turn until the thrower has had an opportunity to lift forcefully upward; with this waiting time, success will surely occur. An added version of this stunt is to do it with the performer in a handstand position, then falling down into the thrower's hands, and then doing the forward somersault.

14. *Ankle Pick-Up.* The performer lies on his back and extends the legs straight up, placing the hands on the mat behind the shoulders. The thrower steps in close to the performer's hips and grasps the uplifted ankles with the thumbs on the inside of the ankles. The performer bends his knees slightly and then ex-

straddle position and his hands flat on the mat, palms upward, while the performer stands on the thrower's hands. As the thrower lifts upward with his hands, the performer executes a backward somersault. The thrower gives an assist to the performer in the completion of the backward flip. A spotter should stand at the side to assist the performer.

16. *Assisted Front Somersault.* The performer stands between two spotters, all facing the same direction. The inside hands of the spotters grasp the wrist of the performer, and with the outside hand the performer's upper arms are grasped. Then after a few steps the performer jumps into a forward somersault, and the spotters, lifting on their respective arms, assist the performer in the completion of the flip. Be sure the spotters do not lift too fast or too high, because this prevents the performer from turning into the

ASSISTED FRONT SOMERSAULT

somersault action. Also, the spotters should continue to lift the performer even after the somersault has been completed. This will allow for a soft landing on the feet instead of slamming into the mats.

CHAPTER THREE / *balancing*

We all have seen children in the playground, front lawn, or sandy beach kick upward into a momentary handstand, and each second that the balance is held is a moment of joy for them. It is great fun and a matter of warm pride to accomplish a balance of some sort with a moderate degree of proficiency. Besides this fun aspect, balancing does contribute a great deal to the physical development of the growing boy or girl. Very little equipment or space is required; the regular tumbling mat is satisfactory for all degrees of balancing stunts. Surely an activity that offers so much return on so little investment of equipment and space should be given serious consideration in the physical education program.

Balancing as such does not lend itself to organized competition, although it plays a large part in other gymnastic competitive events, such as floor exercise and parallel bars.

values

The specific values of balancing activities are:

1. Balancing develops coordination and agility. The ability to maneuver the body in an upside-down position and to land correctly on the feet requires a great deal of coordinated action from the entire body.

2. Strength and endurance are developed by many balancing stunts. Many balances call for holding the body in positions that depend on muscular action for support, particularly of the abdomen and shoulders. Presses often depend on strength in the arms and shoulders.

3. Balance and a sense of relocation are essential in balancing stunts and are gained through consistent practice. Poise and orientation can be developed through balancing activities.

4. Balancing develops confidence and

sureness in the ability to handle the body. This is a value that all growing boys and girls should experience.

5. In executing the doubles balancing stunts, a certain degree of teamwork is necessary. This value is developed as one performer depends on another to do his part of the stunt.

6. Balancing is fun and enjoyable because it is a natural and self-motivating activity.

7. Balancing provides a chance for the small boy or girl to gain needed recognition. Very often the smaller person has an advantage in balancing over the larger person, which is different from many sports.

organization

Balancing needs little equipment. Tumbling mats and space are about the only essential requirements, and even if tumbling mats are not available the activity can still be conducted if handled with close supervision and caution. Any area can be used, including a gymnasium, classroom, school corridors, and playgrounds. The important item in this respect is to provide ample space for each student.

There is little difference in the organization and conduct of tumbling and balancing. Only the differences will be noted here, and the reader is asked to refer to the preceding chapter on tumbling for the general plan.

Balancing can be taught by the mass method or by the squad method. Unlike tumbling, it requires no more space for advanced stunts than for beginning stunts. Balancing work requires a lot of practice for most people, so time should be allotted for it. However, variety is also needed to maintain interest. Tum-

bling and a mixture of singles and doubles balancing can make a good contribution to variety. It is not necessary for singles balancing to precede doubles balancing. Both can be presented in the same lesson.

For singles balancing, the students should work in pairs, with one performing and the other spotting. For doubles balancing, groups of three or four are best, with two students performing the stunt and the other students spotting.

Students should be encouraged to perform stunts with good form inasmuch as this teaches, and indicates control of, the stunt as well as adding to the beauty of it.

program of instruction

The following stunts are recommended for learning in the approximate order in which they appear. The singles work will be presented first followed by the doubles balancing stunts.

SINGLES BALANCING

1. *Squat Head Balance*. Start this stunt from a squat position with the hands on the mat and the inside of the knees resting on the elbows. From this position lean forward and place the head on the mat. Lift the toes from the mat so that the balance is on the head and hands, thus placing the performer in the squat head balance.
Variation: Do a squat head balance and then lift the knees off the elbows, touch them together, and then place back on the elbows. For a challenge, see if the students can do this several times without losing their balance.

2. *Squat Hand Balance*. This is similar to the squat head balance except the

SQUAT HEAD BALANCE

mat, and lift the feet into the balance position. Maintain the balance by working with the arms and pressing with the fingers.

Variation: While doing a squat hand balance, lift the knees off the elbows, touch them together, and then place back on the elbows. For a challenge, see if the students can do this several times without losing their balance.

3. *Head Balance*. This stunt consists in balancing on the head and hands with the feet straight overhead. One method of moving into the head balance is from the squat head balance position. After reaching the balancing point on this fundamental stunt, raise the feet upward over the head. Do this slowly and the balance will be maintained more easily. Another method is to place the head and hands in the proper position on the mat and simply kick one leg up, and follow with the other into the head balance position. Be sure to maintain a triangular formation with the head and the hands and keep the back neatly arched. Also, rest the head on the forward part and not the very top or back side of the head.

It is suggested that a spotter be used while learning this stunt. The best position for the spotter is to the side and slightly behind the performer. To come down from this stunt, either duck the

head does not touch the mat and the entire balance is maintained by the hands. Start from a squat position with the arms shoulder width apart, with the inside of the knees resting on the elbows. Lean forward, keeping the head off the

SQUAT HAND BALANCE

HEAD BALANCE

head and do a forward roll or return the legs to the mat in the same manner as they were put in position.

Variation: While doing a head balance, lift the hands from the mat and clap them together and then place them back on the mats and maintain the head balance. For a challenge, see if the students can clap their hands several times before placing the hands back on the mats to maintain the head balance.

4. *Forward Roll to Head Balance.* Do a forward roll, and on reaching the feet remain in a tuck position and place the hands on the mat, well ahead of the feet, lean forward, and reach outward with the head before placing it on the mat. Then slowly move the feet up into the balance position. Rushing into the balance out of the roll will simply cause the performer to fall forward into another roll.

5. *Head Balance—Arms Folded.* Start from a kneeling position with the arms folded in front of the chest and resting on the mats. Place the head beyond the arms and kick upward into the balance position.

6. *Head and Forearm Balance.* From a kneeling position place the forearms

SPOTTING A HEAD BALANCE

HEAD BALANCE—ARMS FOLDED

HEAD AND FOREARM BALANCE

FOREARM BALANCE

BACKWARD ROLL TO HEAD
BALANCE

flat on the mat, with the thumbs of the hands almost touching each other. Place the head in the cup formed by the thumb and fingers of the two hands and kick upward into the head and forearm balance. This same stunt may also be done with the fingers interlaced behind the head. In either method be sure that the forearm and head form a good tripod.

7. *Forearm Balance.* From a head and forearm balance, lift the head off the mat and maintain the balance with the forearms alone. The position may also be attained by placing the forearms on the mat and kicking upward into the balance position without the head touching the mat at all. Keep the upper arms as vertical as possible and the lower arms nearly parallel to each other.

8. *Backward Roll to Head Balance.* From a sitting position on the mat, roll backward as in a backward roll. When the back of the head touches the mat, place the hands beside the head and extend the legs upward. Continue the roll to the top of the head, arch the back, and at the same time, slide the hands backward to the tripod position to stop the momentum of the moving body and to secure the head balance.

9. *Hand Balance.* This stunt consists in simply balancing oneself in an inverted position on the hands. It is a fascinating stunt but requires a great

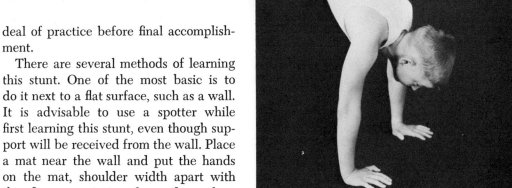

HAND BALANCE

HAND BALANCE AGAINST WALL

deal of practice before final accomplishment.

There are several methods of learning this stunt. One of the most basic is to do it next to a flat surface, such as a wall. It is advisable to use a spotter while first learning this stunt, even though support will be received from the wall. Place a mat near the wall and put the hands on the mat, shoulder width apart with the fingers pointing forward, a short distance from the wall. With head up and eyes focused on the wall, kick upward until the feet rest on the wall. While kicking into the hand balance be sure to keep the head up to prevent the body from rolling into the wall. From this resting position push gently away from the wall with one foot in order to slowly move into a free supporting hand balance. The action is a back-and-forth motion from a free hand balance to the wall hand balance.

Another method consists in working in an open area with the use of a spotter. Execute the stunt in the same manner and let the spotter grab the legs and hold the performer in a hand balance position. Little by little the spotter can release the legs of the performer and finally a free supporting hand balance

will be accomplished. It is most important that the spotter work extremely close with the performer and safely hold him in position. A safe recovery may be made from an overbalance by turning the body a quarter turn and landing on the feet. In the final hand balance, remember to keep the head up (eyes looking forward slightly), back arched, and hands pointed forward, with fingers gripping the floor and arms straight.

10. *Walk on Hands.* Walking on the hands is sometimes easier than holding a fixed hand balance, although a controlled walk is really more difficult. After getting into a hand balance, simply lean forward, and before overbalancing too far, move one hand at a time forward a short distance. A constant lean will provide a smooth walk. Avoid taking too large a step with the hands.

14. *Double Elbow Lever.* Start from a kneeling position with the hands on the floor so that the fingers point toward the knees. Lean forward and place the

DOUBLE ELBOW LEVER

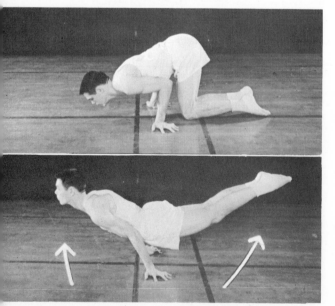

right hip on the right elbow and then the left hip on the left elbow. From this position extend the legs backward until they are straight, then raise them slightly from the mat. The body then will be supporting itself in a double elbow lever position.

15. *Single Elbow Lever.* Start from a kneeling position with the right hand on the floor, fingers pointing toward the knees, and the right elbow inside the right hip. The left hand is on the floor, extended beyond the head. Extend the legs backward, either together or in a straddle position, and raise the feet from the floor, thus placing most of the weight on the right elbow. Gradually shift the entire weight to the right elbow and slowly lift the left hand from the floor. The body then will be supporting itself in a single elbow lever position. (See picture in Chap. 4)

16. *One Arm Handbalance.* To learn this difficult stunt, start from an ordinary hand balance. Slowly shift weight from two arms to one arm and at the same time lift the other hand from the floor. Keep the balancing arm straight and strong, with the other hand ready to add support from the floor if necessary to maintain balance. The legs may be kept together or in a straddle position. Practice is the key to the final learning of the one arm handstand. (See picture in Chap. 4)

DOUBLES BALANCING

Doubles balancing is a very enjoyable activity and can readily supplement a singles balancing program. Many of the stunts are relatively easy, and with a third or fourth person to assist and spot, the activity can become fun and exciting. Some of the stunts could include:

CHEST BALANCE

1. *Chest Balance.* Start this stunt with one partner kneeling on all fours. The other partner slides his arms under the kneeling partner's chest and places his chest on the kneeling partner's back. Then the top man kicks upward in a similar manner as if kicking into a head balance, and finishes in a chest balance position on his partner's back. The arms may also be placed with one arm along the leg and the other along the arm.

2. *Hold Out Facing Out (Thigh Stand).* Start this stunt by having both persons face the same direction. Then the bottom person squats down, bends forward, and places his head between the top person's legs and lifts him (using the legs and not the back for lifting) into a sitting position on his shoulders. The top person then places the feet on the bottom person's thighs, with toes pointed downward, and the bottom man places his hands just above the top man's knees. The bottom man leans backward and removes his head from between the legs and finishes by holding the top person on his thighs with his arms straight. The top person straightens upward and forces a neat arch in the body with the arms out horizontally, head and chest erect. To dismount from this

position, the top man simply drops forward to his feet. The spotter should stand in front of the performers in assisting in this stunt.

One may also mount into the position by jumping up onto the bottom man's thighs with bottom man lifting by the hips. (See page 36.)

3. *Hold Out Facing In.* The two partners stand facing each other. The top

THIGH STAND

THIGH STAND

person circles his hands behind the bottom person's neck while the bottom one places his hands behind the top person's hips. The top man then proceeds to step upward onto the thighs of the bottom man with the toes facing outward, keeping the hips over the feet as he steps up. When a solid balance position is reached, each right arm is brought across

the other's chest and a sure grip is secured on the other's wrist. From this position, both men lean backward slightly and finish up in the hold-out-facing-in position. Some find it easier to grasp right arms as part of the starting position and simply step up onto the bottom man's thighs and proceed to lean into the hold out facing in.

HOLD OUT FACING IN

KNEE AND SHOULDER BALANCE

4. *Knee and Shoulder Balance.* One partner is in a supine position with the hands and knees raised and the feet on the mat close to the buttocks. The top person places his hands on the knees and his shoulders in the bottom man's hands. From this position, kick upward into a knee and shoulder balance. Be sure that the top person's arms are kept straight throughout this stunt and that contact is made with the shoulders into the bottom man's hands before kicking upward into the balance. The spotter can stand by the side of the performers to assist in reaching the balance position.

FRONT SWAN ON FEET

5. *Front Swan on Feet.* One partner lines in a supine position with the legs and hands raised. The top man faces his partner and places his pelvis on the bottom man's feet, with the latter's heels angling in toward the stomach and the toes outward. The men grasp each other's hands. Then the top person leans forward into an arched balance position on the feet. Hold the hands until the balance is secure and then release the grip and lift the arms gracefully to the side supported by the bottom man's feet.

6. *Back Swan on Feet.* This is similar to the front swan except the top man is balanced on his back. The top partner backs into the upraised feet of the bottom man and leans backward into the back swan on feet. The bottom man's heels are inward and the toes pointed outward; the feet rest on the hips and the small of the upper man's back.

BACK SWAN ON FEET

7. *Foot to Hand Balance.* The bottom man lies on his back with hands beside his head and legs raised upward. The top person stands lightly on the bottom man's hands and grasps the uplifted feet. The top person jumps upward slightly and pushes downward on the bottom man's feet. Simultaneously, the bottom man lifts the hands straight upward to a straight arm position. When this foot-to-hand position is secure the top person releases the bottom man's feet and stands up in a comfortable standing position.

8. *Two High Stand.* The partners stand facing in the same direction with

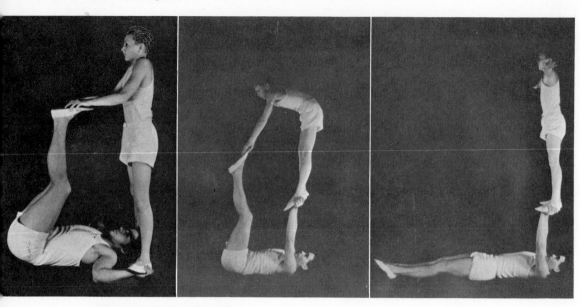

FOOT TO HAND BALANCE

the bottom man's hands resting just above his shoulders and the top man behind him, grasping the bottom man's hands as in a handshake. The top man then moves to the side of the bottom man and the bottom man squats down a little. From this position, the top partner places his right foot on the bottom man's thigh and proceeds to climb up-ward onto the shoulders. The bottom man pulls with the arms and keeps both arms firm and strong while the top man is approaching the final position. When the top man's foot is on the far shoulder of the bottom man, the other foot is removed from the bottom man's thigh and placed on the other shoulder. The hands are still clasped, and after a good

TWO HIGH STAND

SHOULDER BALANCE ON FEET

balance position is obtained the hands are released and the bottom man's hands are placed behind the top man's knees, just above the calf. The top man's shins should be resting on the back side of the bottom man's head, and the bottom man's hands then in effect pull downward and forward on the top man's legs. This makes for a solid two high stand. To dismount, the bottom man lifts his right hand, the top man grasps it and proceeds to leap forward, turning slightly to his right as he leaps to the ground. Another method is to simply jump forward off the shoulders to the mat. As skill progresses, the two persons may want to finish the dismount by doing forward rolls after the top man lands on the mat.

Be sure to work with one or more spotters on this stunt. The spotter should be behind the top man while he is climbing up to the shoulders and assist by pushing upward under the buttocks.

9. *Shoulder Balance on Feet.* The bottom man is in a supine position with the hands and feet raised. The top man stands behind the head, grasps the bottom man's hands, and places his shoulders in the bottom man's feet. The

LOW ARM-TO-ARM BALANCE

top man then jumps upward in a tuck position and continues to press upward into the shoulder balance on the feet. Pressure is applied to the hands in order to complete the press to the balance. When the shoulder balance on the feet is secure, the hands are released and the top man places his hands on the lower legs of the bottom man and continues to hold the shoulder balance on the feet. This same balance can be done in the opposite direction, with the top person starting from a position behind the buttocks.

10. *Low Arm-to-Arm Balance.* The bottom man is in a supine position with the arms up and the legs straight out on the mat, while the top man straddles the bottom man's waist, leans forward, and places his upper arms in the bottom man's hands. The top person grasps the back side of the bottom man's arms; he then jumps upward into a tuck position and continues to press into a low arm-to-arm. This position can also be reached by kicking upward with one leg, followed by the other. Keep the head up and grasp the arms firmly for support. This stunt can also be done from knee and shoulder balance with top man transferring one arm at a time from the bottom man's knees to his arms.

A good combination is to have both men lying in a supine position, head to head, grasping each other's arms. The top man executes a back extension up to a low arm-to-arm balance.

11. *Low Low Hand-to-Hand Balance.* The bottom man is in a supine position with the arms along his sides. Bend the arms and raise the hands upward, keeping the elbows on the mat. The top man stands, straddling the bottom man's head and places his hands in the bottom man's hands. The top man then kicks upward

LIFT TO OVERHEAD BACK ARCH

into a hand balance on the partner's hands. Work closely with a spotter on this stunt. Remember to allow the bottom man to do most of the balancing by shifting the hands and arms. The top man should simply maintain a rigid position.

12. *Low Hand-to-Hand Balance.* The same as the low low hand-to-hand except that the bottom man's arms are raised straight up from the shoulders. From this position the top man kicks upward into the hand balance position.

13. *High Arm-to-Arm Balance.* The partners stand facing each other with arms raised and each grasps the other person's upper arm. The top man then leaps towards the bottom man and circles his legs around the bottom man's waist. He then swings down between the bottom man's legs and then back upward toward the high arm-to-arm

position. The bottom man swings the top man up and tries to move under him so that the final part of the stunt can be done in a slightly press motion. The top mounter swings freely upward into the high arm-to-arm position allowing the bottom man to move in and hold him up over his head.

14. *Overhead Back Arch.* The bottom person places his hand in the small of the top person's back and holds the ankle with his other hand. The top person then jumps upward into an arch position while the bottom person lifts her overhead. Be sure to hold the top person's ankle as this helps to steady the balance position. Have one or two spotters to assist while learning this stunt.

15. *Overhead Swan.* The bottom person places his hands on the hips of the top person and then the top person jumps upward into the arch position

LIFT TO OVERHEAD SWAN

BACK EXTENSION TO LOW
ARM-TO-ARM

LOW LOW HAND-TO-HAND

overhead. Finding the center of balance of the top person is very important in maintaining the Overhead Swan. At first the top person can hold onto the bottom person's arms while overhead, and as balance becomes secure the hands are released.

PYRAMIDS

Combinations of balancing stunts can be put together to form pyramids. Because of the great number of possible combinations, no attempt will be made to cover specific pyramids. Instead, general principles will be given and the readers can use their own imagination and creativity.

1. The usual shape of pyramids is either a convex curve with the peak in the center or a concave curve with a peak at each end.

2. The performers may be arranged in such formations as a line or a circle and may utilize apparatus or equipment such as parallel bars, vaulting bucks, ladders, chairs, tables, and flags.

3. For large pyramids the group may be arranged in units, each of which could be a pyramid in itself. In this case the highest unit would be in the center, with the lower units at the sides.

4. If the pyramids are being performed as a part of an exhibition, some attempt should be made to select and arrange the group on the basis of the sizes of the individuals. Ability will be a limiting factor. For example, if a head balance is to be performed on each side of the middle unit, the appearance would be better if two individuals of the same height and build were selected.

5. If the pyramid involves building on top of one another, the stronger and heavier members of the group should be used to form the foundation.

LOW HAND-TO-HAND

HIGH ARM-TO-ARM BALANCE

PYRAMIDS

6. Pyramids are usually formed "by the numbers." The group should be lined up in rows with the top men standing behind the bottom men. Then some sort of signal is given for each step or movement until the pyramid is complete. Another signal should be given to dismount, which usually is done forward and may include a forward roll when hitting the mat. The pyramid need not be held for a very long time. The instructor, through watching the performance, can judge the amount of time that would be most effective.

7. Often a lack of ability may be compensated by having one person held in a balance position by another person. For example, two performers may do hand balances facing each other and have their legs held in place by a third person standing between them. Also, such stunts as merely standing on a kneeling partner's back or on the backs of two people in a push-up position make suitable parts of a pyramid requiring no particular ability.

An example of a pyramid involving simple singles balancing stunts is:

squat hand balance—head balance—forearm balance—hand balance—forearm balance—head balance—squat hand balance.

An example of a pyramid involving simple doubles balancing stunts is:

knee-shoulder balance—hold out, facing out-two high balance—hold out, facing out—knee-shoulder balance.

Pictures of various pyramids are included to help stimulate the imagination of the instructor.

CHAPTER FOUR / *floor exercise*

The floor exercise event can be one of the most exciting and creative activities in gymnastics. The range of ideas and the scope of imagination connected with this event are unlimited. A performer can execute stunts of great flexibility, of tremendous strength, of soft agility, of keen tumbling and balancing, and of imaginative rhythm. It has been only in recent years that this event has been used to any extent in American gymnastics, but it is receiving greater enthusiasm with each ensuing year of competition.

The floor exercise area is 12 meters (39.44 feet) square. The surface used is either the floor or, as recommended by national governing bodies, a thin resilient pad. The area is generally bordered with an inch line of either paint or tape. To leave the area while performing the floor exercise routine is an indication of poor planning and results in a reduction of points from the judge's score. With this in mind it is imperative that the area be properly marked as an aid to the performer.

Current rules governing this event call for a minimum of 50 seconds and a maximum of 70 seconds for the completion of the floor exercise.

values

The specific values received from working this event are:

1. The tumbling values already covered in the tumbling chapter are similar in that floor exercise develops timing, agility, and the musculature of the legs.

2. The values received from balancing are the development of a keen sense of balance and coordination. The minute control of intricate balance positions calls for the utmost in coordination and cooperation of all the muscles in the body.

3. The strength movements executed in floor exercise develop power and strength, particularly in the upper body.

4. The flexibility movements develop suppleness to its highest degree.

5. The creativity of the exercise calls for keen imagination and expression not found as readily in the other events.

organization

In first learning floor exercise movements it is highly recommended that a tumbling mat be used. After many successful completions on the mats, the stunts may be attempted on the floor. National rules require a special floor exercise pad, but lacking this, mats should be used for learning. Floor exercise is different from other gymnastic activities in that it is taught in part in a class situation. The skills of tumbling and balancing that make up floor exercise are taught in classes, and these methods have been covered in the preceding chapters. However, when basic tumbling and balancing skills have been learned, some time can be taken from the class period to put together some combinations of stunts. A basic feeling for the event is cultivated this way, and as skill progresses more difficult stunts may be introduced.

Because of the creativity, originality, and individuality that is desired in this activity, the best work can be done with individuals, particularly at the more advanced stages. However, elementary floor exercise can be given by mass instruction methods. Large groups can go through elementary movements together and, with practice, can use such synchronized routines for exhibitional purposes. Such exercises as swinging the arms into a front scale, into a forward roll, to a V seat, or side body roll can be used for mass work. Be sure to allow ample room between the students.

program of instruction

Instruction in floor exercise involves three basic steps:

1. Individual Stunts.

2. Combinations: As a person learns a new stunt, he should be challenged to combine it with another stunt as smoothly as possible. Because a stunt must be learned well in order to combine it with another, the use of combinations in the teaching progression stresses proper execution and increases the safety of performance. In addition, the smaller combinations serve as building blocks for longer routines. Combinations can be suggested by the instructor or coach or created by the performer.

3. Routines: Ultimately a pupil should strive to combine stunts into a routine. Competition is based on routines, required or optional. The approach to optional routines is one of problem solving. Certain requirements involving time and the types and number of movements are presented as a problem for the performer to solve creatively within his own capabilities. The instructor, coach, and pupil can coordinate their thoughts on the development of a particular routine. For sample routines refer to the end of the chapter.

Floor exercise routines generally consist of a mount or starting stunt, followed by the body of the routine consisting of stunts of all types, and finally a finishing stunt, often called a "dismount." For an effective opening, the mount is usually explosive or dynamic in nature. The majority of performers start with some movements in the corner and then run and execute a tumbling routine across the square. If a performer isn't an effective tumbler, he may start with an equally impressive strength or balance stunt. The same effect is attempted in the finishing stunt, and many performers use a run and finish with tumbling stunts. For the middle of the routine, it is desirable to have a good representation of stunts from each category. Descriptions and learning techniques are given by categories in the following pages.

FRONT SCALE

BALANCING STUNTS

The balancing stunts consist of any movement that has an element of stationary pose to it. Stunts such as head balance, hand balance, and scales belong in this group.

1. *Front Scale.* Scales are probably the easiest balancing moves that can be learned, but unless they are done gracefully, it is best to omit them from the routine. The easiest scale is done by starting in a standing position and then slowly leaning forward so that the upper body lowers to a position parallel to the floor and at the same time the right leg is elevated to make a straight line with the chest, also parallel to the floor. The arms are held in swan position with the head up and the back arched, or the right arm is held along the side of the body and the left arm extended forward, parallel to the floor. The leg is extended backward in a taut, yet smooth, position with the toes pointed.

2. *Side Scale.* This type of scale can

SIDE SCALE

be done to the side by leaning to the left and lifting the right leg. The left arm is held close to the head and extended out to the left with right arm along the body down toward the knee. From here the performer may execute a cartwheel into a handstand, and so on.

3. *Needle Scale.* This is done by simply lifting the right leg up into the

NEEDLE SCALE

V SEAT

SINGLE ELBOW LEVER

air to the side of the performer, the ankle of the lifted leg is grasped with right hand, and the entire leg is pulled in as close to the body as possible.

4. *Knee Scale.* An elementary move is to do a one knee scale from a kneeling position. Simply lift one leg back and lower the chest parallel to the floor. This is very similar to the forward scale except that the performer is resting on one knee with the shin and instep adding to the support.

5. *V Seat (Balance Seat).* This consists in merely sitting on the floor with the legs elevated and straight. Thus the body assumes a V position. The hands may be on the floor behind the performer or raised out to the side.

6. *Double Elbow Lever.* See description and pictures in Chapter 3.

7. *Single Elbow Lever.* Similar to the two-arm version, except that the weight of the body is on one elbow. Steady the balance with the free hand and then lift it from the floor, holding it straight out in a line with the legs.

8. *Planche.* This stunt is started in a straddle position with the arms between the legs and with the fingers on the floor pointing backward. Lean forward slightly and lift the legs upward into the planche position as is pictured. Practice this stunt by placing the feet on low parallel bars and holding the position momentarily. Also, practice by lifting the legs up into the position and then holding only for a second, and so on. This is a difficult but very impressive stunt once learned.

9. *Hand Balance.* This is probably one of the most commonly used stunts. For techniques of learning an ordinary hand balance, refer to Chapter 3. There are many different methods of moving into the hand balance position, and some of them will be covered in the next section

PLANCHE

on strength balance moves. For greater difficulty, this stunt may be done with the following variations:

(a). *Wide Arm Hand Balance.* From an ordinary hand balance the arms are moved to a wide arm position by moving the hands to the sides with a finger-creeping movement.

(b). *Yogi Hand Balance.* After complete control of the hand balance position is reached, slowly bring the head forward between the arms and allow the hips to move in the opposite direction, with the legs piking downward slightly. This awkward-looking handstand has been named a Yogi handstand because of the unique position of head, hips, and legs.

(c). *One Arm Balance.* From an ordinary hand balance, slowly shift weight from two arms to one arm and at the same time lift the other hand slowly from the floor. Keep the balancing arm straight and strong with other hand ready to add support from the floor if necessary to maintain balance. The legs may be together or spread in a straddle position. Practice is the key to learning the one arm hand balance.

10. *L Seat On Hands.* From a sitting position with the hands on the floor at the side of the hips, lift the legs and

WIDE ARM HAND BALANCE

ONE ARM BALANCE

STRADDLE SEAT

BENT ARM PRESS TO HAND BALANCE

BENT ARM STRAIGHT LEG PRESS TO
HAND BALANCE

body upward and hold this L seat with the hands supporting the entire body.

11. *Straddle Seat On Hands.* Sit on the floor with the legs in a straddle position. Place the hands on the floor between the legs and then lift the entire body upward, supporting the weight by the hands and arms alone.

STRENGTH BALANCE MOVES

These stunts are generally called "presses," and as implied they consist in moving into balance position with an element of strength or power required.

1. *Squat Press to Head Balance.* From a squat balance with the knees resting on the elbows, place the head on the floor and slowly raise the hips and legs upward into a head balance.

2. *Bent Arm Straight Leg Press to Head Balance.* From a kneeling position, place the head on the floor and lift the hips upward, keeping the toes on the floor with the legs straight. From this pike position slowly lift the legs upward into a head balance position.

3. *Head Balance to Hand Balance.* From a head balance position bring the legs downward slightly so that the body is piked a little. From this position extend the legs upward and at the same time push hard with the arms. Continue upward until the body is in a hand balance position. A spotter can be of assistance on this stunt in lifting the hips upward into the hand balance position.

4. *Bent Arm Press to Hand Balance.* From a squat position on the floor press upward into a hand balance. The legs at the start of this stunt may be either between the arms or resting on the elbows. In pressing to the hand balance position be sure to move the hips upward and forward to a position above the hands and then extend the legs to a

full hand balance. A spotter can assist by holding the performer's hips and steadying them as the stunt is attempted.

5. *Bent Arm Straight Leg Press to Hand Balance.* From a pike position on the floor, with the arms bent and the hips high and toes resting on the floor, press upward with the legs straight into a handstand position. Be sure to move the hips forward and upward to a position above the hands before extending the legs upward.

6. *Ball Through Arms to Hand Balance.* Start from a sitting position on the floor with the hands at the side of the body. Elevate the body with the hands and then pull the knees into the chest and on through the arms. Continue the movement through and on up into the hand balance. This stunt can also be done supporting the weight on the fingers of the hands.

7. *Tiger Press.* From a forearm balance position lean forward, shifting the weight toward the hands, and then press upward into a hand balance position. This is a stunt that calls for great strength in the arms. A spotter can assist by grasping the performer's ankles and lifting upward.

8. *Arched Roll to Hand Balance or Head Balance.* Start by lying prone on the floor with the hands at the sides of the body near the hips. Lift the chest upward and from this position roll downward and forward onto the chest and up toward the hand balance. Remember to rock forward onto the hands and with the momentum of the roll push hard with the arms and finish in the hand balance or the more intermediate position of the head balance.

9. *Press to One Arm Handstand.* This stunt is done by only a few gymnasts, one being Gil Larose who is pictured here. Start by placing one hand in close

BALL THROUGH ARMS TO HAND BALANCE

PRESS TO ONE ARM HANDSTAND

STRAIGHT FALL

STRADDLE LEAP

to the forward foot with the other leg elevated toward the handstand position. From here press sideward into the one arm balance as is pictured and then hold for the required two seconds. Notice the position of the extended arm and the straddle legs to assist in holding the balance. This stunt is very difficult and requires considerable strength and balance for its final accomplishment.

AGILITY STUNTS

This area of floor exercise is one in which an imaginative person can create many new and different stunts of agility that fit in well with a floor exercise routine. These stunts generally arouse much interest and appreciation of participants as well as of spectators.

The following are a few of many stunts that can be done in this group:

1. *Pirouette*. From a standing position leap into the air, turning the head and shoulder to the left and pulling the right arm across the front of the chest, and execute a full turn (pirouette) of the body. Keep the body erect and straight throughout the turn. For more difficulty a double pirouette may be executed.

2. *Straight Fall.* This generally follows a tinsica or handspring. The momentum is simply continued, and the performer falls downward toward the floor with one leg elevated. The body is caught with the arms, and by flexing slowly and smoothly, the chest continues downward to the finish position.

3. *One Half Turn Fall.* From a standing position, fall backward and immediately execute a half turn to the left and continue to fall toward the floor with the front of the body facing the direction of the fall. Catch the weight of the body with the arms and flex them softly with the fall. Finish in the position of a straight fall. This stunt often follows a tumbling stunt such as a back somersault.

4. *Straddle Leap.* Leap into the air, raising legs in straddle position parallel to the floor, and touch the ankles with the hands or place the arms straight downward between the legs.

5. *Flying Leap.* Take off from one leg and leap into the air and execute a half turn of the body and land on the other foot in a balance position with the arms out to the side with the upper body parallel to the floor, similar to a forward scale.

6. *Single Leg Circle.* Start from a squat position with the hands on the floor in front of the body and with the left leg stretched out to the left side of the body. Bring the left leg forward and around in front of the body, lifting one arm at a time as the leg passes under. Continue the swing of the left leg behind and under the right leg, which is continually flexed, and finish up in the starting position. This stunt is generally done two or three times and thus has a pinwheel action. Be sure to keep the left leg straight, with the toes pointed, throughout the stunt.

SINGLE LEG CIRCLE

WIDE ARM FORWARD ROLL

BACK ROLL TO STRADDLE

7. *Single Leg Circle to Elbow Lever.* Execute two or three single leg circles and near the end of the final one extend the right leg back with the left and drop both hips into the elbows and finish in a double elbow lever.

8. *Back Roll to Straddle.* Execute a backward roll, and when the weight is on the hands spread the legs and continue the roll, finishing in a straddle stand position.

9. *Front Support with Full Turn.* From a front support position, with the arms straight and legs extended backward, push hard with the arms and at the same time bring one leg up slightly. Support the body on the flexed leg and execute a full turn of the body and land back on the hands again in a front support position.

10. *Wide Arm Forward Roll.* Do a forward roll with the arms out to the side, keeping them in this position throughout the roll and on up to the feet as is pictured in the three photos. This type of roll has been required for some international competition.

11. *Straight Leg Roll.* This consists in executing a forward roll with the legs straight throughout the stunt. It is important to push hard with the hands as the body completes the roll, because this helps the performer to roll up to his feet. Remember to keep the head and shoulders forward during the latter part of this stunt.

12. *Double Tap Handstand into Forward Roll.* Kick into a hand balance and immediately hop forward, with both hands maintaining the hand balance position, then execute a forward roll, with legs either straight or in a tuck position.

13. *Twisting Handstand into Forward Roll.* Kick up in a cartwheel action to a momentary one arm handstand. Then turn on the supporting arm, and after a

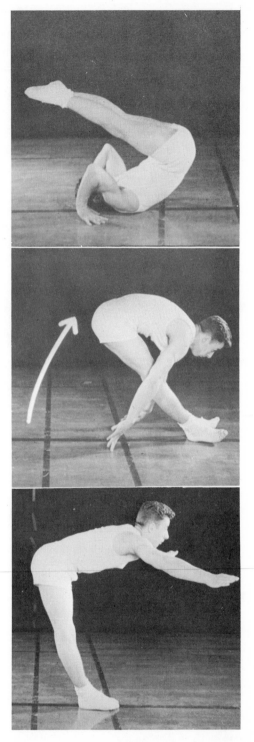

STRAIGHT LEG ROLL

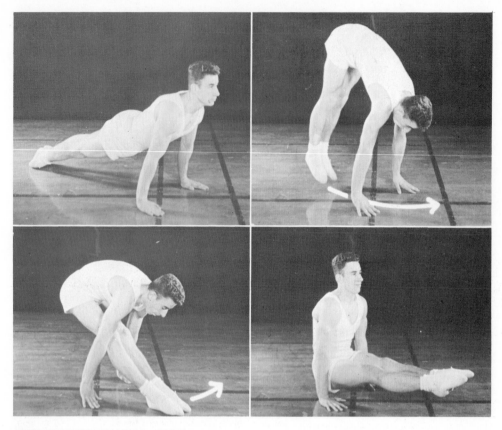

SHOOT THROUGH TO L SEAT

half turn is completed, execute a forward roll. This also can be done by placing the right arm across the body and on the floor with the fingers turned toward the left foot and in front of it. The left arm pulls inside of the right arm in front of the right foot, fingers facing it, and at the same time the body completes a half turn to the left and then a forward roll is executed.

14. *Shoot Through to L Seat*. From a front support position with the arms straight and legs extended backward, lower the hips slightly. Then raise the hips quickly and push with the hands. Shoot the legs through the arms and finish in an L sitting position, supporting the body with the arms.

15. *Headspring to Straddle Seat on Floor*. Execute a high headspring and immediately after the whip action has started, pike the body strongly and spread the legs and land on the floor in a straddle sitting position. Try this stunt several times on a mat before attempting it on the floor. It can also be done to a sitting position with legs together.

16. *Double Around to L Seat*. Start in a front rest position. Flex the hips slightly and then bring the legs around the left arm. Lift the hand as the legs pass under it and quickly drop it to the floor so as to catch the body in an L seat position. This can also be done by straddling the legs on outside of arms in passing them forward, landing in an L seat position.

17. *Half Twisting Back Dive to Roll.*

Start from a standing position and leap backward and execute a half turn of the body landing on the hands and continue into a forward roll. It is important to lift the legs and hips upward as the stunt is executed and then the forward roll can be done smoothly. A spotter can be of assistance by lifting up under the performer's hips during the first part of the stunt.

Variation: Upon completion of the back dive half twist, land on the hands and hold the hand stand position momentarily before going into the forward roll.

18. *Neckspring with Half Twist.* Execute a high neckspring, and immediately after the whip of the legs has started, execute a fast half twist. After the twist, land on both hands with the feet extended to a front resting position. It is important to do the spring high in order to complete a clean half twist.

19. *Cradle with One Half Twist.* Start out as a slow and deliberate back handspring. Upon landing on the hands, tuck the chin in toward the chest and lower the body slowly to the back of the neck and shoulders. At the same time, the legs swing up into a pike position similar to the start of a neckspring. Then whip the legs upward and forward, pushing hard with the hands, and execute a half twist of the body, landing on the hands, the legs and feet extended to a front resting position.

20. *Back Handspring to Hand Balance.* Execute a slow, deliberate and long back handspring, with the feeling of "just making it" to the hands. Stall the feet behind the body as much as possible, and after numerous attempts, the feeling of holding a balance position out of the back handspring will emerge.

21. *Valdez.* Start from a sitting position with the left hand placed on the floor behind the back, with the fingers

DOUBLE AROUND TO L SEAT

HALF TWISTING BACK DIVE TO ROLL

CRADLE WITH HALF TWIST

VALDEZ

pointed away from the body. Keep the right leg straight, with the left leg bent and the left foot near the buttocks. Raise the right hand over the head. With a push off the left foot, a throw backward of the right arm, and an upswing of the right leg, the performer executes a quick back bend motion into a hand balance position. It is imperative that a spotter be used while first learning this stunt.

FLEXIBILITY STUNTS

There are several stunts that are grouped in the flexibility category, and these stunts demand a great deal of looseness and suppleness of the joints and muscles. Many of these stunts are not particularly difficult, but they require time and constant practice to accomplish them.

1. *Regular Splits*. This simply consists of standing with one leg ahead of the other and slowly lowering the body downward into a split position. By placing the hands on the floor on each side of the body, a small cushioning effect is produced. This stunt can be done with the following variations:

    a. From a hand balance fall sideward to the split position.

    b. From a hand balance bring one leg through the arms to a split position.

    c. From a hand balance snap the feet down to the mat and then bounce back to the hands, lifting the legs upward, and upon landing on the hands, snap one leg through the arms to a split position.

    d. Back handspring to the feet and then back to the hands and immediately pass one leg through the arms to a split position as in variation "c."

    e. Back handspring into an immediate split position. Upon landing on the arms, bring one leg down quickly and pass it through the arms to a split position.

    f. Back somersault to a split position. Lift a backward somersault as high as possible and just prior to landing on the feet, move the legs apart and drop into a split position, catching the body with the hands.

2. *Straddle Splits*. Splitting action can be done sideward with the legs out to the sides, the upper body forward parallel to the floor, and the arms outstretched. This stunt may be combined very nicely with a front fall. After landing in a front fall position, bring one leg around to the side and twist the body in the same direction so that the straddle split position can be assumed.

3. *Head to Knees*. Start in a standing

REGULAR SPLIT

STRADDLE SPLIT

position and then bend forward and place the hands behind the thighs and continue bending forward until the head touches the knees or shins. Constant practice will produce the flexibility necessary for this stunt.

ROUTINES

Creativity, imagination, and resourcefulness can be developed in the sport of gymnastics by the individual's construction and performance of his own sequence of stunts. The following are suggestions of combinations that can be enlarged upon within the pupil's ability.

1. Start in corner, do side scale, and move on to cartwheel action into a handstand. Hold momentarily and drop into a forward roll (legs bent or straight). Stand and then run a few steps across area and execute a cartwheel and front handspring to a front fall. Bring one leg up under body to squat position with other leg straight behind and from here execute two single leg circles and then come to stand. Walk along side of area and do a double tap handstand into forward roll to a straddle stand position. Press to either a headstand or handstand, holding momentarily, then do a forward roll with bent knees into a lounge position into corner. Turn and finish with a run across diagonal of area and do a roundoff, bouncing into the air with a straddle leap to stand.

2. Start in corner and jump to handstand, immediately dropping to a chest roll, and then push to a straddle stand, bending forward with the arms outstretched parallel to floor. Press to a headstand or handstand and then do a forward roll to a stand. Along the side do a handspring and then a dive and roll to stand and then a front fall. Bring

one leg up under the chest and execute two single leg circles, then extend both legs back, resting on the toes, then whip both legs up and snap both feet to floor coming to a stand. Across the diagonal of the square do a front handspring into a headspring to a forward roll to headspring to straddle seat. Bring chest forward toward the knees and then sit up straight and execute a partial valdez to a stand on the feet. Do a front scale while in the corner and then turn and finish routine with a run along side and execute a roundoff–straddle leap into air to a stand.

3. Stand in corner at attention position. Swing arms in circular manner crossing in front of body and place right leg to side in straddle stand position with the arms out to the sides and the chest leaning forward parallel to the floor. Press to a handstand (bent arm press) and hold momentarily. Roll forward with legs straight or bent and then run a few steps to a roundoff–back handspring. Execute a half turn and drop to a front fall position. Place both feet back, dip hips slightly, and then whip hips up and over to a forward roll to sitting position. From here execute a valdez on to the feet and then along one side of the area do a front handspring, dive, and roll to a lunge position in corner. Lift one leg and execute a front scale. Place both feet on floor and then turn and face diagonal corner. Run and execute a roundoff–back handspring into a high bounce with legs into straddle position and then drop to a stand.

4. Stand in corner and do a jump to a handstand position into a forward roll and then back handspring to a stand. Run across the diagonal and execute a roundoff–back handspring–back flip to a backward roll to a stand in corner. Along the side do a running front somer-

sault to a diving forward roll, stepping into corner, and then execute a half turn to stand facing the center of the area. Place one leg to side into a straddle stand position (or do a split). Press to a handstand and roll forward to stand. Run toward far corner, executing a roundoff–back somersault.

5. Stand several feet from corner and do a back dive with half turn to a handstand position. Roll forward, turn around, and run diagonally and execute a roundoff–back handspring–back somersault–back handspring; snap the feet down and back to handstand to forward roll to another back handspring to feet, step toward corner and then with half turn swing into a handstand. Slowly lower the legs into a straddle position on the upper arms. From this position, lift legs back up to a handstand or simply drop back to the seat and execute a backward roll to feet. Along one side, run and execute a diving forward roll (with full twist if possible) and then do a front scale. Then turn and run diagonally to finish with a roundoff–back handspring–back somersault in pike position.

CHAPTER FIVE / *trampolining*

Trampolín is a Spanish word meaning "diving board" and refers to just that in many of the Latin American countries, Spain, and Mexico. In Germany the word refers to a springboard or to juggling. Little has been written about the beginning and the progress of the sport of trampolining. A French circus acrobat of the middle ages, whose name, "du Trampoline," may also be legendary, is said to have first started working on the springboard and leaping board and then visualized the possibility of doing tumbling stunts on the safety net suspended under the flying trapeze acts. He reduced the size of this net and then performed on it, with a unique repertoire of flips, twists, and turns. This net gradually was reduced to approximately its present size.

After this start, the trampoline grew in popularity and soon each circus had its "bounding bed" act.

After this initiation, many YMCA directors, physical education teachers, and gymnastic coaches adopted the main idea of the bounding-bed construction and built them for their gymnasiums and camps.

After some years of research and development, the "Nissen Trampoline" was patented and manufactured in quantity in 1939. At the present time several companies manufacture trampolines and different-sized models have been introduced.

The trampoline consists of a sturdily constructed table-high frame approximately 9′ x 15′, within which is attached, by means of elastic cord or metal springs, a heavy canvas or woven webbing sheet that serves as a performing surface. The junior-size trampoline stands about 2′ high and is about 5½′ x 9′. The giant-sized trampoline has a frame that is approximately 10′ x 17′.

In recent years trampolining has been accepted as an official event in national gymnastic meets. It has proven to be very popular with spectators as well as with participants. Competitive rules vary but at present can be summed up as follows: Competition is composed of one sequence or routine consisting of at least eleven principal parts, which is the same as eleven stunts. The routine must include forward and backward twisting and somersaulting along with bed work other than the feet.

TRAMPOLINE

values

The specific values of working the trampoline are:

1. More than in any other activity, trampolining develops a sense of relocation.

2. The many movements made while in the air display the development of timing, rhythm, and coordination.

3. Trampolining requires and develops confidence and self-reliance.

4. The trampoline, along with tumbling, excels among gymnastics activities in developing the legs.

5. Trampolining is one of the most enjoyed activities in gymnastics. Perhaps the inherent desire to bounce, or the ease with which the bouncing is done, is responsible for the fun in participating in this activity. Enjoyment motivates intensive participation.

organization

AREA AND EQUIPMENT

The trampoline can be used in a class without occupying too much space. Just a few feet of space on each side of the trampoline is all that is needed, although the ceiling should be of sufficient height to allow free bouncing. Depending somewhat on the age of the class, the minimum ceiling height should probably be about 15'. The area immediately surrounding the trampoline should be clear of obstacles that would hurt a person falling off the device. If sufficient mats are available, an additional safety precaution would be to put mats on the floor around the trampoline.

If more than one trampoline is available for the class, it would be advisable to put them a few feet apart and parallel to one another. This would concentrate the activity in one area. Wherever the activity is located in the gymnasium, it should be within clear view of the teacher. Sometimes it is helpful to have a platform between two trampolines the same height as the trampolines. This would allow close supervision of a class involving only two trampolines.

TEACHING METHODS

If the trampoline instruction is to be profitable, there should be no more than six to ten students to each trampoline. Any more than ten will prevent the students from getting enough time during the class period to practice the stunts. If the class is too large for the number of trampolines, other gymnastic activities could be carried on elsewhere. This would be done best by dividing the class into squads and rotating the squads during the period.

One of the problems facing the instructor is organizing for best use of the trampoline by the class. Too often an instructor will allow one student to monopolize this equipment while the other students only stand and watch. The watchers lose interest and are apt to engage in "horseplay." The following suggestions may aid in efficient organization:

1. Make it clear that those standing around the trampoline are spotters and have an important job to perform.

2. Plan your schedule beforehand to insure that each student will have some time to practice on the equipment. A system of rotating the students from spotter to performer back to spotter is highly advisable.

3. Practice one stunt at a time. It is much wiser to have all students in your group learn at least one stunt than have part of the group learn several while the remainder have learned nothing. A good rule of thumb for beginners is to allow no more than thirty seconds per man per turn. In this way you are sure to give everyone a chance to perform.

Demonstrations should progress from the simple stunts to the more difficult. Sufficient time should be spent on each stunt before the student is allowed to progress to the next. However, this may become a problem because some students may have more ability than others and consequently will progress faster.

You probably will find it advisable to rearrange the group so that you are teaching groups of equal ability rather than groups of unequal ability. This not only makes teaching easier but creates a better learning situation for your students.

As an instructor, undoubtedly you have some degree of proficiency in trampoline stunts. This should enable you to perform your demonstrations easily, but remember that because it is easy for you to demonstrate, it is not as easy for the beginning student to follow the demonstration. Accordingly, you should demonstrate the stunt several times until you are sure the students have grasped what you are trying to show them. While this may take a bit more time initially, in the long run it is quicker. After you have demonstrated a stunt, be sure to ask the group if they understand what they are going to try to do. Once the group appears to have grasped the point of the demonstration, give them the opportunity to practice the stunt. Don't start another demonstration—you will only confuse them.

Because trampolining is a self-testing activity, it is probably best evaluated by some form of stunt chart. Attractive, well-kept charts are good for motivating the students also. If checking individual stunts is too time-consuming, well-spaced routines could be used to check achievement and progress. For more advanced classes, it would be possible to judge the students in competitive routines, taking into account form and continuity as well as difficulty.

SAFETY

One precaution that should be noted in trampolining is safety. This does not mean trampolining is dangerous. If properly used, the trampoline is not. Instructors should remember that the dangerous element in trampolining is the illusion of foolproofness that is created by the soft springy bed. Students may easily get the feeling that they cannot get hurt. This can lead to taking unnecessary chances and result in injury. Showing off can be dangerous. If, however, you closely supervise trampoline activities, these stunts can be learned with little or no danger.

Good equipment properly maintained is basic to all other safety precautions. Trampolines are sturdy, well-constructed pieces of equipment, built to last for many years, but like all other types of equipment, misuse can damage them. Therefore, it is important that you as instructor take precautions to insure that they are used properly. The following points should prove to be of value:

1. The trampoline should never be left unsupervised. When you have finished with it, it should be folded up and stored away. Too often, trampolines have been damaged and people hurt because the trampoline was left out and was used by inexperienced students who thought it would be fun to bounce on.

2. Never allow students to wear street shoes when using the trampoline.

3. "Horseplay" should never be allowed on a trampoline—it is not designed for such use.

4. Inspect the trampoline before and after it has been used. This not only protects the trampoline from further damage, but is an excellent means of preventing accidents.

As to actually conducting the class for trampolining, there are some basic safety hints that should be adhered to:

1. There should be a minimum of two spotters, one at each end of the trampoline. If more are available, space them around the trampoline.

2. Safety pads should be provided for the metal frame of the trampoline.

3. The progressive order of learning the stunts should be closely adhered to.

4. Learn early how to "stop" the bounce by flexing the knees immediately upon landing on the canvas. This will prevent an uncontrolled bounce off the bed.

5. To prevent possible injury, come to a complete stop before dismounting and place your hands on the frame to support yourself as you crawl off.

6. Remember that in bouncing, control is more important than height.

7. To prevent losing control the trampolinist should bounce for short periods of time.

8. Horseplay should not be tolerated.

9. Not more than one student should bounce until after they have become proficient at single trampolining.

10. A hand or overhead safety belt should be used in learning the more difficult stunts.

program of instruction

Instruction on the trampoline involves three basic steps:

1. Individual Stunts.

2. Combinations. As a person learns a new stunt, he should be challenged to combine it with another stunt as smoothly as possible. Because a stunt must be learned well in order to combine it with another, the use of combinations in the teaching progression stresses proper execution and increases the safety of performance. In addition, the smaller combinations serve as building blocks for longer routines. Combinations can be suggested by the instructor or coach or can be created by the performer.

3. Routines. Ultimately, a pupil should strive to combine stunts into a routine.

HALF PIROUETTE

Competition is based on routines, required or optional. The approach to optional routines is one of problem solving. Certain requirements involving the types and number of movements are presented as a problem for the performer to solve creatively within his own capabilities. The instructor, coach, and pupil can coordinate their thoughts on the development of a particular routine. For sample routines refer to the end of the chapter.

Before beginning a discussion of the stunts, it is important to understand the basic trampoline activity of bouncing. Bouncing on the canvas of the trampoline is similar to bouncing on a spring board or diving board. The feet should be kept about shoulder width apart while on the bed. The legs should be kept together while in the air. The knees should be bent slightly when contacting the canvas and the legs straightened while in the air. One should lift with the arms on the upward bounce of the body and drop the arms when coming down in preparation for the next upward bounce. The body should be kept straight, the head up and eyes forward.

Some preliminary bounces and lead-up stunts before actually attempting the trampoline stunts are as follows:

1. *Half Pirouette.* Bounce straight up into the air and execute a half turn, twist, or pirouette so that the body is facing the opposite direction upon landing. In twisting, pull one hand across the waist and the other hand behind the head.

2. *Full Pirouette.* Same as the half pirouette except complete a full turn.

3. *Tuck Bounce.* Bounce straight up, and when off the bed draw the knees up to the chest and grasp the shins with the hands. This places the body in a tuck or ball position. On the way down release the tuck and land in a standing position.

4. *Pike Bounce.* Bounce straight up, and while in the air lift the legs so they are parallel to the bed. While in this position the hands should touch the ankles. Remember to keep the legs straight throughout the performance of this stunt. On the way down snap the legs down and land in a standing position. A variation of this stunt is to spread the

legs in straddle position while in the air.

These few preliminary bounces and lead-up tricks serve as "feelers" and will aid tremendously in acquiring confidence and courage for the more advanced stunts.

5. *Seat Drop.* Land on the bed in a sitting position with the legs fully extended forward so the entire back of the legs contacts the canvas simultaneously. The trunk is slightly inclined backward from the vertical. Hands are flat on the bed 6 to 8 inches in back and to the side of the hips, with the fingers pointed toward the feet with the arms slightly bent. Return to the feet. In first learning, try from a low bounce and also spread the legs when landing in the seat drop.

6. *Front Drop.* Land on the bed in a prone position. Extend the arms forward with the elbows extended sideward and the palms of the hands downward. The following contact points should land simultaneously: palms, forearms, abdomen, and thighs. Try this first from a hands-and-knees position and then from an upright standing position.

7. *Back Drop.* Land on the bed in supine position with the legs straight and vertically inclined. Place the hands

TUCK BOUNCE

PIKE BOUNCE

SEAT DROP

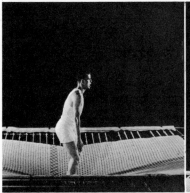

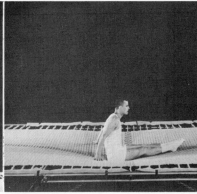

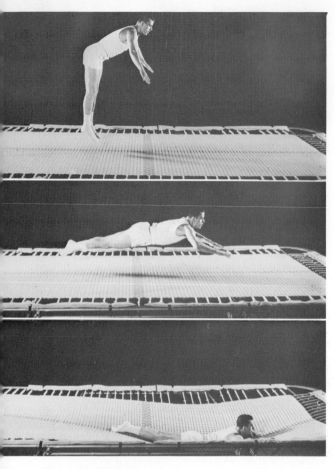

FRONT DROP

BACK DROP

either on the thighs or free of the legs but near them. Keep the chin on the chest. Try the first few by leaning backward from a standing position and lift one leg up to help tip the body into the back drop position.

8. *Knee Drop.* Land on the bed in a kneeling position with the contact point being the knees, shins, and instep. Be sure to keep the body directly above the knees when landing in the knee drop position. In first learning this stunt keep the bounce extremely low and do not allow the back to arch too much upon landing on the knees. An arched back has a tendency to snap the performer forward, which results in a strain of the back muscles.

9. *Half Twist to Back Drop.* Begin as if going into a front drop and on leaving the bed throw one arm across the waist and turn the head in the same direction, thus twisting the body into a half turn. Land in a back drop position.

10. *Half Twist to Front Drop.* Start as if going into a back drop and on leaving the bed execute a half twist of the body by pulling one shoulder back and piking the body slightly. Look into the twist and when facing the bed extend the legs and prepare for the front drop position.

11. *Back Drop to Front Drop.* In first trying this stunt it is suggested to do a back drop and shoot forward to a hands-and-knees position. This should be tried several times before attempting the final stunt. It is important to obtain a solid landing in the back drop position with the legs up at an open pike position. From this position a kip or kick is obtained by extending the legs forcefully forward and upward. Upon leaving the bed, the shoulders are rolled forward and the legs are tucked under the body. When the body has rolled over to an almost parallel position above the bed,

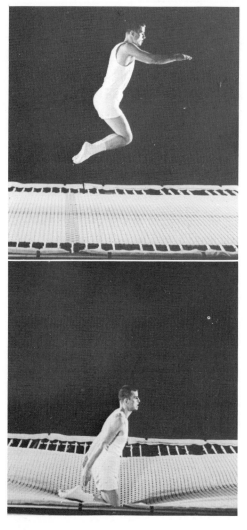

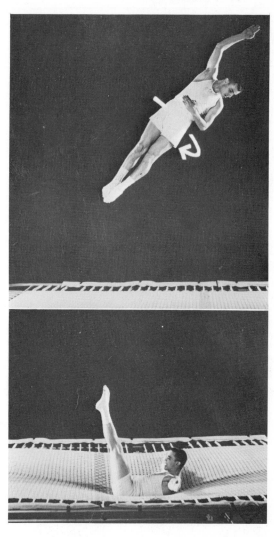

KNEE DROP

HALF TWIST TO BACK DROP

HALF TWIST TO FRONT DROP

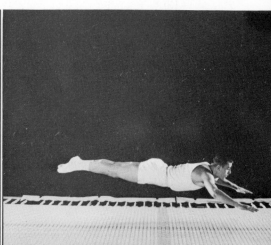

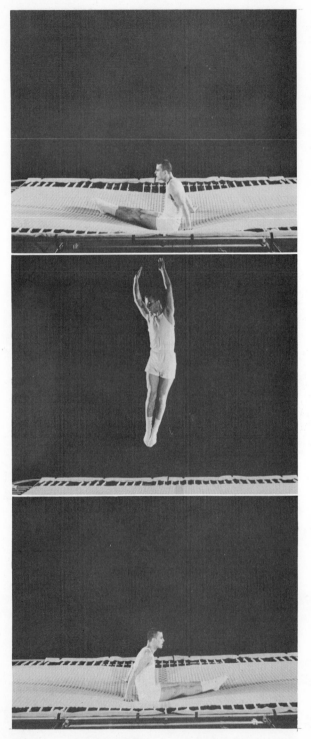

SWIVEL HIPS

extend the legs backward and place the arms forward and sideward in preparation for the front drop position.

12. *Front Drop to Back Drop.* From a front drop landing, push with the forearms and thrust the body backward by tucking the legs into the chest and forcing the chest backwards. Continue on over until in back drop position and then open the tuck and land on the back.

13. *Basic Routines.* At this stage of your learning program you are ready to try to put a few of these basic stunts into small routines. Some of these are:

    a. Seat Drop–Knee Drop–Seat Drop-Feet
    b. Front Drop–Knee Drop–Seat Drop–Knee Drop–Front Drop
    c. Knee Drop–Half Twist–Seat Drop
    d. Front Drop–Seat Drop–Front Drop–Feet
    e. Front Drop–Half Twist–Seat Drop
    f. Front Drop–Half Twist–Back Drop
    g. Back Drop–Half Twist–Front Drop
    h. Knee Drop–Seat Drop–All Fours–Front Drop–Back Drop–Feet

14. *Swivel Hips.* From a seat drop landing lift the arms over the head and extend the legs downward. Twist the hips a half turn and swing the legs under the body in a pendulum fashion. After the half twist is finished, flex the hips into a seat drop position and land on the seat. For the first few times do a seat drop and execute a half twist, land on the feet, and then continue on to another seat drop. Do this several times until the "feel" of the stunt is acquired and then attempt the entire swivel hips.

15. *Seat Full Twist to Seat.* This stunt is first done from a sitting position on the bed. The body is rotated in the direction of the twist and the hands are placed on the bed near the hips in the direction of the twist. The hands support the body and the complete full twist is

SEAT FULL TWIST TO SEAT

executed and the seat drop position is again assumed. This should be done several times to acquire the feel of the full twist. The seat drop full twist to seat drop is done from a standing position, then drop to a seat drop landing in a slightly leaning backward position. Extend the body and go into the twist by thrusting one arm across the waist with the other arm behind the hips. Keep the body extended throughout the twist and upon completing the twist, pike the body and land in a seat drop position.

16. *Front Dive to Back Drop.* This consists of diving over to a back drop landing. Remember to keep your eyes on the bed until about two feet above it and then duck the head and land on the shoulders. Keep the hips forward so that a good back drop landing is obtained.

17. *Half Turntable.* After landing in a front drop position turn in one direction by pushing hard with the arms in the opposite direction of this turn. Upon bouncing off the bed, tuck the knees into the chest, keep the head low, and look

HALF TURNTABLE

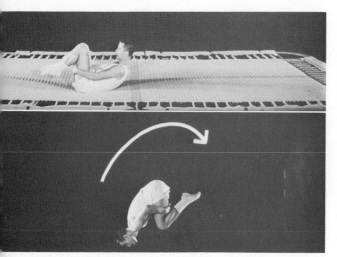

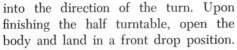

BACK PULLOVER

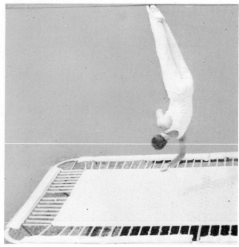

BACK PULLOVER: VARIATION WITH
HALF TWIST

into the direction of the turn. Upon finishing the half turntable, open the body and land in a front drop position.

For those having difficulty learning this stunt try a one quarter turntable and then progress to the one half turntable. For greater difficulty try a complete turn of the body, thus executing a full turntable. This stunt involves a good push with the hands and a tight tuck of the body to complete the 360° turn.

18. *Back Pullover.* This stunt is a back drop or hip landing and a pull backward into a back pullover to the feet. In first learning this stunt, try several backward rolls from a squat position. Place the hands over the shoulder on the first few tries to assist in pushing the body over the head. After the backward roll has been done satisfactorily several times, then the same roll is done from a standing position. The technique here is simply to squat and roll on over into a backward roll. With the standing start the body generally obtains a small bounce on landing on the hips prior to the backward roll. After a few of these have been attempted, then try with a

couple of bounces. Land on the hips in a slightly tucked position. From this position pull back under the thighs with the hands and continue on over to the feet. Gradually increase the height of the bounce as the stunt becomes perfected.

This stunt has several variations, including back pullover to a front drop; back pullover to a back drop landing; and a back pullover with one half twist to back drop.

19. *Cradle.* This stunt is started from a back drop landing, and as the body bounces forward, as if rolling over to a front drop position, one arm is thrust across the waist and the head is turned into the direction of the arm thrust and a half twist is executed. The stunt continues into a backdrop landing. It might be helpful to learn this in two stages: back drop to feet continuing on forward with one half twist to back drop.

20. *Front Somersault.* It is suggested that the front somersault be learned from an all-fours landing and then the knee drop landing. However, before this, several forward rolls should be done to ac-

quire the feeling for the somersault. Then try it from an all-fours landing. Simply land in a "doggie" position and duck the head and turn over to the back. Next try it from a knee drop landing. Upon landing on the knees with the arms over the shoulders, throw the arms forward and under and duck the head turning the body over into the somersault. Remember in executing the front somersault from the knees to the feet to lift the arms up and forward as the legs drive down into the bed. Look into the direction of the flip and then grasp the shins with the hands and pull the knees into the chest into a tight tuck. Hold on to the tuck until the somersault is almost

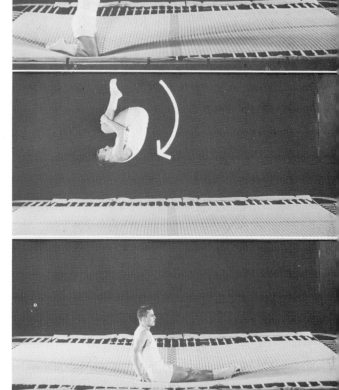

FRONT SOMERSAULT

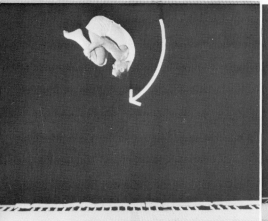

KNEE FRONT SOMERSAULT

HAND SPOTTING

SAFETY BELT SPOTTING

BACK SOMERSAULT

completed and then extend the legs downward toward the bed, leaving the arms up and forward of the chest. Next do the front somersault from the feet. This may be accompanied by a spotter, bouncing along with the performer or using a safety belt.

21. *Back Somersault.* On the take-off, raise the chest into the air and press away from the bed with the legs and at the same time lift the arms up past the chest and tilt the head backward to look into the back somersault. After leaving the bed, bring the knees up to the hands and the hands should grasp the shins and pull the body into a tight tuck. Continue the back somersault and when the somersault is near completion release the tuck and extend the legs downward for the landing. A preliminary move for a back somersault is to have a spotter stand on the bed to the side of the performer with the right hand behind the performer's neck and the left hand holding at the hips. Have performer lift into the air in a facsimile of a back somersault, but the spotter should hold the performer and place him back to the bed in the direction from which he came. The performer goes through the action of placing his head back, eyes looking toward the ceiling, arms and knees up toward the chest. The spotter momentarily holds the performer in this tuck position and then pushes him back to the bed in the direction he came, landing on his feet. After several of these are attempted, the performer should attempt the entire stunt, with adequate spotting. Another method similar to the one described above is for the spotter to stand on the bed directly behind the performer, with his hands on the waist. Use the same technique of holding the performer in the air while he has his head back, arms up, knees to the chest, and

74

PRELIMINARY TECHNIQUE FOR LEARNING BACK SOMERSAULT

so on. Again the performer is pushed back to the bed in the direction he came.

22. *Barani.* A barani is a front somersault in a pike position with a half twist. The best way to learn this is by doing a knee bounce and going into a handstand and executing a half twist and continuing over to a knee drop position again. This is somewhat like a roundoff from the knees. After doing this several times, try to finish on the feet. Remember in doing this stunt to get a strong lift of the hips at the start and thrust the body into a good forward momentum movement before executing the half twist. Be sure that the legs describe an arc over the head and not to the sides as is often the case with beginners. Next try the round-off from the knees to the knees without touching the hands, and the stunt will then be a knee barani. Do several of these and finally try the barani from the knees to the feet and then attempt the final stunt, which is the barani from the feet to the feet.

KNEE BARANI TOUCHING HANDS

KNEE BARANI

BARANI

There are several other ways that the barani can be learned and these will be mentioned briefly.

One method is to try a front somersault with a half twist using the twisting belt. By doing the front somersault in pike position and then executing a sharp half twist, a barani can be learned. Because this stunt is somewhat "blind," the twisting belt is essential for safety.

Another proven method is for two persons to stand on the bed facing the same direction, grasping hands behind the front person's hips. The forward person then does a front somersault through the arms of the spotter. After the somersault has passed through the arms, the spotter crosses his arms, which in turn twists the performer into a half twist or barani action. The performer then continues the flip and finishes facing the spotter.

Another method is to have the spotter stand to the left side of the performer, with his right hand partially under the waist and the left hand behind the neck. After the third bounce, the performer starts into the barani action and the spotter pushes downward with the left hand and holds the performer up slightly with the right hand. After the initial forward barani action has started, the spotter then places both hands on the hips of the performer and actually turns and assists the execution of the barani motion. This should be tried after the performer has tried several knee baranies, touching the hands, and even the two-foot barani again, touching the hands so the general feeling of the forward motion and the twist is established.

23. *Three-Quarter Back Somersault to Front Drop.* This consists in doing a back somersault for three quarters of the way over and then landing in a front drop. In trying this stunt for the first time, land on the hands and knees instead of the stomach. This will prevent unnecessary jarring or straining of the back because of improper landing. On the take-off the arms are lifted straight up, and the hips seem to slide forward and upward. The head goes back to look into the stunt. Try to spot the stunt and open up flat for the front drop landing.

24. *Front One-and-One Quarter Somersault to Front Drop.* Try a few front

HAND SPOTTING OF BARANI

somersaults that are turned a little too far and land on the feet leaning forward. After acquiring the feeling of going a little too far on a front somersault then try the complete stunt. Hold on to the tuck a little beyond the opening point for a front somersault and extend the legs backward and thrust the arms forward in preparation for the front drop landing. It is suggested that this stunt be learned with the use of an overhead safety belt. For more difficulty, a half twist just before finishing will put the performer in a back drop position.

25. *Back One-and-One Quarter Somersault to Seat Drop.* Execute a back somersault and hold on to the tuck a little beyond the point of opening up to the feet. Upon reaching this point, extend the legs forward and place the hands behind the hips and keep the shoulders forward. Land in a seat drop position.

26. *Back One-and-One Quarter Somersault to a Back Pullover.* Complete a back somersault and continue toward a seat drop position but land on the hips

with the body in a semi-tuck position. From this landing, continue into a back pullover to the feet. Pull with the hands under the thighs upon landing on the hips as this aids in completing the pullover.

27. *Kaboom.* In doing this stunt, land in an extended backdrop position with the legs raised about a foot above the

FRONT 1 1/4 TO FRONT DROP

FULL TWISTING BACK SOMERSAULT

bed. Immediately upon landing on the back, drive the heels forcefully into the bed keeping the legs straight. The heels bounding into the bed serve to toss the body backward into a flip. Upon leaving the bed, the knees are brought into the chest and the kaboom is completed.

28. *Cody.* This stunt is a back somersault executed from a front drop position. Upon landing on the stomach, get a feeling of sinking low into the bed. The knees should be bent. Push hard with the arms and force the chest up and back. Upon leaving the bed, grasp the shins and pull the body backward into a tight tuck. Complete the somersault to the feet. This can be done easier after a three-quarter back somersault to the stomach.

29. *Twisting Backward Somersault.* The basic mechanics of the full twisting, double twisting, and triple twisting somersaults are very similar. The take-off for all three twists resembles the take-off for a back somersault layout. As the number of twists is increased (full, double, triple) the somersault should become more stalled. On the take-off, the arms should lift straight over the head, a little further apart than shoulder width. There should be very little bend at the elbows. The straight-arm position will give more force and momentum to the twist when the arms are finally folded into the body. When the arms are extended all the way overhead before a twist to the left, the right arm should be pushed out to the side and swept across the abdomen up toward the chest. The performer should think of keeping his elbow straight at the beginning of the sweep and as the arm reaches across the left side of the body, it should be folded into the chest. The tighter the arm is drawn to the chest, the more force the twist will have. Little

force is required for the full twisting back somersault.

Simultaneous with the right-arm sweep is the movement of the left arm, which is bent slightly and forced backward and down in the direction of the twist. As the twist progresses, the left hand and arm are folded into a position directly in front of the chest. As mentioned before, a tight wrap-up of both arms will increase the speed of the twist.

Upon completion of the twist, the arms are thrust forcefully from the body, which serves as a means of stopping the twisting action.

It is highly recommended that a twisting belt be used in learning the twisting back somersault.

Remember while twisting to keep the body in a firm position with toes pointed, legs straight, stomach taut, and so on. A sloppy, loose appearance is undesirable for its own sake as well as for its interference with the performance.

30. *Back Drop Ball Out to the Feet.* Land on the back and get a sharp kick off the bed by extending the legs quickly. After the initial start, pull the body into a ball and complete the somersault to the feet. For the first few times the performer will land in a seat drop position but finally will finish in a standing position. This may also be done from a dive to a back drop landing and from there into the one and one-quarter somersault (or ball-out) to the feet.

31. *Front One and Three-Quarter Somersault to Back Drop into Front One and One-Quarter Somersault to Feet.* After the completion of the first somersault, continue the spin but attempt to see the bed for just a fraction of a second; then duck the head and land in a

DOUBLE-TWISTING BACK SOMERSAULT

DOUBLE BACK SOMERSAULT

back drop position. From the back drop position execute a front one and one-quarter somersault to the feet. The last one and one-quarter should be tried alone at first, either from a high dive to the back drop and then the stunt, or from a back drop bounce into the front one and one-quarter to the feet as previously explained. For safety's sake, the one and three-quarter front should first be attempted in an overhead safety belt.

32. *Back Double Somersault.* After a power take-off, lifting the chest and arms into the air with the head up, bring the knees forcefully up toward the chest. The hands then grasp the shins and pull the body into a tight ball. Continue the backward spin until the second somersault is almost completed, then open the tuck by releasing the knees and dropping to the feet. This stunt should be learned in an overhead safety belt. To accelerate the somersault action, bring the head into the chest after the initial revolution has begun. This serves to tighten the ball or tuck, which will increase the speed.

33. *Rudolph.* Start the somersault in a slightly piked position with the arms out to the sides. After the body is well in the air throw one arm down and across the front of the thighs and continue upward toward the chest with the other arm pushing backward. Turn the head in the direction of the twist. The body extends to a straight layout position while it is twisting and then pikes downward to the bed for the finish. To stop the twist thrust the arms out to the sides after the one and one-half twist is completed. This stunt is done best by lifting the somersault almost straight up, which gives the performer the feeling of underturning (or stalling) the somersault. The use of a twisting belt is advisable in learning this stunt.

34. *Randolph.* This stunt is similar to the one and one-half twisting front somersault except another full twist is added. Height and a more pronounced stall of the somersault is necessary for the accomplishment of this stunt, along with a tighter pull of the arms into the body for a faster twist.

35. *Fliffis.* A fliffis is a combination of a double somersault backward or forward with a twist added. Because of the difficulty of these stunts it is advisable to use an overhead twisting belt in learning. Some of the possible combinations are:

(a.) *Front Fliffis with Late Twist*
(Late Fliffis)

Do a double front somersault, and on the second flip execute a one-half twist. To learn this in an overhead twisting belt try a front one and one-half somersault and open up with the body suspended above the trampoline by means of the belt. At this point the one-half twist is executed and the entire trick is then completed. Try the entire stunt by doing a fast one and one-half flip and then look for the canvas and at the same time execute a one-half twist to the feet. A slight forward lean into the stunt is helpful. After numerous successful completions in the belt, try it without the belt. The following are some preliminary stunts or progressive steps in learning the stunt:

1. Do several low and fast twisting baranies.
2. Do several one and three-quarter somersaults to back drop so that you can see the opening spot for the half twist.
3. Do several back drop ball outs with barani twist to feet.
4. Do the stunt with the use of the twisting belt.

(b.) *Front Fliffis with Early Twist*
(Early Fliffis)

Execute a barani and then quickly grab a tuck and go directly into a backward flip. This makes for a double front somersault with a one-half twist on the first flip. Some progressive steps in learning this Fliffis:

1. Do several baranies.

RUDOLPH

BARANI OUT FLIFFIS (LATE FLIFFIS)

2. Do several baranies to a back drop into a back pullover. Do this stunt low and hard. Try this several times and after you have the twisting movement perfected, try the entire stunt in the overhead belt.

(c.) *Back Full Fliffis*
(Early full twist)

This is a double back somersault with a full twist in the first flip. This is done by forcing an overturning full twisting back flip into a tuck back flip to the feet. The progressive stunts are:

1. Do several back full twisting somersaults to a back drop back pullover.
2. Try the complete stunt in the twisting belt.

(d.) *Back Full Fliffis*
(Half In-Half Out Fliffis)

This is a back double somersault with a half twist in the first somersault and a one-half twist on the second somersault. To accomplish this stunt do an overflipping one-half twisting back somersault followed with another one-half twisting flip of the barani type. In short this is a half twisting back somersault with a barani out to the feet. The progressive stunts are:

1. Do several overflipping half twisting back somersaults to the stomach.
2. Continue the stunt mentioned above but carry it over to the back.
3. Try the complete stunt in the twisting belt.

(e.) *Early One and One-Half Twisting Front Fliffis.*

This consists in doing a double front somersault with a one and one-half twist on the first somersault followed immediately with a back somersault. Progressive stunts are:

1. Do several overflipping one and one-half twisting front somersaults to a back drop back pullover (Rudolph to a back pullover).
2. Try the complete stunt in the twisting belt.

(f.) *Late One and One-Half Twisting Front Fliffis.*

This consists in doing a double front somersault with a one and one-half twist on the second somersault. The progressive stunts are:

1. Do several front one and three-quarter somersaults to the shoulders with a Barani ball-out.

HALF IN-HALF OUT FLIFFIS

RUDOLPH FLIFFIS

BACK 1 3/4 SOMERSAULT TO FRONT
DROP TO DOUBLE CODY

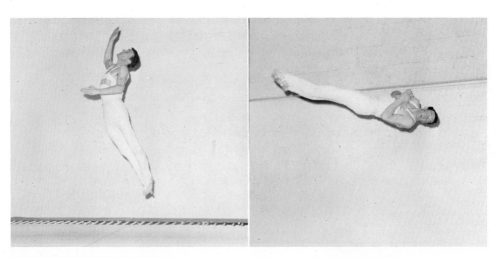

DOUBLE TWISTING CODY

2. Try the same stunt, but instead of a Barani ball-out execute a one and one-half twisting somersault to the feet.

3. Try the complete stunt in the twisting belt.

(g.) *Double Full Fliffis*

Execute a back one and one-half twisting somersault and then on the second flip do a barani to the feet. The lead-up for this is a back one and three-quarter somersault with an early one and one-half twist; land in a back drop position. Then try entire stunt in the belt.

36. *Back One and Three-Quarter Somersault to Front Drop to Double Cody.* When the body is near the one and one-half somersault spot open the tuck by extending the legs sharply upward and the chest downward. Keep the body in a straight or even very slightly piked position as it continues to rotate towards the front drop landing on the bed. Just prior to landing on the bed bend the knees thus landing in a full front drop position with the hands to the side of the shoulders, stomach full into the bed and the knees bent. From this position the technique is similar to the cody somersault discussed previously only the push is somewhat harder and with the added height the double cody is executed.

37. *Double Twisting Cody.* Upon landing on the front drop from a back one and three-quarter somersault the cody is started in a layout position. After the body has moved well into the cody somersault the arm is swung across the chest with the opposite shoulder moving backward into the direction of the twist. Upon completion of the single or double twisting cody pike the body sharply downward to the bed. Common fault on the twisting cody is to start the twist too soon which hinders the somersault

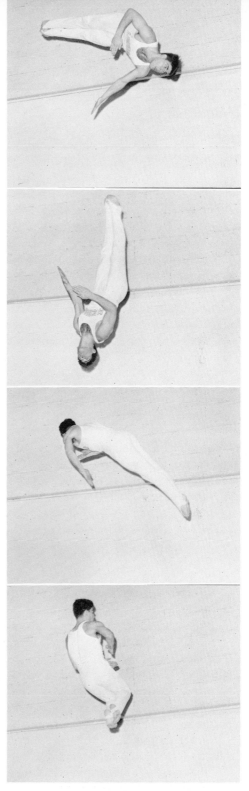

FORWARD DOUBLE SOMERSAULT
WITH BARANI IN AND FULL
TWIST OUT

action resulting in a landing on the face, all fours, etc.

38. *Barani in Full Twist Out Double Somersault.* Consists of executing a fast barani in the first somersault with the legs in pike position and then continuing the twist with a back somersault with a full twist. It is imperative that the barani and the full twist are done in the same direction. The position of the legs in the full twisting back somersault are drawn up towards the stomach (puck position) in order to increase rotation of the 2nd somersault. It can also be executed with the legs bent in the barani and straight in the full twisting second somersault. As skill increases attempt both somersaults with legs straight in pike position.

ROUTINES

Creativity, imagination, and resourcefulness can be developed in the sport of gymnastics by the individual's construction and performance of his own sequence of stunts. The following are simply suggestions of combinations that certainly can be enlarged upon within the pupil's ability:

1. Knees—Seat—Swivel Hips—All Fours—Front Drop—Half Turntable —Back Drop—Cradle—Feet.
2. Back Pullover—Feet—Seat Drop— Swivel Hips—Knee Drop—Front Somersault to feet.
3. Back somersault (tuck)—barani— tuck bounce—half twist to back drop—half twist to feet—straddle leap—three-quarter back layout to front drop to full turntable to feet.
4. Rudolph—back somersault (tuck)— barani—back (tuck)—back somersault layout position with full twist —barani—three-quarter back somersault to front drop to cody (tuck).

5. Fliffis—barani—back somersault— double back—rudolph—back somersault—back with double twist—back —forward one and three-quarter to back drop with barani (or rudolph)—ball-out to feet.

Continue general theme of increasing difficulty as performer gains in proficiency.

Good luck and finish those routines with top form!

Examples of two routines that were required for a recent world trampoline meet:

COMPULSORY EXERCISE MEN

1. Double back somersault. (tuck)
2. Barani to back landing.
3. ¾ back somersault. (Back pull over) (pike)
4. Back Somersault. (tuck)
5. 1½ twisting front somersault.
6. Back somersault. (pike)
7. Back somersault with full twist.
8. Barani. (pike)
9. ¾ back somersault to stomach. (layout)
10. 1¼ back somersault. (cody) (free)

COMPULSORY EXERCISE WOMEN

1. 1¼ back somersault to back. (tuck)
2. Forward ½ somersault ½ twist to back.
3. ¾ back somersault. (back pull over) (tuck)
4. Back somersault. (tuck)
5. 1½ twisting-front-somersault.
6. Back somersault. (pike)
7. Back somersault with full twist.
8. Barani. (pike)
9. ¾ Back somersault. (layout)
10. 1¼ back somersault. (cody) (free)

CHAPTER SIX / *side and long horse*

Friedrich Jahn is credited with inventing the side horse with pommels in the early 1800's. This apparatus lends itself both to vaulting and to support work. The vaulting phase is somewhat easier and less dependent upon strength and as a result generally precedes the support work.

The side horse is a leather-covered cylindrical body of about 14 inches in diameter and 60 to 63 inches in length. The horse has two pommels or handles near the center about 17 to 18 inches apart. The height of the horse may be adjusted from approximately 3' to 5', although the regulation height for competitive purposes is 4' to the top of the pommels.

The long horse is the same as the side horse with the pommels removed; as the name implies, it is used along its length, instead of across. In competition, the height from the floor to the top of the horse is 4'5".

Organized competition for men is held in long horse vaulting and side horse support work. In the former the gymnast executes two different vaults with the better of the two scores counting. This event differs from the others in that the judge considers form only, the difficulty having been predetermined from a table of difficulties. The side horse support work competition consists of swinging movements, without stops or holding of position, and scissors, forward and backward (one of these at least twice in succession). All three parts of the horse must be used and double leg circles must predominate.

values

The specific values of working the side horse are:

1. Side horse work develops strength

THE SIDE HORSE

in the upper part of the body, particularly the arms and shoulders.

2. A person needs agility for the vaulting stunts and develops it from this type of work.

3. Coordination, rhythm, balance, and a sense of timing are all factors developed particularly by support work. The constant shift in weight and cutting action of the legs in a limited space make these values especially important.

4. The side horse provides an outlet for activity for many kinds of handicapped people. Because most stunts involve action of the upper body, a person with an impediment in the legs can safely work on this piece of apparatus and receive much joy and recognition from it. Records show that men who have been paralyzed from the hips down have been champions.

organization

AREA AND EQUIPMENT

The side horse itself occupies very little space in the gymnasium. Usually two 5′ x 10′ mats are sufficient to cover the area under the horse, with one on each side. However, when vaulting, more mats may be desired at the landing area to cover more space and to give added thickness. Room for a short run must be provided when vaulting. When using the horse as a long horse, even more room must be provided for running.

TEACHING METHODS

Only one person may work a side horse at one time. Most schools do not have more than two side horses so the activity does not lend itself to the mass method of instruction very well. However, most stunts, particularly the vaults, do not take much time to perform, so that large squads or small classes could be kept busy at one piece of equipment without undue waiting. A vaulting buck, which is a short side horse without pommels, can be used for vaulting and many of the support stunts and is very helpful as a lead-up to the side horse itself. A balance beam with mats hung over it can be effectively used as a multiple vaulting apparatus.

Because only one person can work the side horse at one time, it is easy to supervise this activity. Thus the squad method of instruction fits in nicely. The side horse can be one teaching station of a gymnastic unit with the squads rotating during the period.

A good method of supervising vaulting is to have the students line up and then the instructor can demonstrate the stunt. Following this, the first student in line performs the stunt with the instructor spotting. After a man performs a stunt, he spots for the next one in line. In this way the instructor is free from spotting and can make corrections when necessary. Side horse work is probably best evaluated by means of a stunt chart, although actual competitive routines could be used in advanced classes.

SAFETY

Support work requires little spotting in the beginning stages because missing a stunt seldom means falling from the apparatus. However, close spotting is necessary for the vaulting stunts where it is very easy to catch a foot on the horse, causing a fall. The following are some general safety hints to consider when working the side horse:

1. In vaulting exercises set the side horse as low as possible at first and gradually increase its height.

2. Be sure to post a spotter on the far side of the horse and near enough to prevent serious falls by the performer.

3. Learn the proper technique of taking off from both feet before attempting even the fundamental vaults.

4. Be sure to learn the technique of pushing downward with the hands in passing over the horse on the vaults.

5. It is advisable to have a double thickness of mats on the landing side of the horse.

6. Always work in a progressive manner in learning the stunts. Start with the easier vaults and support stunts and progress toward the more difficult as skill is acquired.

program of instruction

Instruction on the side horse involves three basic steps:

1. Individual Stunts.

2. Combinations. As a person learns a new stunt, he should be challenged to combine it with another stunt as smoothly as possible. Because a stunt must be learned well in order to combine

SPOTTING

it with another, the use of combinations in the teaching progression stresses proper execution and increases the safety of performance. In addition, the smaller combinations serve as building blocks for longer routines. Combinations can be suggested by the instructor or coach or can be created by the performer.

3. Routines. Ultimately a pupil should strive to combine stunts into a routine. Competition is based on routines, required or optional. The approach to optional routines is one of problem solving. Certain requirements involving the types and number of movements are presented as a problem for the performer to solve creatively within his own capabilities. The instructor, coach, and pupil can coordinate their thoughts on the development of a particular routine. For sample routines refer to the end of the chapter.

Side horse work can be divided into two categories: the vaulting activity and the support activity. Vaulting will be treated prior to the support work, although the two activities are sufficiently different in nature so that one is not dependent on the other. The stunts as

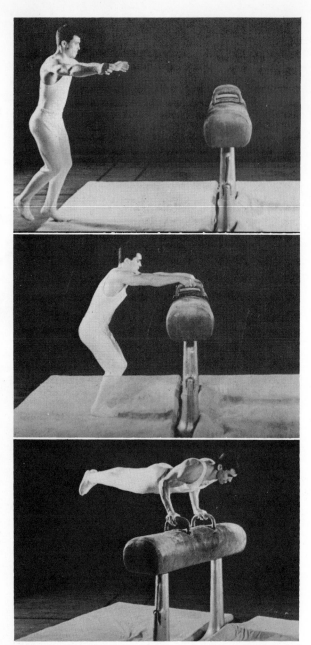

THE APPROACH AND TAKE-OFF

listed under each category are arranged in a progressive order of learning.

VAULTING WORK ON THE SIDE HORSE

Before attempting the vaulting stunts it is exceedingly important for.the performer to learn the art of taking off into the vault. A lead-up for this may be by

90

running to the horse and taking off from both feet and reaching for the pommels with the hands. Bounce off the feet, leap into the air, and grasp the pommels with the hands, flexing the arms only slightly, and let the feet ride upward behind the body. Do not pass over the horse but instead return to the same side of the horse from where the run started. This warm-up stunt will acquaint the performer with such principles of vaulting as: proper running approach, correct hurdle, and the take-off, using both feet. After this has been done a few times the student is ready for the first series of vaulting stunts. When the idea of the vault is gained, it may be done first with a walk approach, then a jogging approach and finally a run. However, many teachers find that such a gradual progression for each stunt is not necessary, particularly with the first few vaults.

The first three vaults can be done either to the right or left, and it is recommended that the performer learn to do the vault both ways.

1. *Front Vault.* Upon taking off, grasp the pommels with the hands, turn toward the horse and lift the legs to the left, passing them over the top of the horse toward the other side. The front of the body should face the horse throughout the stunt, and an attempt should be made to force an arch in the body while passing over the top of the horse. As the body passes over the horse and starts toward the mat, drop the left hand, hold on with the right, and proceed to land on the mats with the ride side of the body closer to the horse.

2. *Flank Vault.* Upon taking off extend the body to the left and pass over the horse with the flank side of the body closest to the horse. Land on the mat on the other side of the horse with the back toward the horse close to the pommels.

3. *Rear Vault.* Upon taking off, grasp

FRONT VAULT

FLANK VAULT

the pommels with the hands and lift the legs to the left. Turn the body so that the back side passes over the horse in a sitting position. Release the left hand first and then the right in passing over the horse. After dropping with the right hand, grasp the pommel with the left hand to steady the landing on the far side of the horse. Finish facing in the direction of the neck with the left side of the body nearest the horse.

4. *Squat Stand Leap.* Upon taking off, bend the knees and land in a squat position with the hands on the pommels. From this position leap forward by removing the hands from the pommels, lifting the arms and pushing off with the feet. Land in a standing position on the mats.

5. *Squat Vault.* On the take-off, reach with the hands for the pommels, and as the body passes over the horse with the knees in a squat position, push downward with the arms. Land on the other side of the horse upon completion of the squat vault. For more difficulty add a half turn before landing on the mat.

REAR VAULT

WOLF VAULT

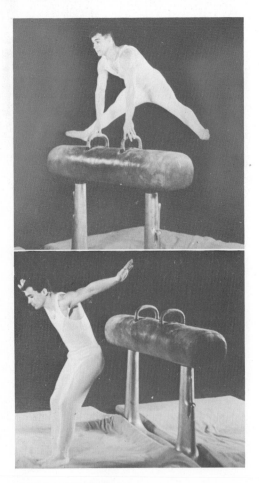

STRADDLE VAULT

6. *Wolf Vault.* Upon taking off, grasp the pommels and pass one leg in a tuck position between the pommels, with the other leg over the end of the horse in a straight and extended position. Upon passing over the horse, bring both legs together and land on the mat with the back toward the horse.

7. *Straddle Stand-Jump Dismount.* Jump into a straddle stand on the side horse with the feet on the outside of the pommels. Lift the arms and jump forward off the horse and land on the mat on the other side of the horse.

8. *Straddle Vault.* Upon taking off, place the hands on the pommels and push downward forcefully. Release the hands as the legs pass over the horse in a straddle position. Be sure to keep the head and chest up as the vault is executed. After passing over the horse, bring the legs together and land on the mats with the back toward the horse.

9. *Thief Vault.* This vault is begun with a take-off from one foot. Run at the horse and at a distance of about 3-4 feet from the horse lift one leg up and thrust it forward between the pommels and immediately bring the other leg up adjacent to the lead leg so both feet pass over the horse ahead of the body. As the hips pass over the horse, grasp the pommels momentarily with the hands and continue the vault by pushing downward, keeping the body in flight as the feet come down for a landing on the mat.

10. *Rear Vault with Half Twist.* Just after passing over the horse in a rear vault to the right push the pommel with the right hand and turn inward toward the horse. Complete a half turn of the body and land on the mats facing the opposite direction from that as passing over the horse. A mass drill for this stunt consists in having all the students stand, facing the same direction, with the right

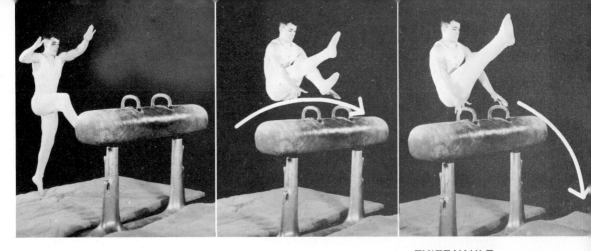

THIEF VAULT

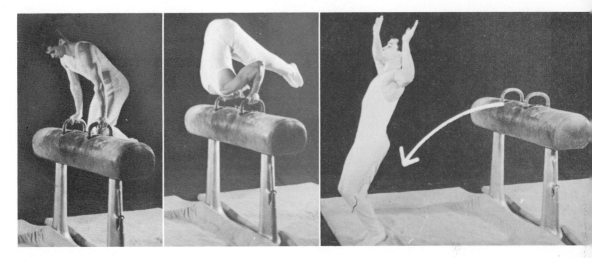

NECKSPRING FROM KNEE STAND

hand by their side as if grasping an imaginary pommel. Explain that all of them should feel they have just passed over the side horse in a rear vault position. Then they all should push with the right hand and execute a half turn in the direction of the right hand. This will give them the feel of the half twist to the right. Do this several times prior to actually attempting the stunt on the horse itself.

11. *Stoop Vault.* Upon taking off from both feet grasp the pommels with both hands and lift the legs and hips high. Then snap both legs downward between the pommels in a straight leg position. Continue the stoop and land on the mats

on the other side of the horse. A practice drill for this is to stand on the horse between the pommels and kick into a partial handstand with the hands on the pommels. As soon as the feet are up in the air, snap them down through the arms into the stoop dismount.

12. *Neckspring from Knee Stand.* This stunt is done from a kneeling position with the hands on the pommels. With a firm grip on the pommels, the performer lifts his hips into the air and tucks the head back under so that the back of the neck rests on the horse. The body should be in a pike position with the legs extended backward and the hips forward beyond the horse. Lean in the direction

93

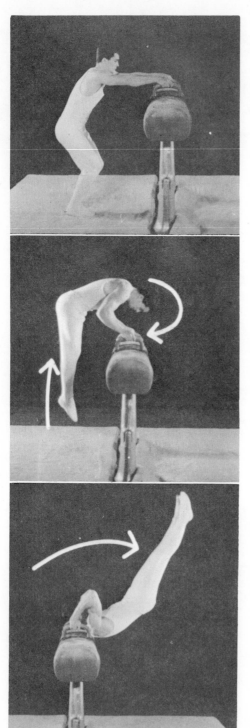

NECKSPRING

of the hips and then whip the legs over toward the mats, push with the hands, and continue the neckspring to the feet. Land in a standing position on the mat on the far side of the horse. Spotters can be particularly effective in helping the performer by grasping his arms and assisting him through the neckspring. Continue to hold the performer's arms even after he lands on the mat for the first few times. This will prevent over-flipping, which would cause a fall on the face.

13. *Neckspring.* This is done in a similar manner as the neckspring, from a kneeling position, except it is done from a run. After the take-off, the performer grasps the pommels and leaps into the air with the hips high. He then ducks his head and places the back of the neck between the pommels. Allow the body to continue over the horse in a pike position; when it reaches the point where the hips are past the horse and the body feels as if it is off-balance, whip the legs sharply over toward the mats. At the same time, push hard with the hands and land in a standing position.

14. *Headspring.* Same as the neck-spring except the top of the head is placed on the horse instead of the neck. It is important to emphasize the delaying of the whip action of the legs until the hips are well past the horse.

15. *Handspring.* Same as the head-spring except the head does not touch the horse and the weight is supported by the arms in a semi-flexed position.

LONG HORSE VAULTING

Long horse vaulting is an exciting event in which a performer runs at the horse, lands on a beat board, sails into the air and pushes on the horse with the hands while executing a vault, such as a stoop, straddle, hecht, or handspring.

To prepare for long horse vaulting, simply remove the pommels, turn the horse lengthwise, obtain a beat board for take-off, and the event is ready for action. The more recently used beat board is one that Olympic teams have been using and is called a Reuther system board. This board, built in Germany, has more spring and makes the long horse vaulting a more exciting and easier activity. As mentioned, the vaulting is done from the beat board over the entire length of the horse. Some of the vaults that can be done and techniques of performing them will be described, but before this a few words should be said regarding the proper take-off from the beat board.

Tips on Proper Take-Off from Beat Board. One of the most important phases of long horse vaulting is the proper take-off from the beat board. This takes courage, timing, and considerable practice. First the performer places himself at a good distance from the horse and beat board, the exact spot being determined with practice and repetition. From this position the run should start with a couple of trotting steps and as the horse is approached, should become a fast and confident run. The gaze includes beat board, horse, and surroundings rather than only the beat board. As the board is approached, take off from one foot into a hurdle and then bring the other foot up and proceed to land on both feet. Be sure to land on the part of the beat board that will provide the maximum amount of spring. Land strongly on the board with the body more in an upright position than in a forward leaning position. Remember that the run will provide the forward force, but it is up to the performer to make sure he obtains a

LONG HORSE VAULTING

maximum spring upward from the board. Many beginners have a tendency to simply dive over the horse with no thought of obtaining a beautiful lift or flight throughout the vault. Try one of the fundamental vaults such as straddle vault many times while trying to cultivate style and ease of performance. Proper take-off from the board cannot be overstressed. Remember to hit the board solidly, and take off with the thought of obtaining height and loft and not just skimming over the top of the horse. Also try to swing the feet high into the air before executing the particular vault in mind. The landing should also be practiced diligently because this provides the final impression, and an unsure landing can detract considerably from an otherwise fine vault. Try to land solidly in one spot and avoid if possible any additional hopping or jumping around after landing on the mat. Bend the knees to absorb the shock of hitting the mat and spread the arms forward or sideward to maintain balance. When a secure position is obtained, straighten to a position of attention.

Competitive Vaulting. As stated earlier the gymnast performs two vaults in succession and both vaults are scored with the better vault counting. The gymnast

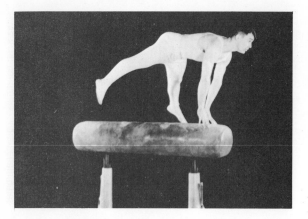

STRADDLE VAULT

must perform two different vaults. Judging takes into consideration four factors: difficulty, placement of hands in the proper zone, flight of the body throughout the vault, and the landing along with sureness and precision of the vault. For placement of the hands, the long horse is divided into five clearly marked zones: the near end, middle, and far end zones are 15¾ inches, and dividing these three zones are two smaller ones 7⅞ inches long. In order to obtain maximum credit for the vault, the competitors must place both hands clearly in the zone at either end with one exception, and that is the cartwheel where the last hand down

must be placed in the far end zone. Should any part of the hands extend behind or ahead of the proper zone, a deduction of one point per zone will be incurred.

Regarding the flight of the body, a deduction is made for the angle of the stretched body with the top of the horse, if less than 30°. The following table gives the degree of difficulty for each vault:

1. *Straddle Vault.* With the take-off and landing in mind, the vault itself consists in simply landing with the hands on the far end of the horse and then straddling the legs forward outside of the hands. Continue the straddle until the horse is passed and land on the mat in a standing position. Try to elevate the legs before cutting them downward for the straddle. Upon doing this vault from the croup (near end) place the beat board at a further distance from the end of the horse. Keep the body in more of an upright position and push hard with the arms in order to comfortably pass over the entire horse.

2. *Squat Vault.* Similar to the straddle vault except that the legs are tucked into the chest and between the arms as they pass over the end of the horse.

TABLE 6–1.

Vault	Neck (Far End)	Croup (Near End)
Straddle Vault	7.5	7.5
Squat Vault	8.0	8.0
Stoop (with knees bent at start)		9.0
Stoop (with knees straight)	9.5	10.0
Stoop (with one-half turn)	10.0	
Scissors (with one-half turn)	9.8	9.0
Cartwheel (handstand pivot)	9.0	
Cartwheel (giant)	9.8	
Handspring (body stretched or piked)	10.0	10.0
Hecht	10.0	10.0
Hecht (with one-half turn)	10.0	10.0

3. *Scissors with Half Turn* (Rear Straddle). After the two foot take-off, the hands are placed in a line parallel to the length of the horse at the far end, the right hand ahead of the left hand. The legs start off as in a straddle vault, but the right leg suddenly cuts over the horse to the left side, then the left leg over to the right side. This turns the performer around so that he is in a straddle position, with the rear of the body leading the way. The vaulting body forces the hands to be released as the performer passes over the neck of the horse. Land in a standing position facing the end of the horse. Place the right hand on the end to steady the landing.

To learn the mechanics of this scissors vault, it is recommended that the stunt first be tried from a standing position on the end of the horse rather than with a running take-off from the board.

4. *Stoop Vault.* After the take-off, land on the hands on the far end of the horse with the legs in an almost hand balance position. From this position, pike downward forcefully with the legs, push hard with the hands, and lift the chest so the body is extended prior to landing on the mat. The legs are straight throughout the stunt.

In doing this from the croup (near end) the legs may be either bent or straight at the start. In the stoop vault, with knees bent at start, the legs are straightened after they pass over the point of support of the hands. When keeping the legs straight throughout the stoop vault from the croup, emphasis is placed on a forceful takeoff from the board and a strong push with the arms resulting in an elevation of the hips, which allows the legs to pass over the croup without bending.

5. *Handstand Pivot Cartwheel.* After the take-off, land with the hands to-

SQUAT VAULT

SCISSORS WITH HALF TURN

STOOP VAULT

HANDSPRING

HANDSTAND PIVOT CARTWHEEL

gether in the middle zone. Continue the swing of the feet up to the handstand position. At this point reach out with one arm, execute a quarter turn of the body, and place the reaching hand on the neck. From here allow the momentum to carry the performer into a cartwheel. Dismount off the end.

6. *Giant Cartwheel.* Similar to the handstand pivot cartwheel except that upon taking off the beat board, the performer sails into a cartwheel position by placing one hand in the middle zone and from there continuing with the other hand so that it is placed on the end of the horse. This provides the giant cartwheel action and will carry the performer over the entire horse in a cartwheel fashion to a landing position on the mat sideways to the horse.

7. *Handspring.* Take off from the board and reach for the far end with the hands. Allow the feet to carry forcefully on upward into a hand balance position. Continue the swing of the feet over the head and finish out the front handspring vault. A spotter is essential while first learning this stunt. It is also suggested that this vault be tried at first from a

standing position on top of the horse. From here simply reach downward with the hands to the end of the horse and kick the legs up into the handspring action over the end. The following material is included as an addendum because of the diagrams that so clearly demonstrate the latest techniques.

THE ORGANIZATION OF THE JURY FOR LONG HORSE VAULTING

1. The four judges will place themselves in such a way that two of them can observe the vault frontways and particularly the trajectory. The other two judges will especially concentrate on the first phase of the vault.

2. The two judges assigned to check the position of the hands will place themselves one on either side of the horse.

3. The judge-referee places himself diagonal with the front end of the horse to be able to observe the vault in its entirely and without his vision being obstructed.

FORM AND TECHNICAL EXECUTION OF THE VAULTS

1. Vaults in which the hands are placed on the neck of the horse.

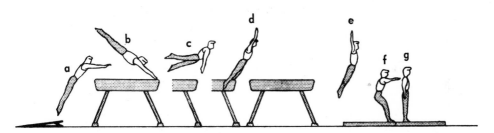

1. VAULT, BODY STRETCHED ABOVE THE HORIZONTAL, STRADDLING LEGS LATERALLY TO STAND REARWAYS. (STRADDLE):   7.50 PTS.

2. VAULT, BODY STRETCHED ABOVE THE HORIZONTAL, PASSING THE LEGS, TOGETHER BUT BENT, BETWEEN THE HANDS AND THEN STRETCHING THE BODY BEFORE LANDING TO STAND REARWAYS. (SQUAT VAULT):   8.00 PTS.

*This material reprinted with permission of George Nissen.

3. VAULT TO HANDSTAND, 1/4 TURN TO RIGHT, PLACING LEFT HAND ON THE NECK AND TURNING LATERALLY IN FREE FLIGHT, TO STAND LEFT SIDEWAYS. (THE VAULT CAN BE EXECUTED INVERSELY). (HANDSTAND PIVOT CARTWHEEL VAULT): 9.00 PTS.

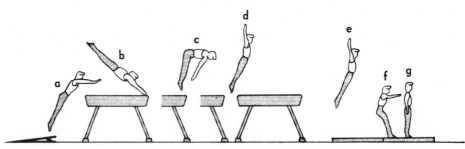

4. VAULT, BODY STRETCHED ABOVE THE HORIZONTAL, THEN BEND THE BODY IN ORDER TO PASS OVER THE NECK, WITH LEGS STRAIGHT AND JOINED AND THEN STRETCH THE BODY BEFORE LANDING, TO STAND REARWAYS. (STOOP VAULT): 9.50 PTS.

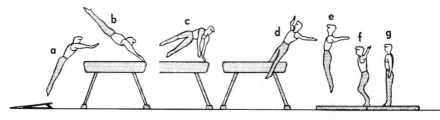

5. VAULT, BODY STRETCHED ABOVE THE HORIZONTAL, CROSSING THE LEGS WITH 1/2 TURN, TO STAND FACING THE HORSE. (SCISSORS VAULT WITH 1/2 TURN): 9.80 PTS.

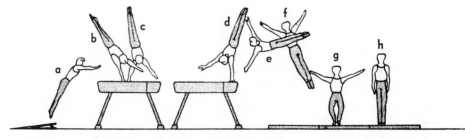

6. VAULT, WITH 1/4 TURN TO LEFT OR RIGHT DURING THE FLIGHT, TO A SIDE HANDSTAND, THE HANDS BEING PLACED ON THE HORSE SUCCESSIVELY OR SIMULTANEOUSLY, THE FORWARD HAND ON THE NECK, AND TURN LATERALLY IN A FREE FLIGHT, TO SIDE STAND. (GIANT CARTWHEEL): 9.80 PTS.

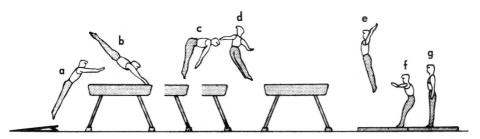

7. SAME AS # 4 EXCEPT THAT AS THE LEGS PASS OVER THE NECK YOU EXECUTE A
1/2 TURN LEFT OR RIGHT AND THEN STRETCH THE BODY, LANDING TO STAND
FACING THE HORSE. (STOOP VAULT WITH 1/2 TURN):   10.00 PTS.

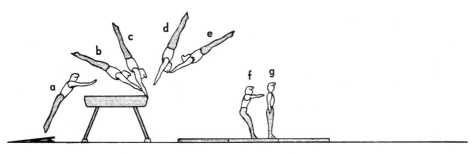

8. VAULT, TO A MOMENTARY HANDSTAND SUPPORT AND TURN OVER WITH A FREE
FLIGHT, TO STAND REARWAYS. (HANDSPRING):   10.00 PTS.

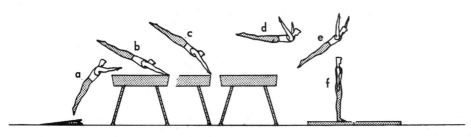

9. VAULT, BODY STRETCHED ABOVE THE HORIZONTAL, LEGS TOGETHER AND STRAIGHT,
CONTINUE THE FLIGHT OVER THE HORSE WITH THE BODY LAID OUT, AND LAND
TO A STAND REARWAYS. (HECHT):   10.00 PTS.

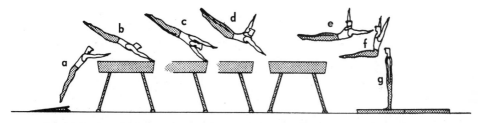

10. SAME AS # 9, EXCEPT THAT DURING THE FLIGHT OVER THE NECK EXECUTE 1/2
TURN TO STAND FRONTWAYS. (HECHT WITH 1/2 TURN):   10.00 PTS.

II. Vaults in which the hands are placed on the croup.

11. VAULT, BODY STRETCHED, LEGS STRAIGHT AND STRADDLED LATERALLY TO STAND
REARWAYS. (STRADDLE):   7.50 PTS.

12. VAULT, LEGS TOGETHER AND BENT, STRETCH THE BODY AND THE LEGS BEFORE
LANDING, TO STAND REARWAYS. (SQUAT):   8.00 PTS.

13. VAULT, CROSSING THE LEGS WITH 1/2 TURN, TO STAND FRONTWAYS, LEGS TO-
GETHER. (SCISSORS WITH 1/2 TURN):   9.00 PTS.

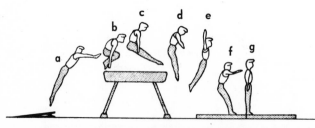

14. VAULT, LEGS BENT AT THE START THEN STRETCHED FORWARD DURING THE FLIGHT,
STRAIGHTEN THE BODY BEFORE LANDING, TO STAND REARWAYS. (STOOP VAULT,
LEGS BENT AT START THEN STRAIGHT DURING FLIGHT):   9.00 PTS.

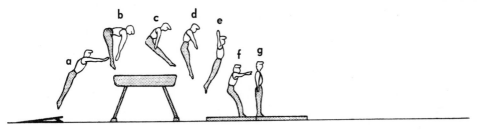

15. VAULT, BENT BODY, LEGS STRAIGHT, STRETCH THE BODY BEFORE LANDING, TO STAND REARWAYS. (STOOP):   10.00 PTS.

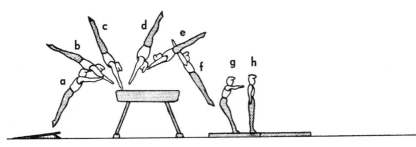

16. VAULT TO A MOMENTARY HANDSTAND SUPPORT AND TURN OVER WITH A FREE FLIGHT BODY LAID OUT, TO STAND REARWAYS. (HANDSPRING FROM THE CROUP):
                                                          10.00 PTS.

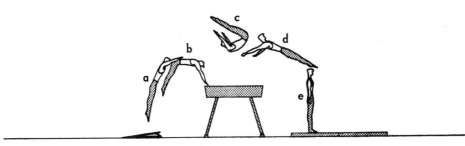

17. VAULT, PLACE THE HANDS ON THE CROUP MOMENTARILY, SOMERSAULT, EXTEND BODY BEFORE LANDING, TO STAND REARWAYS. (YAMASHITA):   10.00 PTS.

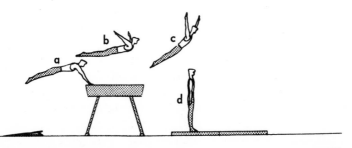

18. HECHT FROM THE CROUP (SAME DESCRIPTION AS # 9):   10.00 PTS.

19. HECHT WITH 1/2 TURN FROM THE CROUP (SAME DESCRIPTION AS #10): 10.00 PTS.

NOTE: Regarding vaults Nos. 3 (handstand pivot cartwheel) and 6 (giant cartwheel), only the forward hand is to be considered in evaluating the placing of the hand.

SUPPORT WORK ON THE SIDE HORSE

Support work is the activity of performing stunts while on the horse, with the performer supporting himself by the arms with the hands on the pommels or ends of the horse. This type of work is more difficult than vaulting, but the participation will be as enjoyable as the vaulting phase of side horse work if a person progresses effectively.

It is important to remember a few general hints for the successful learning of support work:

1. Be sure to work from the shoulders, thus supporting oneself with straight arms, and keep the chest up.

2. Learn soon to shift the weight from one arm to the other in a rhythmical manner.

3. Learn everything in small parts first and later incorporate the stunts into a presentable routine.

Some of the vaults that have been described under side horse vaulting can be used as mounts or dismounts in beginning support work. For mounts, the vault would be done from a stand and without releasing the hands, and for dis-

mounts the vault would be done from a support position on the horse rather than a take-off from a beat board. Such vaults as front, flank, rear, squat, and straddle are usable.

Other support stunts are as follows:

1. *Single Leg Half Circle.* From a front rest position supporting the body with the arms, hands on the pommels, and the front of the body leaning on the horse, swing the right leg over the end of the horse. While the right leg is swinging over the end of the horse, shift the weight of the body toward the left arm and release the right hand. Immediately after the leg has passed over the pommel, the right hand then regrasps the right pommel. Swing the right leg slightly to the left and then pass it backward over pommel and the right end of the horse. Regrasp the right pommel with the right hand and finish up in the original starting position of a front rest support position. This stunt can be done to the left with the left leg. Most of the stunts described hereafter can be done either to the left or right, although for brevity's sake the instruction for the most part will cover the right only. The

20. *Direct Tromlet.* This stunt consists of a side travel from the center of the horse to support position with both hands on one pommel followed by an immediate double in without touching the end of the horse with a hand. This necessitates a good support position on the one pommel as the immediate double in is performed.

21. *Reverse Stockli.* This stunt is best described by visualizing a motion picture of a double in, run in reverse in the projector. Thus from a front support position in the center of the horse, pass the legs under the left hand, regrasp and shift the weight to the left arm. Execute a half turn to the right, pivoting on the left arm and swinging the legs over the right pommel. Continue the backward turn, placing the right hand on the left end of the horse and continue the double leg circles.

22. *Moore (Czech).* As the legs swing backward in a flank circle, start turning the body inward toward the horse and reach back with the left hand and place it along the right. Swing the legs around the right end of the horse and raise the hips in order to pass the legs over the far pommel. After the legs clear the horse, grasp the far pommel with the right hand and continue flank circles.

23. *Russian.* This stunt consists in a continuation of the Moore movement from the first pommel over the second pommel in a layout position. As one passes over one end of the horse, he promptly reaches for the other pommel with the leading hand in preparation of the layout movement over the second pommel. A strong flank circle prior to the Russian and a low layout position of the body during the stunt are essential for its accomplishment.

24. *Loop Dismount.* The loop dismount is performed on one end of the horse out of flank circles. It consists in doing a flank circle around the end of the horse while facing its length. Remember to keep the weight centered over the hands. For greater difficulty, two or more loops on the end may be performed before dismounting.

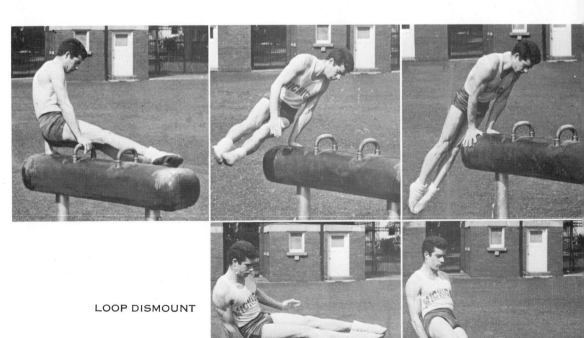

LOOP DISMOUNT

LOOP DISMOUNT
WITH HIGH LEG LIFT

LOOP DISMOUNT ENDING IN A
FRONT LAYOUT POSITION

ROUTINES

Creativity, imagination, and resourcefulness can be developed in the sport of gymnastics by the individual's construction and performance of his own sequence of stunts. The following are simply suggestions of combinations that certainly can be enlarged upon within the pupil's ability:

1. Start at right end with left hand on pommel and right hand on end of horse. Squat vault through arms to rear support, bring right leg half circle to right, left leg half circle left. Then bring right leg half circle right and left leg half circle left, but do not cut the left hand. Instead, finish with the legs straddling the pommel. Bring right leg back in a half circle, shifting right hand to right pommel, and then as the left leg is half circled to the left, the left hand is shifted to the left pommel. Execute alternate half leg circles, starting with the right leg, and finish with a front vault dismount.

2. With hands on the pommels, execute a flank circle across the right end half way to rear support. Continue the left leg over the left pommel, followed by a half circle back with the right leg to the right. Swing the left leg in a half circle over the left pommel and then execute scissors to the right. Then bring the left leg over the left end to a rear support and continue it to the right by cutting it under the right leg to complete the single leg circle (with the left leg). Continue the swing over the left end to join the right leg in front again. Execute a right leg half circle right and a left leg half circle left, finishing with a rear vault over the right end of the horse to a stand on the mat.

3. The performer stands facing the right end of the horse with his right hand on the end and the left hand on the pommel. He then jumps to a support position with the right leg passing over the end of the horse. Execute a scissors over the left pommel. Leaving the left leg in front of the horse, bring the right

leg around the end turning to the left and continue the right leg over the horse grasping the far pommel with the right hand and the left hand remaining on the left pommel. From here execute a scissors to the left, then right, and then left. Bring the right leg to the front of the horse, bringing the left leg back, and execute a reverse scissors. Bring the right leg around to a straddle position on the right hand pommel. Then bring the right leg back, turning the body to the right, and place the left hand on the end of the horse. Continue to circle the legs into a single or double rear dismount.

4. Start at right end of horse with left hand on pommel and right hand on right end of horse. Execute a double leg half circle and continue the right leg by cutting it under the left leg and continue it completely around to join the left leg in front, and then execute a double in movement to the saddle (between the pommels) and then circle the left leg back over the pommel to the left. Bring the right leg back over the right pommel and then execute a scissors by bringing the left leg over the end of the horse with the scissors to the right. Bring the left leg to the front of the horse and swing the right leg back over the right end of the horse. Execute a reverse scissors to the left. Bring the right leg back over the right end and then bring the left leg over the left end in a half circle. Bring the right leg around the right end of the horse and continue it over the far end of the horse (left end) and execute a single leg circle around it with the right

hand placed on the end of the horse. Continue the single leg circle over this end of the horse to a dismount stand on the mat.

5. Start at right end of horse and jump into a double leg circle. After one full circle then execute a double leg circle in (double in) to the center of horse and there execute a double leg circle—stop both legs in back with the right leg continuing over the right end of horse and then into a scissors to the left side of horse, then execute a scissors to the right side, then bring left leg over the left end of horse and bring right leg back over right end of horse and execute a reverse scissors over the left end of horse. Bring right leg back over right end of horse and then the left leg over the left end to the front of the horse and then bring right leg around right side of the horse and execute double leg circles. After two circles execute a double out to the left and on the end execute a loop dismount to the mat.

6. Start with loop around end of horse and then do a side travel to the pommels and continue on to other end and then do a double in to pommels to flank circles. After two circles stop in back of horse and bring right leg around right end and do two regular scissors and then bring left leg over the left end of the horse to front of horse and bring right leg back and execute a reverse scissors and then commence regular flank circles and after two circles do a side travel to end and then two loops on end to dismount.

CHAPTER SEVEN / *horizontal bar*

Friedrich Jahn introduced the horizontal bar in Germany about 1812. In his famous playground he visualized the high bar as being like the branch of a tree. Knowing how children like to play on a strong level branch he thought that they would be keenly interested in working, swinging, and performing on this high bar. His expectations were fulfilled, because soon after its introduction it was well accepted by children and adults alike. Now it is still one of the most popular gymnastic events.

The horizontal bar (often called the high bar) is suspended parallel to the floor by two mental uprights 8' to 8' 4" apart. Many bars are adjustable so that they can be lowered and raised to heights that best fit the needs. For competition the bar should be at a height of 8' to 8' 3" from the top of the mat.

In competition a routine is composed of continuous swinging and vaulting movements, including giant swings.

values

The specific values of working the horizontal bar are:

1. The high bar develops strength in upper parts, of the body, especially the arms, shoulders, chest, and back muscles.

2. A good hand grip is essential to working the high bar. Constant work will strengthen the fingers and hands and insure a good grip.

3. Because of the rapid circling of the bar by the performer, a sense of relocation must be developed to reduce any dizziness caused by this action.

4. Courage and confidence in the ability to handle the body is developed from working at a considerable height with the body weight supported only by the strength of the fingers.

5. Rhythm and coordination are developed through constant practice, which in turn reduce the demand for great strength in many stunts.

116

organization

AREA AND EQUIPMENT

The area required for the horizontal bar is fixed in that it uses fittings in the floor when raised. Much thought should go into the placing of these fittings when being put into the floor for the first time. Proper placing will prevent interference with other activities that may be conducted at the same time. Several styles of high bars are available. The wall type, which is supported by cables on one side and the wall on the other side, is easily taken down and stored against the wall. It does have a drawback in that work must be performed close to a wall. Other styles are supported on both sides by cables, which may come from the ceiling or entirely from the floor. These possibly take up more floor space but are clear of building obstructions.

Mats should be used under the high bar and should extend a minimum of 10 feet on either side of the bar. The area should be clear of obstructions for about 20 feet on either side of the bar, and the ceiling should be at least 15 to 17 feet high depending upon the height of the students.

TEACHING METHODS

Only one person should work the high bar at one time. Thus the mass method of instruction will not work well as most schools will not have more than two high bars. Many of the beginning stunts can be tried several times, if missed the first time, without dismounting from the bar, but this could make the class proceed slowly. However, high bar work requires a great deal of energy and wear on the hands, which calls for longer rest periods between stunts. Often it is advisable to teach two stunts at a time to conserve strength. For example, a person may mount by means of a single knee swing-up. While he is in this position, he may as well try a single knee circle backward rather than merely swinging down from the bar. Thus, the squad method of instruction best fits this activity. Probably the high bar will be one teaching station of a gymnastics unit with the squads rotating during the period.

The high bar can be supervised best from underneath the bar along one upright. From this position, the instructor is able to see the mistakes as they are made, give manual assistance when needed, and closely spot the performer.

Evaluation of high bar work is easily done by means of a stunt chart. Competitive routines would also be useful in evaluating more advanced classes.

SAFETY

Great care should be exercised in maintaining safety on the high bar. Because the bar is fairly high off the floor and the activity involves swinging around the bar supported most of the time only by the hands, the danger of falling can be great. This is not to say that the high bar is a dangerous piece of equipment, but it requires close adherence to the safety rules. In many cases the stunts do not progress gradually, so each one must be thoroughly learned before proceeding. It is highly important that the stunts be tried in an orderly, progressive manner. The instructor should always be at hand to assist the performer through the learning stages of the stunts.

The following is a list of safety rules for working the high bar:

1. Check the cables and make sure they have been attached securely. This should apply also to the nuts and bolts holding the bar in place and the turnbuckles on the cables.

2. Use plenty of mats around the bar for safety and dismounting purposes.

3. Always use high bar chalk (carbonate of magnesium) on the hands.

4. Keep the bar clean of excessive chalk and rust by using emory paper or steel wool to rub the bar.

5. Grasp the bar with the thumbs circling the bar in one direction and the fingers in the other.

6. With a few exceptions, always go around the bar in the direction in which the thumbs point.

7. Always have at least one spotter while learning new stunts to prevent slips or falls. Two spotters are preferred, with one of them being the instructor.

8. In working on an adjustable bar, work low at first and gradually increase the height.

9. It is advisable to work the bar for short periods of time because the wear and friction on the hands causes blisters that often tear. When the hands are sore it is suggested that they be soaked in warm water and then rubbed with skin ointment.

10. It is also suggested that hand guards be worn to prevent unnecessary blistering and tearing. These hand guards may be of leather, lamp wick material, or gauze.

program of instruction

Instruction on the horizontal bar involves three basic steps:

1. Individual Stunts.

2. Combinations. As a person learns a new stunt, he should be challenged to combine it with another stunt as smoothly as possible. Because a stunt must be learned well in order to combine it with another, the use of combinations in the teaching progression stresses proper execution and increases the safety of performance. In addition, the smaller combinations serve as building blocks for longer routines. Combinations can be suggested by the instructor or coach or can be created by the performer.

3. Routines. Ultimately, a pupil should strive to combine stunts into a routine. Competition is based on routines, required or optional. The approach to optional routines is one of problem solving. Certain requirements involving the types and number of movements are presented as a problem for the performer to solve creatively within his own capabilities. The instructor, coach, and pupil can coordinate their thoughts on the development of a particular routine. For sample routines refer to the end of the chapter.

Two types of grips are normally used: the overhand, or regular, grip and the underhand, or reverse, grip. On the regular grip the hands circle the bar with the fingers going over the top of the bar and the backs of the hands facing the performer. In the reverse grip the hands circle under the bar with the palms of the hands facing the performer. Less commonly used is a mixed grip, which consists of one hand in the overhand grip and the other hand in the underhand grip. Normally the bar is grasped with the hands shoulder width apart. However, for a few stunts a wider or narrower grasp may be desirable.

While first working the horizontal bar it is advisable, if possible, to lower the bar to approximately shoulder height. Later, as skill progresses and as the

half giant swing. Flex the hips slightly and then whip the legs up and over the head and at the same time extend the arms so that the full swing is started in an almost straight hand balance position. Continue the swing downward and under the bar with the body fully extended. On the back end of the swing, pull with the arms and lift the hips upward slightly. This will force the body upward into another hand balance position and from there on into another reverse giant swing. Remember not to kip or pull with the arms too soon but instead wait for the moment when the body has almost reached the peak of the backward swing, then pull in toward the bar and allow the shoulders and head to shift over the bar and the feet to swing upward into the handstand position.

16. *Squat Dismount.* From a reverse giant swing, when the legs are rising above the horizontal bar, quickly pull the knees in toward the chest, bending the legs, and pass them through the arms above the bar. Push off with the hands, keeping head and chest up, and continue on downward to a standing position on mats. This also can be done in a straddle position while passing over the bar.

17. *Straddle Dismount from Kip.* Execute a regular kip and then lift the hips up above the bar and at the same time sharply bring the legs in a straddle position over the bar. Be sure to get a good push with the hands while straddling over the bar and keep the head and shoulders up as much as possible.

18. *Regular Flyaway.* A regular flyaway from the horizontal bar is one of the prettiest and yet one of the more difficult dismounts to master. Perhaps one of the easiest methods of learning this stunt is to use the "skin-the-cat" approach. By this is meant that the first time a performer tries a flyaway he

REVERSE GIANT SWING WITH OVERHEAD BELT

STRADDLE DISMOUNT FROM KIP

should simply hang on the bar and then pull the legs up and between the arms into a skin-the-cat position and then drop off to the feet. After a few times the stunt is then tried with a small swing but at all times the principle is the same in that a quick skin the cat is performed. The knees are bent and a slight pull of the arms is effected. This principle is continued with the swing slightly in-

REGULAR FLYAWAY

REGULAR FLYAWAY
(WITHOUT BELT)

creased with each try. Upon gaining confidence and sureness, the flyaway is tried with more swing and later from a cast and finally from a giant swing. As swing increases, the body is extended to a layout position instead of a tuck. The spotters can assist by grasping the performer's wrists and helping him through the early stages of the dismount.

Another method of learning the flyaway is to swing on the bar with an overhead safety belt and then drop at the forward end of the swing straight downward with the feet. Increase the height at each attempt, thrusting the hips forward, pushing with the hands. After several of these have been tried, then from a cast off the bar, swing outward and upward and attempt to simply sit in the air with the spotter holding the body above the mats. The performer may either tip over backward or extend forward to the feet. This feeling of lofting the body upward into a backdrop or sitting position with the legs above the chest is important in learning the flyaway.

19. *Reverse Flyaway.* This is normally done from a reverse giant swing. After the body swings downward, the performer pikes slightly, and on passing the

uprights he thrusts his legs and hips into the air. At this time he releases his hands, ducks his head, and turns a reverse somersault in the air, landing on his feet. This may be done with the body in a tuck or pike position. In learning this dismount an overhead safety belt is recommended. The performer tries this stunt at first from a high power swing with the hands in a regular grip. After the technique of dropping and turning over is controlled, the performer executes the reverse flyaway first from a cast from the top side of the bar, with the hands in a reverse grip position and yet still in the safety belt. Remember, do not pull in toward the bar upon releasing it and lift the hips and legs upward for maximum height and flight.

This same stunt can be done with a half twist, which is executed after the reverse somersault has been started. Another method, which also includes a half twist, is to execute a barani type dismount, involving an early twist from the bar and a barani movement to the feet.

20. *Vault.* This stunt consists of a rear vault over the top of the bar with a releasing of the hands and then regrasping with both hands. This may be learned from a power swing, with the performer in an overhead safety belt. Facing the bar, the performer should grasp the bar with the right hand in an overgrip and the left hand in an undergrip. So that the legs may pass conveniently over the length of the bar, the hands should grasp the bar toward the right upright. With the hands fairly close together and the safety belt securely fastened around his waist, the performer executes a high back uprise swing. As the legs swing past the uprights, the body turns and the legs are elevated upward to assume a pike position with the legs parallel to the bar. At the same time, the arms continue to pull and then thrust

VAULT

the body up and over the bar. As the performer passes over the bar, the hands release their grip and the body turns inward (which is left) toward the bar with the hands passing in front of the chest, and he quickly regrasps the bar. This stunt when learned is used occasionally as a mount, although the vault may more often be used within a routine with the technique varying as follows:

From a reverse giant swing, when the body flows upward approaching the handstand position and slows to a stalled position, the left hand is at this time changed from a reverse grip to a regular grip and the right hand is passed under the left arm and grasps the bar in a reverse grip. Then the body reverses direction and swings back down under the bar with the body turning to the left. At this point the performer finds himself in a position similar to a back uprise into a vault, thus the action continues to the regrasping of the bar. This method of doing a vault from a reverse giant swing has been found to be safe and effective.

The vault may also be done from a reverse giant swing with the right hand changing from a reverse grip to a regular grip after the body has passed over the top of the bar. With this mixed grip, he

DISLOCATE

then swings downward and simply executes a back uprise into the vault.

Another method is out of regular giant swings. After the body has passed over the bar, reach under the left hand with the right hand and regrasp the bar in a reverse grip. The body continues downward and turns to the left, and after passing the uprights the performer again finds himself in a position similar to a back uprise vault.

21. *Regular Giant Cross Over to Reverse Giant Swings.* As the performer passes over the bar in a regular giant swing, the right hand crosses over the left arm and grasps the bar in a regular grip near the left hand. The body continues in this crossed arm position downward and past the uprights. At this time the body turns to the right and swings

upward to a reverse giant position, and at the same time the left hand is released and regrasps in a reverse grip position. After this exchange of the hands, the performer continues over the top in a reverse giant swing.

22. *Reverse Giant Swing Pirouette to a Regular Giant.* As the performer reaches a handstand while doing a reverse giant swing, he pushes with the right hand and turns his body to the left. To complete the pirouette he grasps the bar with his right hand in a regular grip and continues downward in a regular giant swing.

23. *Straddle Cut and Catch.* At the forward end of a swing bring both legs upward between the arms in a pike position. When the body swings upward and reaches its peak, the legs are strad-

dled out to the sides and the hands are released. After the legs have cleared the bar the hands then quickly regrasp the bar and the swing is continued. A good spotting technique is for the coach to stand directly behind the performer and away from the bar slightly so that if the performer misses the bar on the regrasp, the coach can catch him by the hips and place him safely onto the mat.

24. *Dislocate*. From a reverse giant swing as the body swings above the bar, bring the legs between the arms either in a tuck or pike position. The performer should attempt to keep his arms locked in stooping into the bar and if possible keep his legs held tightly against his chest. In this position he does a seat circle without the legs touching the bar, and as he starts over the top of the bar the legs are extended forcefully overhead and the arms push downward. The entire body is fully extended so that the body appears to be in a partial handstand position with the hands in a dislocated grip. From here the shoulders are dislocated and the performer swings downward and finishes the dislocate into either a back uprise to regrasp to regular grip or back uprise to regrasp to reverse grip into reverse giants or continues the swing with the hands in the L position into dislocated giant swings (Eagle Giants).

In learning this stunt an overhead safety belt is recommended, with the performer starting the stunt from a sitting position on top of the bar. With the hands in a reverse grip the performer swings his legs upward and away from the bar. This extends the body outward to approximately a 45 degree angle. The shoulders are dislocated and the swing continues downward with the hands in the dislocated or L position. The spotter attempts to hold the performer with the belt so that the dislocation of the shoulders will take place above the level of the bar, at which time the body weight is not fully supported by the shoulders and arms. After the dislocation, the spotter gently lowers the performer

EAGLE GIANTS

DISLOCATE HALF TWIST

INVERTED GIANT SWING

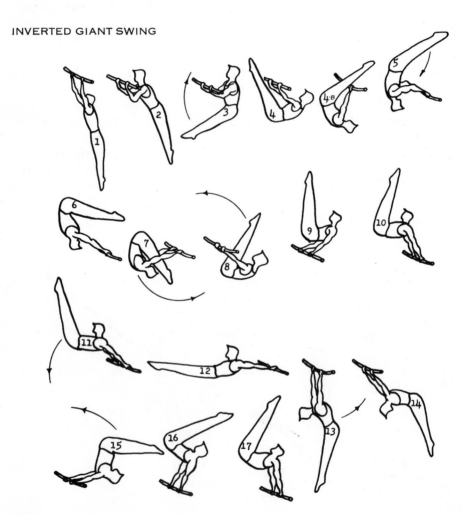

downward to prevent his grip from slipping.

Another method of doing the dislocation is using a reverse grip to power upward into almost a handstand position. From here, quickly bring the legs downward and between the arms either in a pike or tuck position. In this position the performer circles under the bar and on upward into the dislocate action.
Variation:

Dislocate with half twist is a variation of the dislocate stunt, and as pictured, the half twist is done over the top of the bar and a regular giant swing position is assumed.

Another variation of the dislocate maneuver is to stoop in and proceed as if going into a dislocate, only do not dislocate and continue once around in the "undislocated" or inverted giant position. After performing one complete inverted giant, proceed to dislocate and continue on into an eagle giant swing. Notice the complete extension of the body at the bottom of the swing and

GERMAN GIANT SWING

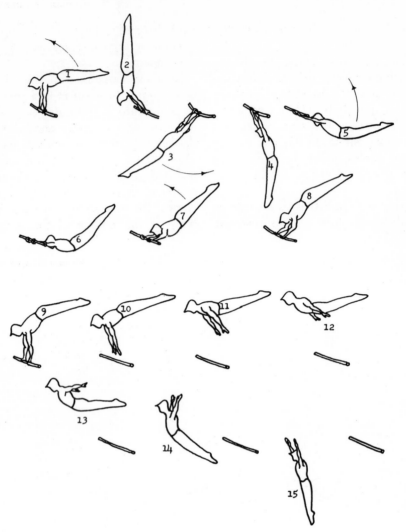

HECHT DISMOUNT

then the tight pike as the performer passes over the top of the bar. Keep the arms at shoulder width. Spot this stunt numerous times in an overhead rigging and also with hand spotting prior to attempting alone. The hand spotting can be effectively done by standing on a side horse placed under the high bar near one upright.

25. *German Giant Swing.* From a rear support position on top of the bar with the hands in a regular grip, the legs are swung upward and backward with the shoulders leaning backward slightly, but kept as high as possible. The legs continue on over backward beyond the head with the arms pushing downward forcefully; the body, in the German position fully extended, swings downward and beyond the uprights. After passing the uprights, the legs are swung upward strongly into a pike position, and the performer continues on over to the top of the bar. Be sure to have a strong change

of the grip on the latter part of the stunt from a hang to a support position. It is recommended that a safety (overhead) belt be used in learning this stunt. Another variation of this stunt is to pass through the first part of the German but on the upward swing, release the hands and execute a half twist. Upon completion of the half twist, regrasp the hands in a regular grip position and continue back downward to a kip. This also can be done to an immediate back kip circle.

26. *Hecht Dismount.* An advanced dismount involving flying over the top of the horizontal bar, which is spectacular and beautiful, is called the hecht dismount. As pictured, this dismount is performed out of a reverse giant swing. Notice the small pike of the body at the bottom of the swing and then the arch followed by still another pike prior to pushing off with the hands. With the proper momentum and beat, the performer should be able to pass over the bar in a complete layout position. It is highly recommended that this stunt be done numerous times in an overhead rigging.

ROUTINES

Creativity, imagination, and resourcefulness can be developed in the sport of gymnastics by the individual's construction and performance of his own sequence of stunts. The following are suggestions of combinations that can be enlarged upon within the pupil's ability:

1. (Low Bar). Hip pullover—back hip circle—underswing dismount forward.

2. (Low Bar). Jump into single leg swing up—single leg circle backwards—continuing swing under bar—single leg swing up—bring leg that is over bar back to a front support position—swing legs to back dismount.

3. Single leg swing up—bring other leg over to sitting position into a black double knee circle—drop below bar into a hock swing dismount.

4. Kip into a back hip circle—into under bar swing, executing a half turn at front end of swing into a single leg swing up into a front leg circle; place backs of both knees on bar and execute a hock swing dismount with half twist.

5. Back uprise to back hip circle—underbar swing with half turn at front end of swing into kip—forward hip circle, cast to three-quarter regular giant swing—drop kip to sole circle dismount.

6. Reverse kip—drop back and bring legs between arms to drop kip—forward hip circle, cast back to a cross-over into a back uprise—back hip circle into underswing—dismount forward with a half turn.

7. Back uprise to back hip circle—underbar swing to kip; cast into regular giant swings (2)—cross over to reverse giant swings (2)—jump change to back hip circle to drop kip; cast into a flyaway.

8. Jump to reverse grip and execute a power swing and then a reverse giant swing. After one reverse giant swing, stoop the legs between the arms and execute a dislocate and then hop to reverse giant swing again and after one reverse giant swing execute a vault (by either turning one hand over as the body passes over the bar or by changing the hands on this side of the bar and then swinging back and under the bar for the vault—see vault description in text). After the vault do a reverse kip into a half German giant, executing a half twist to a regrasp of the bar (on the upward swing of the half German giant swing). From here do a kip into an immediate straddle dismount.

CHAPTER EIGHT / *parallel bars*

Parallel bars were first introduced by Friedrich Jahn in the early 1800's. He hoped through this apparatus and the others that he invented to strengthen the degenerated muscle groups of the body and thus perhaps to liberate man from the shackles of an overcivilized environment that had enfeebled him.

The parallel bars consist of two parallel hand rails made of the finest grained hickory connected to uprights supported by a metal base. All are firmly connected, with no undue shaking allowed. The bars are adjustable in width and in height, which allows convenient adjustment for the students of different age groups and sizes. For collegiate competition the bars should be from 5'4" to 5'8" high. The bars are 11'6" long with an inside width of 16" to 22". A competitive routine includes a series of predominately swinging and vaulting movements combined with exercises of strength and holding of positions.

values

The specific values of working the parallel bars are:

1. The parallel bars develop strength and power in the arms, chest, and back.

2. Balance is essential in parallel bars work and is developed by it.

3. The maneuvers call for great coordination and timing.

4. Confidence is developed on the parallel bars as the fear of falling between the bars is overcome.

organization

AREA AND EQUIPMENT

The parallel bars are easily moved and thus can be set up in any part of the gymnasium. Because the stunts do not require the performer to start or finish far away from the bars, the area needed would be that taken by the bars themselves plus about 5 feet on all sides. Mats should be under and around the bar. 5′ × 10′ mats will fit along the sides and ends, but underneath and between the uprights is more of a problem. The same sized mats cannot be placed here without curling up or overlapping, which may cause injuries. The best solution is a special mat to fit the area. These can be obtained from the companies that supply parallel bars.

TEACHING METHODS

Normally only one person can work the parallel bars at one time, but during the elementary skills period, two performers may work at the same time. When doing dips, one student may work at each end. For a series of straddle seat travels along the length of the bars, a second performer could begin before the first one has finished at the other end. Performers generally proceed rapidly so no undue waiting should result with large squads.

The instructor should carefully supervise the activity at the beginning stages because most students have a fear of falling between the bars. However, this fear is quickly overcome, and with confidence the performer executes the stunts with little danger of injury.

Work on the parallel bars can be evaluated by using a stunt chart. Because of the great variety of stunts possible, it is easier and less time-consuming to make up simple routines for checking purposes. For more advanced classes, regular competitive routines make a good test.

SAFETY

In order to carry out a successful program of instruction on the parallel bars,

a few safety hints should be followed:

1. Check the equipment to see that it is firmly supported on the floor and that the uprights are in a secure position.

2. The area around and under the bars should be safely padded with mats.

3. In first working the parallel bars, the bars should be lowered as far as possible. This makes for safe performance and convenient spotting. For balancing stunts, a set of low parallel bars is extremely valuable to use.

4. One or more spotters should be present at all times to assist the performer through the more involved stunts.

5. For stunts done in the middle of the bars, the spotter should stand to one side of the bars. In helping the performer, he should be careful not to allow the arm to be caught across the bars with the weight of the performer on the arm; thus, most of the spotting should be done under the bars.

program of instruction

Instruction on the parallel bars involves three basic steps:

1. Individual Stunts.

2. Combinations. As a person learns a new stunt, he should be challenged to combine it with another stunt as smoothly as possible. Because a stunt must be learned well in order to combine it with another, the use of combinations in the teaching progression stresses proper execution and increases the safety of performance. In addition, the smaller combinations serve as building blocks for longer routines. Combinations can be suggested by the instructor or coach or can be created by the performer.

3. Routines. Ultimately, a pupil should strive to combine stunts into a routine. Competition is based on routines, required or optional. The approach to op-

STRAIGHT ARM SUPPORT

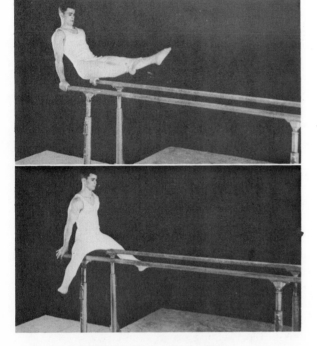

JUMP TO STRADDLE SEAT

UPPER ARM SUPPORT

tional routines is one of problem solving. Certain requirements involving the types and number of movements are presented as a problem for the performer to solve creatively within his own capabilities. The instructor, coach, and pupil can coordinate their thoughts on the development of a particular routine. For sample routines refer to the end of the chapter.

There are three common starting positions:

(a) Straight arm support—jump onto the bars with a hand on each bar. The arms are straight and run along the sides of the body. Keep the head up, chest out, body slightly arched, and the toes pointed.

(b) Straddle seat—from a straight arm support position, swing the legs forward between the bars. As the legs swing slightly above the bars, separate them and place one on each bar, ending in a straddle seat position with the legs and back straight and the head and chest up and the hands behind the legs.

(c) Upper arm support—the body is supported between the bars by the upper arms, which are over the bars. The hands grasp the bars ahead of the shoulders and the elbows are spread out to the side. The body should be able to swing freely from this position.

To become a successful performer on the parallel bars, it is important to progress slowly through the fundamental and strengthening stunts. As skill and strength improve, the more advanced stunts may be tried with complete confidence. The following is a description of some of the stunts that may be done on the parallel bars, given in recommended order of progression. For variation, many of these stunts can be done in the opposite direction from the one described.

1. *Dips.* Jump onto the bars in a straight arm support position facing toward the center of the bars. In this position, flex the arms and drop downward until the elbow joint is less than a right angle. After reaching the bottom with the arms flexed, push the body upward into the straight arm position. Do several of these dips at one time to increase arm strength.

2. *Swing.* Jump to a straight arm support position on the ends of the bars. Bring the legs up slightly and extend the body into an arched position. Swing the legs downward and then backward and forward in a series of swings. Be sure to keep the arms straight and make the *shoulders* the fulcrum of the swing. Swing low at first and gradually increase the height of the swing. Control is especially important as the swing becomes larger.

3. *Swinging Dips.* Swing in a straight arm support position, and when the feet are at the end of the backward swing, flex the arms and drop to a dip position. Remain in this dip position as the legs swing forward. Just as the feet reach the end of the forward swing, push the arms straight and finish in a straight arm position. This same stunt can be done backward by dropping into the full dip position at the end of the front swing and pushing up at the back end of the swing. To do this stunt on lowered parallel bars, it may be necessary to bend the knees so that the feet will not hit the mats.

4. *Swinging Dip Travel.* The first half of this stunt is done just like the swinging dips. As the body is swinging forward from the dip position, push vigorously

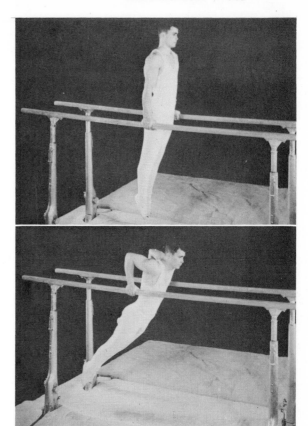

DIP

SWING

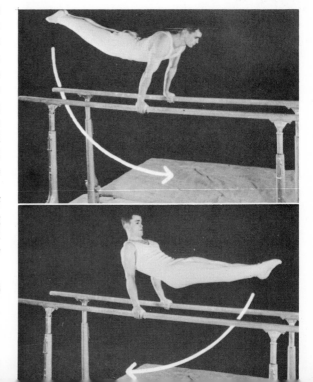

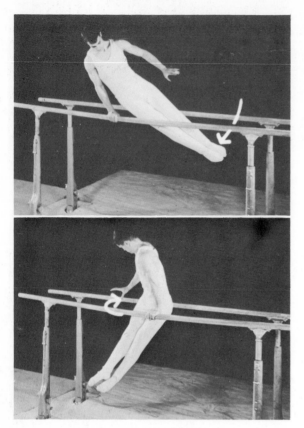

FRONT SUPPORT TURN

with the arms in an upward and forward direction. The hands leave the bars momentarily, the body travels or hops forward, then the hands regrasp the bars, and the body finishes in a straight arm support position.

5. *Straight Arm Walk.* Walk the length of the bars in a straight arm sup-

port position, keeping the arms straight, head up, body arched. As one hand leaves the bar to take a step, shift the weight to the other hand. Be sure to take small steps with the hands.

6. *Front Support Turn.* From a straight arm support position in the center of the bars, lean to the right and shift the left hand to the right bar, bringing the front of the thighs to rest against the bar. Keep the body straight and back slightly arched. Continue the turn by reaching back with the right hand and grasping the vacated bar, thus ending in a straight arm support position.

7. *Half Twist Change (Scissors from a Straight Arm Support).* Here is another simple method of turning around. From a straight arm support position, swing both legs backward, execute a half twist of the body, and bring the right leg over the left bar and the left leg over the right bar. After finishing this scissor action, turn the body into a straddle seat position facing the opposite direction.

8. *Front Dismount.* Swing in the center of the bars from a straight arm support position. As the body reaches the peak of the backward swing and the legs are above the bars, push hard with the left arm and swing the body over the right bar so the front part of the body is closest to the bar. After passing over this bar, drop toward the mat, grasping the bar with the left hand as the right hand releases the grip. Land on

FRONT DISMOUNT

REAR DISMOUNT

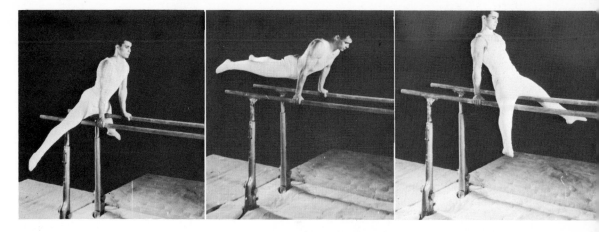

STRADDLE SEAT TRAVEL

SIDE SEAT HALF TURN TO STRADDLE SEAT

the mat with the left hand steadying the landing by holding onto the closest bar.

9. *Rear Dismount.* Swing in the center of the bars in a straight arm support position. As the body swings forward and the feet reach a point above the bars, push with the left hand and swing the body over the right bar so the rear of the body is closest to the bar. After passing over the right bar, regrasp it with the left hand as the right hand lets go.

10. *Straddle Seat Travel.* From a straddle seat position, lean forward and place the hands on the bars in front of the legs. As the weight is shifted to the straight arms, swing the legs backward above bar level; then bring them together and swing them forward between the bars. At the front of the swing, separate the legs again and place them in a straddle seat position in front of the hands. Travel the length of the bars in this manner.

11. *Side Seat Half Turn to Straddle Seat.* This stunt is a simple method of turning around and is done in the following manner. From a straight arm support position in the center of the bars, swing both legs forward over the right bar and end up in a side seat position.

145

SINGLE LEG CUT OFF-FORWARD

SINGLE LEG CUT ON

DOUBLE LEG CUT ON

FORWARD ROLL TO STRADDLE SEAT

Release the right hand and place it on the left bar and bring the right leg across from the right bar over to the left bar. Bring the left hand back to the right bar and finish in a straddle seat position facing the opposite direction. This can also be done by swinging to a side seat position on the inside of the right bar. Execute the half turn by bringing the right hand to the left bar and turning the body to a straight arm support position.

12. *Single Leg Cut Off—Forward.* From a straight arm support position on the end of the bars facing away from the bars, swing the body backward. At the back end of the swing, raise the hips and swing the right leg outside the right bar. On a forward swing, release the right hand and land in a standing position on the mat. Remember to keep the shoulders well forward of the hands so there is a definite forward lean into the dismount, which will help to keep the cutting leg from hitting the bar.

13. *Single Leg Cut On.* Stand on the mats facing the end of the bars and grasp them with the hands. Jump toward a straight arm support position and as the body moves upward, separate the

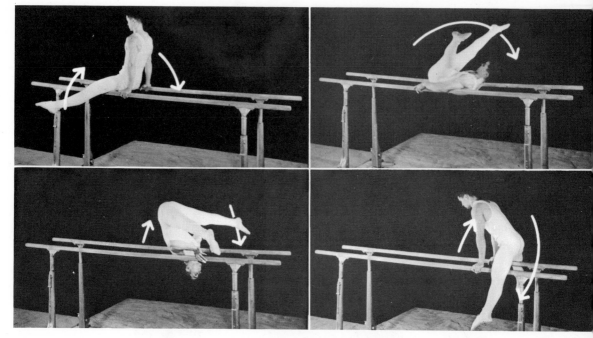

BACKWARD STRADDLE SHOULDER ROLL

legs and pass the left leg outside the left hand. The left leg passes over the bar to the inside of the bars while the performer releases the left hand. After the leg has passed over the bar, regrasp the bar and finish in a straight arm position. When first attempting this stunt, cut the leg across the bar; regrasp the bar but land in a standing position on the mat until the proper cutting action is achieved. The spotter may assist by standing behind and lifting at the waists.

14. *Forward Roll to Straddle Seat.* Start from a straddle seat position and grasp the bars in front of the thighs. Lean forward and place the upper arms on the bars with the elbows out to the side. Raise hips, keeping the body in a pike position. As the hips pass over the head, release the hands, keeping the elbows out to the side, and grasp the hands behind the back. The roll is continued to a straddle seat position.

15. *Backward Straddle Shoulder Roll.* From a straddle seat position, lean backward onto the arms and execute a backward roll. Grasp the bars over the shoulders and continue the roll to a straddle seat.

16. *Back Roll Off Both Bars Dismount.* Start from a sitting position on one bar with the hands grasping it on each side of the hips and the body facing away from the bars. Lean backward so the back rests on the other bar and bring the legs up and over the head. When the feet are as far down toward the mats as possible, release the hands and land on the mats in a standing position.

17. *Lazy Man's Kip.* Grasp the ends of the bars and jump up, placing the feet about half way up on each of the uprights. Swing the body downward, flexing the knees, and hang on with the hands. When the swing reaches the

SHOULDER BALANCE

point where the knees are fully flexed, start the return swing upward by straightening the legs and pulling forcefully with the arms. Continue this pull and shift the wrists from a hanging position to a support position and finish in a straight arm support position.

18. *Shoulder Balance (Upper Arm Balance)*. Start from a straddle seat position and grasp the bars in front of the thighs. Lean forward and place the upper arms on the bars, with the elbows out to the side. Raise the hips and extend the legs over the head. Assume the shoulder balance position with the back arched, head up, and toes pointed, with the elbows out to the side. Either slowly return the body to the starting position or pike the body and roll to a straddle seat. A spotter is important in first learning this stunt.

19. *Single Leg Circle Forward*. From a straight arm support position in the middle of the bars, swing the right leg forward over the left bar. Follow with the right hand. Transfer the left hand to the opposite bar and continue the right leg so it ends between the bars. Finish in a straight arm support position facing the opposite direction. Remember to transfer the body weight to the left bar during the change.

20. *Shoulder Balance—Side Dismount*. From a shoulder balance, lean to the right and push off with the left hand, allowing the body to rotate around the right bar, and land in a standing position on the mat. Hold on with the right hand in order to steady the landing.

21. *Hip Pullover Mount*. Stand at the side of the bars with arms under the near bar and the hands grasping the far bar in a regular grasp. Take a step under the bars and kick upward with the feet, pulling the abdomen into the bar with the legs going on over the top of the bars.

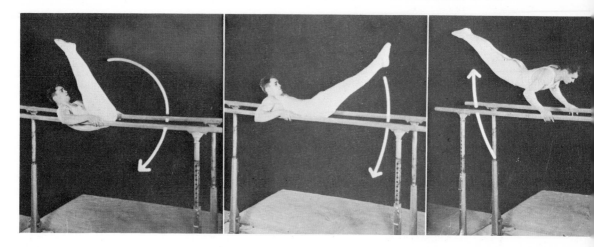

BACK UPRISE

Push body up to a front leaning rest position across the bars. Swing the right leg between the bars and then over the right bar, ending up in a straddle seat position.

22. *Back Uprise.* This stunt must be done with the bars at least as high as the performer's shoulders when standing. From an upper arm support position, swing back and forth a couple of times. On the back end of one of the swings, pull hard with the hands and lift the hips upward. Continue the pull, which brings the shoulders forward, and finish in a straight arm support position. A fairly high swing helps in the accomplishment of this stunt.

23. *Front Uprise.* From an upper arm support position, swing back and forth a couple of times. Toward the end of the forward swing, pull hard with the hands, thrust the hips forward, and lift the feet. Continue the pull, and finish in a straight arm support position. If the performer has difficulty, he could finish in a straddle seat position a few times before attempting the regular ending. A spotter can help by pushing under the hips.

FRONT UPRISE

24. *Scissors Change from Straddle Seat.* Start in a straddle seat position with both hands behind the legs. Swing the right leg between the bars and transfer the left hand to the right bar. As right leg swings vigorously backward, put the weight on the hands. Remove the left

STRADDLE FORWARD DISMOUNT

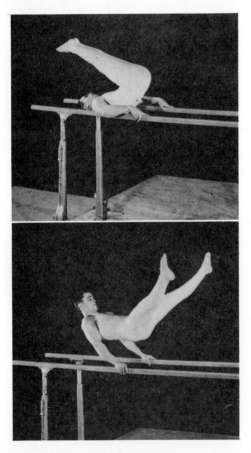

TOP KIP TO STRADDLE SEAT

leg from the left bar and swing it over to the opposite bar, with the right leg moving over to the left bar. Finish in a straddle seat position, facing the opposite direction, with the hands behind the body. An easier version of this stunt is the straddle circle. The performer starts in a straddle seat position with both hands on the bars behind the legs. Swing the right leg between the bar and transfer the left hand to the right bar. Bring the right leg over the right bar to a position next to the left leg. The body is then in a front support position across the bars. Now swing the left leg up and over the left bar and between the bars and continue on up across the right bar to a straddle seat position facing the opposite direction.

25. *Straddle Forward Dismount.* From a straight arm support position on the end of the bars facing away from the bars, swing the legs backward. On the back end of the swing, raise the hips and swing the feet outside the bars into a straddle position. Cut the legs forward sharply, releasing both hands, and allow the legs to pass over the ends of the bars. Finish in a standing position on the mat. Remember to maintain a definite forward lean throughout the stunt. The spotter may grab the performer's shoulder or upper arm and help him clear the bars by pulling forward.

26. *Rear Vault Dismount with Half Twist.* From a straight arm support position between the bars, start the body swinging. On the forward end of the swing, lift the legs up and over one bar as in the rear vault. As the body clears the bar, execute a half twist towards the bar. End in a standing position facing the opposite direction with the near hand on the bar.

27. *Top Kip to Straddle Seat.* From an upper arm support position in the mid-

dle of the bars, raise the legs forward between the bars and over the head so that the body is in a pike position. From this pike position, extend the legs forward and spread them. At the same time pull hard with the arms and finish in a straddle seat position above the bars. Be sure to get the hips high over the bars prior to doing the kip as this will help in the execution of the stunt. A spotter can help by pushing under the hips as the kip is executed.

28. *Top Kip.* This stunt is done the same way as is the top kip to a straddle seat except that the legs are kept together throughout the stunt and thus the finish is into a straight arm support position.

29. *Swing to Shoulder Balance.* Start in a straight arm support position and swing back and forth a couple of times. At the end of the back swing, flex the arms and drop the shoulders forward toward the bars, keeping the body straight. Place the upper arms on the bars, remembering to keep the body arched and head up. Finish in a shoulder balance position.

30. *Top Kip to Shoulder Balance.* As the top kip is completed, keep the body rotating forward. As the momentum causes a forward lean, flex the arms, drop the shoulders to the bars, and allow the feet to rise over the head to a shoulder balance position.

31. *Straddle Leg Cut On to Straddle Seat.* As in the single leg cut on, grasp the ends of the bars and jump upward, straddling both legs over the bars, and land in a straddle seat position on the bars.

32. *Straddle Leg Cut On to Straight Arm Support.* Same as the above except the legs continue over the bars and finish together with the hands grasping the bars in a straight arm support position.

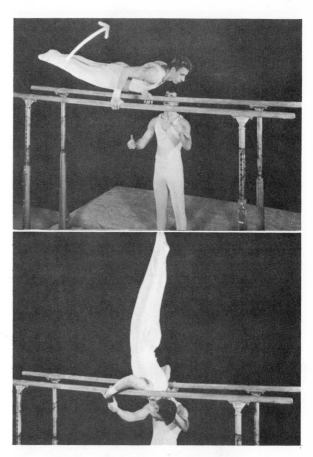

SWING TO SHOULDER BALANCE

STRADDLE CUT ON TO
STRADDLE SEAT

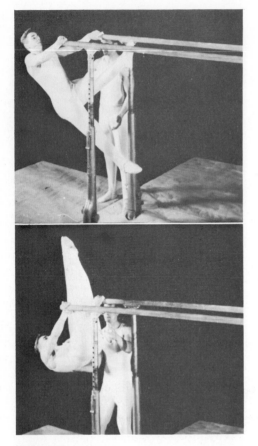

END KIP

BACKWARD GIANT ROLL

The spotter can grab the back of the performer's waist and give him a boost.

33. *End Kip*. With the hands on the ends of the bars, swing the legs forward and up to a pike position, hanging underneath the bar. As the body swings backward after the forward swing, extend the legs upward, pull with the arms, and finish in a straight arm support position above the bars.

34. *Glide Kip*. This stunt may be done from the end of the bars or in the middle of the bars. It is very similar to the end kip except for the glide. At the beginning, skim the feet over the mats until the front end of the swing is reached. Then on the back swing bring the legs up to a pike position, kip upward with the legs and pull strongly with the arms. Finish in a straight arm support position between the bars.

35. *Double Rear Dismount*. From a straight arm support position, swing the body. At the end of the back swing, lift the hips and swing both legs forward over the left bar. Continue the legs over the right bar and down toward the mats, where the dismount finishes in a standing position. Remember to keep the weight of the body on the right arm as the dismount is executed to the right. Keep the hips fairly high throughout the dismount. A spotter may assist by grasping the right arm of the performer, pulling slightly while the stunt is being tried.

36. *Backward Giant Roll (Shoulder Roll)*. This stunt consists basically of completing a full backward roll of the body in a layout position with the upper arms supporting the weight on the bars. From an upper arm support position, with the hands grasping the bars in front of the chest, swing the legs back and forth a few times. Obtain a forceful swing forward and allow the feet to continue on up and over the head. When

the hips reach the height of the bars, push hard with the hands, release the grip, and throw the arms straight out at the sides. With the head back and body arched, allow the legs and feet to continue past the vertical position and down toward the original position between the bars. When the feet are directly overhead and are just starting to continue downward, the hands reach forward and grasp the bars. By grasping the bars, the performer is able to steady the downward flow of the roll. As proficiency increases in this stunt, the backward giant roll may be tried from a shoulder balance position. Two or three of these in a row make for a fine performance.

37. *Cast.* This stunt can be done from a straight arm support position above the bars or from a standing position on the mats between the bars. From a standing position on the mats, grasp the bars with each hand on the inside of the bar and with the fingers circling the top side of the bar. Lean backward and jump up slightly off the mat, keeping the arms straight and bringing the legs up so the body is in a pike position. Allow the body to swing downward between the bars, reaching the full bottom of the swing, and start the upward swing. Just before reaching the peak of the forward swing, extend the body forcefully forward by shooting the legs up between the bars and pulling strongly with the arms. Continue this extension of the body with the legs pressing forward until the shoulders move above the height of the bars. At this point, extend the arms to the side and finish in an upper arm support position. Allow the feet to swing downward and at the back end of the swing execute a back uprise to a straight arm support position. To do the cast from a straight arm support position, raise the legs slightly and

CAST

153

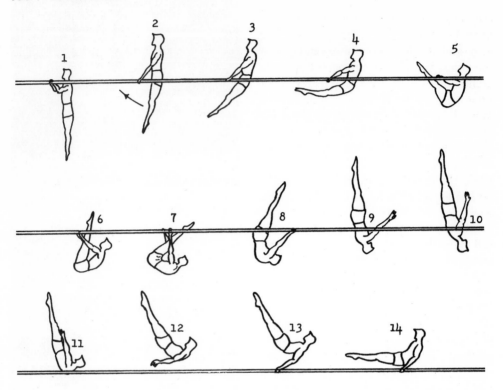

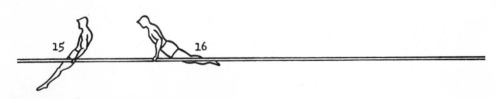

CAST TO A STRAIGHT ARM SUPPORT

drop backward between the bars. This puts the performer in a pike position, swinging beneath the bar, which is correct for completing the cast. This stunt can also be done to a straight arm support position by swinging and extending strongly so that the performer regrasps with the hands on top of the bars and finishes in a straight arm support position.

38. *Dip Half Turn.* Execute a swing-

ing dip movement, and on the upward swing with the body in a slightly piked position, extend an arch in the body, push hard with the hands, and execute a half twist either to the left or right. Hold onto the bar slightly longer, with the hand in the direction of the twist. Upon completion of the half turn, regrasp the bars in a straight arm support position. Try this stunt on the low bars at first.

39a. *Swing to a Hand Balance.* After

learning a hand balance on the low parallel bars by kicking up from the bar, the performer should try a hand balance from a swing on the higher bars. At first, do this on the end of the bars facing outward, so that the performer can land safely if he swings beyond the balance position. This can be done by lifting one hand and twisting the body around to face the bars like doing a roundoff on the mats. As for doing the hand balance, from a straight arm support position swing from the shoulders. with the arms straight. When ready to swing to the hand balance, arch at the front end of the swing and keep the body arched throughout the back swing. Allow the feet to swing over the head, keeping the shoulders over the hands. Flex the arms slightly if needed. If going off balance, grip hard with the hands to maintain the balance and do not give up easily. (*Safety precaution*—in coming down from the hand balance, do not allow the body to swing freely back to the straight arm support position. Slow down the swing with the shoulders and upper back muscles by leaning forward slightly.)

39b. *Press to Hand Balance.* This method is similar to the presses in Chapter 4 under *Strength Balance Moves.*

40. *One Arm Balance.* From a hand balance position, shift the weight to one bar and balance on one arm. The free arm may be held along the body or out to the side with the legs in straddle position or held together.

41. *Moore.* Swing in a straight arm support position. As the body passes the hands on the back swing, lift the hips into the air and pike the body. Reach backward with the left hand toward the right bar and continue to keep the hips high turning to the left so that the body is facing in towards both bars. Allow the

HAND BALANCE

ONE ARM BALANCE

MOORE

feet to swing on the outside of the right bar and grasp the right bar with the left hand fairly near the right hand. After the feet reach the midpoint in the circle around the outside of the right bar, release the right hand and reach across and grasp the free bar. Then let the feet pass over the right bar and swing them down between the two bars. This can be spotted effectively with an overhead safety belt rigging. Simply cross the ropes in the proper direction behind the performer's back and follow the moore through by pulling the rope supporting the performer. This stunt can also be done in a layout manner in that the legs are elevated considerably higher, and an effective flying action is simulated in the moore. This is almost a reverse pirouette movement.

42. *Front Overbar Somersault.* From a straight arm support position, swing several times. When a maximum swing is obtained on the backward swing, lift the hips upward and forward in a pike position. Push off hard with the hands and duck the head. Keep the arms

spread and land on the upper arms and then regrasp with the hands. It should be tried first from a small swing into a simple forward roll. For more difficulty, this can be done to a straight arm catch.

43. *Front Overbar Somersault Dismount.* This stunt is similar to the front overbar within the bars except it is done over one bar in a dismount fashion to the mats. Be sure to look over the dismounting bar just prior to somersaulting. Push with the far hand in order to move the body over the bars toward the mat. Regrasp the bar with the inside hand as quickly as possible in order to steady the landing. While first learning, it is suggested that the bar over which the dismount is attempted be padded. An overhead belt may be used or careful hand spotting applied. For more difficulty, this can be done with half twist.

44. *Pirouette.* From a handstand, shift weight slightly to the right hand, change the left hand forward to the right bar, and quickly change the right hand back to the left bar. End up in a handstand, facing the opposite direction. Keep the

LAYOUT MOORE

FRONT OVERBAR SOMERSAULT
DISMOUNT

FRONT OVERBAR SOMERSAULT
WITH HALF TWIST

body stretched out during the change of
hands so that the shift in weight will take
place without loss of balance. This stunt
should be mastered on the low parallel
bars before attempting it on the higher
bars. This stunt can be done in a reverse
direction, with the left hand reaching
backward behind the right hand, and
then from the handstand on the right
bar, the right hand moves to the left bar
for the completed stunt (reverse pirouette).

45. *Hand balance One Bar—Dismounts.*

A. *Squat Dismount*—After the performer turns forward to a handstand on
one bar, he simply pushes with his arms
and sharply brings his legs down and
between his arms in a squat position. He
continues downward to a standing position on the mat.

B. *Stoop Dismount*—Similar to squat
dismount except that the legs are kept
straight while the body pikes through
for the dismount.

C. *Straddle Dismount*—Again similar
to the above two dismounts except that
the legs are spread into a straddle position with the feet passing outside the
hands while dismounting.

SQUAT DISMOUNT

STRADDLE DISMOUNT

FORWARD ROLL INTO BACK UPRISE,
STRADDLE CUT TO SUPPORT

On all three dismounts there should be two spotters, one at each shoulder of the performer, to help him clear the bar. The spotter actually grasps the performer's upper arm during the early stages of learning these dismounts and pulls the body beyond the bar. The spotter must move forward with the performer so as not to interfere with the dismounting action.

46. *Back Uprise to a Cut and Catch.* From a top kip position on the parallel bars, the body is extended upward and forward as far as possible. The purpose of this phase of the stunt is to get a maximum swing. After the body passes the bottom of the swing and starts upward, the arms start to pull. When the legs are above the bars, they spread quickly, and the hands give a strong quick push before releasing. This enables the legs to pass under the hands and to continue the straddle action to meet in front of the body as the hands regrasp the bars. This stunt may be finished in an *L* position or a swing to a handstand. Another variation is to execute this stunt from a forward roll to a straddle cut into an *L* position.

47. *Stutz.* The performer swings between the bars, and as the feet rise upward at the forward end of the swing, the performer executes a half turn and then regrasps with the hands and swings downward for the next stunt. Be sure to pike at bottom of the swing and then

STUTZ

extend forcefully prior to turning into the stutz action.

For ease of learning and safety, try this stunt with the bars lowered to about waist height and so that the turn can be executed away from the bars at the end. Later the performer may try this stunt with the bars lowered but in the middle of the bars. The spotter may help by standing on a box alongside the bars and help to maintain the height of the legs until the turn is executed. Remember, as you become proficient at the stutz movement, to ride one arm longer than the other as the turn is executed. As this movement is mastered the height may be increased to the point where a handstand can be held after the turn is executed. This then becomes a stutz to a handstand, a very difficult movement.

The back uprise to reverse stutz consists of a back uprise into a reverse stutz movement. As the body rises above the level of the bars, the left hand is quickly shifted to the right bar where it assumes the support of the body while the right arm is shifted to the left bar and the

STUTZ

body turns half way to the right. A good back swing is essential along with an extension of the body as the twist is performed, which allows the hands to regrasp the bars prior to the return swing.

STUTZ TO HANDSTAND

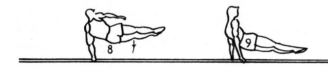

BACK UPRISE TO REVERSE STUTZ

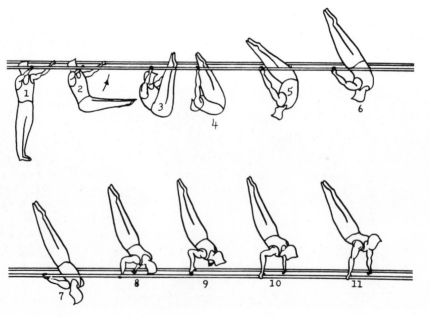

PEACH BASKET

The coach may spot by placing his hands under the performer's hips as the turn is executed.

48. *Underbar Somersault (Peach Basket) to Upper Arm Support Position.* Start this stunt from a standing position between the bars with the hands grasping the inside of the bars. Jump upward and after reaching the top of your height, fall backward with the arms straight and pike the body. When the body passes the bottom of the downward swing and starts up, extend into an arch and at the same time pull with the hands. As the hips rise above the bars release the hands and swing the arms up in between and over the parallel bars, landing on the upper arms and allowing the body to swing forward naturally.

This stunt is actually a preliminary one for the more advanced stunt of an underbar somersault to a straight arm support position. Some pointers are: (1) Keep the hips high throughout the stunt. Do not let them drop too far backward and below the bars; (2) when underneath the bar and executing the last part of the stunt, be sure not to release the hands too soon. An early release of the hands causes the body to travel and prevents a neat looking finish to the stunt.

49. *Peach to Handstand.* This is learned best by executing a cast to the arm pits several times and with each attempt landing higher on the back of the arms in the direction of the shoulders. With the aid of a spotter, the performer should then do a cast to the back of the arms or even to a shoulder balance position. The spotter lifts upward under the performer's back while he is doing the cast movement. When this action is well learned, the performer should try to place his hands on the top side of the bar just prior to landing on the shoulder balance position. The legs are extended straight upward above the shoulders and when the hands regrasp the bar, push upward into the handstand position. This is then done many times with the help of the spotter and finally the complete stunt is executed, with the hands regrasping the top side of the bar and the movement continuing upward into a handstand position. This is one of the finest stunts on the parallel bars— good luck with it.

50. *Back Overbar Somersault to Catch.*

BACK OVERBAR SOMERSAULT TO CATCH

This stunt is executed from a handstand. The body is then allowed to swing downward between the bars with a natural arch. This swing should be free and easy and definitely not tight or tense. The arms should be kept straight and the shoulders should be slightly forward of the hands.

After passing between the arms, the body in a slightly piked position should extend to an arched position, with the head and shoulders extended backward. This is the key spot in the entire stunt. Here we must watch for a few faults, which are as follows: (1) Do not lean forward or backward excessively; (2) Do not bend the arms; (3) Do not release the bars with your hands too soon. (Rather, allow them to be pulled off by the momentum of the swing.)

After the hands are pulled from the bars by the upward and backward momentum of the body, they should reach backward for the catch position. As skill progresses the arms have feeling of dislocating with the hands simply rotating a couple of inches above the bar while executing the stunt. As soon as the bars are caught, allow the body to continue its natural swing and finish in the straight arm support position.

In learning this stunt, it is recommended that an overhead safety belt be used. This eliminates many unnecessary bruises and jolts in learning the fundamentals of the stunt. The overhead belt also overcomes fear of the stunt and develops confidence, which is so essential to the successful gymnast. It is also suggested that this stunt be done first on lowered parallel bars with the suggested height being several inches below the performer's arm pits when he is standing on the mats.

A back somersault to catch can also be hand spotted with two spotters, one on each side of the performer. Example: the left bar spotter places his right hand on the performer's upper arm with the grip around the bicep (twist the arm so thumb faces downward). The left hand grasps the back of the performer's wrist. To spot, the spotters simply carry the performer over by lifting up on his bicep and turning his wrist over so hand regrasps the bar. Should be done with the parallel bars low—about waist height.

51. *Back Somersault to Handstand.* This stunt is similar in action to the back somersault to catch except the swing is more forcefully upward and slightly forward with the hips and the arms are rotated quickly so that a fast regrasp is executed to this handstand position. It is most advisable to execute this stunt in a belt many times prior to attempting alone.

52. *Back Overbar Somersault Dismount.* This stunt is also similar in action to the back overbar somersault to catch excepting that the flip is done off to the side and subsequently over one bar to a standing position on the mat. The same upward thrust of the chest and body is necessary, but at this point the left arm pushes the body over the right bar. After passing over this bar, the left hand quickly regrasps the right bar and steadies the body for the landing. This can be learned in an overhead safety belt with the spotter pulling one rope somewhat stronger, which in turn assists the performer in passing over the dismount bar. This can also be hand spotted by pulling the performer's sweat shirt at his upper arm as he executes the back somersault.

53. *Streilli.* The action on the streilli is a backward roll on the upper arms with a strong push of the hands and arms, swinging the body upward. Regrasp behind the shoulders with the

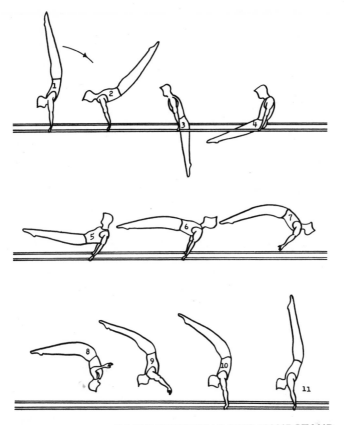

BACK SOMERSAULT TO HANDSTAND

STREILLI (BACK ROLL TO HANDSTAND)

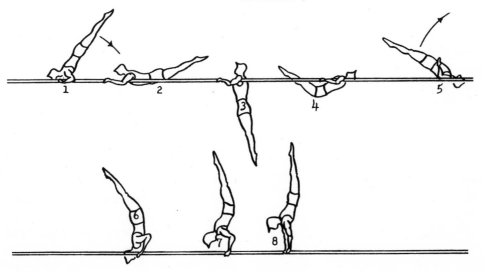

hands. A good streilli movement passes through a handstand position or even holds it. Be sure to pike the body slightly as it swings upward from below the bar and then arch into the handstand.

54. *Full Twisting Stutz.* This stunt, being relatively new, is producing a considerable challenge to the many fine gymnasts throughout the world. On the upward swing of the stutz movement the performer holds on with his left hand, releases his right hand, and turns in the direction of the left arm. Bringing the right arm across the body and under the left arm and back to the right hand bar causes the body to execute a full twist. When a performer misses the stunt slightly he will generally finish with the right hand on the same bar as the left hand and then drop down to the mats over the right bar. Hand spotting seems to be the most advantageous method of spotting and this is done as follows: The spotter stands on the two bars facing the performer and the performer lifts his legs

FULL TWISTING STUTZ

upward toward the spotter's hands. The spotter crosses his arms with the right arm on top of the left arm. With the arms crossed, the right hand then grasps the performer's right ankle and the left hand grasps the left ankle. From here the spotter simply lifts the performer's legs upward and at the same time commences to uncross his arms, which of course twists the performer. The performer during this time holds on with his left hand, releases his right hand, and follows the twisting action activated and continued by the spotter. With the spotter holding the legs well in the air and the full twist near completion, the performer reaches back with his right hand to the right bar for the finish of the full twisting stutz. After many of these have been done to establish orientation with the stunt, then place two spotters on the outside of the right bar and one spotter on the left side on a raised platform at the height of the lowered parallel bars (waist height). Then the performer should try the stunt with the spotter on the raised platform catching his feet and the other two catching the performer in case he falls over the right bar. Also it can be spotted using the twisting belt with one rope in front of arm and other rope in back of other arm.

ROUTINES

Creativity, imagination, and resourcefulness can be developed in the sport of gymnastics by the individual's construction and performance of his own sequence of stunts. The following are simply suggestions of combinations that certainly can be enlarged upon within the pupil's ability:

1. Single leg cut on—swing legs to two straddle seat travels—side seat turn around to straddle seat—forward roll to

another straddle seat and then lift legs and swing backward to front dismount.

2. Jump to upper arm hang, elevate legs to a pike position and then do a top kip to straddle seat—shoulder balance and roll forward to another straddle seat —by swinging one leg between the bars, execute a scissors change to straddle seat —forward roll to straddle seat and then swing legs to straddle dismount off the end of the bars.

3. Jump to upper arm hang—front uprise—swing to shoulder balance—roll out to back uprise—single leg circle forward —shoulder balance and finish with a side dismount.

4. Kip on the end swinging legs backward and then do a swinging dip travel in towards the center of the bars—swing legs backward and drop to upper arm hang and then execute a top kip to shoulder balance—roll forward to a back uprise to a rear dismount with half twist.

5. Jump to upper arm hang—swing to back roll (layout) to straight arm support continue on to cast below bars to upper arm hang into a back uprise straddle cut and catch immediate lay back to upper arms again to front uprise to swing to handstand—pirouette into a stutz dropping to the upper arms again into a front uprise and then a double rear dismount.

6. Peach basket to L position (hold)— press to handstand—swing down to stutz to cast below the bars to back uprise to straddle cut and catch and on up to a handstand—turn to one bar and execute a squat (stoop or straddle) dismount.

7. Peach basket to support then drop below bar to cast to support immediate cut and catch to L position—hold—press to handstand then execute a stutz to cast below bar to upper arms to back uprise cut and catch swing to handstand to back somersault dismount.

CHAPTER NINE / *rings*

The flying and still rings have always had an air of adventure and daring since Francis Amores of Spain invented this apparatus along with the flying trapeze in the early 1800's.

In recent years competition has been limited to still rings where greater strength and control is required. The rings are made of wood and are suspended 18 feet above the floor and placed 18 inches apart. Adjustable straps about 3 feet in length are attached to the rings from steel cables, with a swivel attachment at the point of suspension. For competition, the bottom of the rings should be 7' 10" from the top of the mat. Still-ring work is intended to be done without any swinging of the rings and should combine swinging movements with strength exercises and hold positions.

values

The specific values of working on the rings are:

1. Rings develop strength in the muscles of the arms and chest because of the different presses, levers, and difficult balances.

2. Because the rings must be gripped in the hands, strength in the fingers and a good grip are developed.

3. Ring work develops a sense of timing, rhythm, and beat.

4. Working on the rings develops suppleness within the shoulder joints from stunts involving twisting and turning of the extended arms.

5. Due to the nature of the activity, still rings can be worked by certain handicapped people, giving them enjoyment and a feeling of accomplishment. Most

stunts on the rings involve the upper body, with the legs only being swung to give momentum. Men with legs of limited use have been known to win championships.

organization

AREA AND EQUIPMENT

Because the rings are in a fixed position, they cannot be moved at will around the gymnasium. Where conditions are not satisfactory for suspending the rings from the ceiling, a portable rigging has been adapted by some gymnastic equipment companies. Adequate padding beneath the rings should be provided for the safety of the performer.

TEACHING METHODS

Because only one person at a time can work on the rings and because most schools do not have more than two or three sets of rings, the squad method is best used for instruction. Stunts on the still rings are difficult, and the trials will proceed rapidly because generally one stunt at a time is tried.

While first participating in this activity, the rings should be lowered to approximately shoulder height. As skill progresses, the rings may be elevated to the regulation competitive height.

The instructor or squad leader should constantly stand to one side of the performer while the stunts are being attempted. The instructor can then assist the performer through the stunts and can also catch him in case of a slip or fall.

Evaluation of performers on the rings can be done by means of a stunt chart with competitive routines serving this purpose in advanced classes.

SAFETY

Because of the height involved, spotting is more difficult on the rings than on other pieces of apparatus. Also, the fact that the full body weight is supported by the hand grip leaves some danger of falling. Many stunts involve a strain on the shoulders, which leaves some danger of shoulder injuries if improperly performed. However, if instruction is carried out using a progressive order of learning and the activity is closely supervised, it is not a dangerous activity.

Some hints for the safe conduct of this activity are:

1. Use adequate mats beneath the rings, anticipating possible swinging of the rings while doing the stunts.

2. Use carbonate of magnesia chalk on the hands before working.

3. Use an overhead safety belt rigging when learning difficult stunts and dismounts.

4. Periodically check the rings, straps, cables, and connections for weak spots.

program of instruction

Instruction on the rings involves three basic steps:

1. Individual Stunts.

2. Combinations. As a person learns a new stunt, he should be challenged to combine it with another stunt as smoothly as possible. Because a stunt must be learned well in order to combine it with another, the use of combinations in the teaching progression stresses proper execution and increases the safety

CHIN-UP L POSITION

CHIN-UP ONE ARM TO THE SIDE

INVERTED PIKE HANG

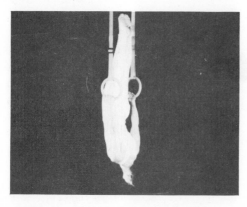

of performance. In addition, the smaller combinations serve as building blocks for longer routines. Combinations can be suggested by the instructor or coach or can be created by the performer.

3. Routines. Ultimately, a pupil should strive to combine stunts into a routine. Competition is based on routines, required or optional. The approach to optional routines is one of problem solving. Certain requirements involving the types and number of movements are presented as a problem for the performer to solve creatively within his own capabilities. The instructor, coach, and pupil can coordinate their thoughts on the development of a particular routine. For sample routines refer to the end of the chapter.

As suggested, the rings should first be worked at approximately shoulder height. Some of the stunts that can be done on the still rings in the recommended order of progression are as follows:

1. *Chin-Ups.* Grasp the rings and simply pull up into a chin-up position. Repeat.

2. *Chin-Ups with Legs in L Position.* Raise the legs to an *L* position parallel to the mats and execute a chin-up.

3. *Chin-Up—One Arm to the Side.* Execute a chin-up and while the arms are in the flexed position, extend one arm to the side, then bring it back and extend the other arm to the side.

4. *Inverted Pike Hang.* Grasp the rings, and bending at the hips, bring the feet up and over the head. Finish in a jacknife position with the knees straight and close to the chest. This is a fundamental starting position for many ring stunts.

5. *Inverted Layout Hang.* Grasp the

INVERTED LAYOUT HANG

rings and bring the feet up and over the head. Finish with the legs straight above the performer between the rings with the feet together, body arched, and arms straight. Hold this position for a few seconds and then return to the original starting position. At first it may be tried with the legs resting on the straps.

6. *Bird's Nest.* Grasp the rings with the hands and pull the feet up and into the rings. Place the instep in the rings and arch the body so the chest is facing the mat. Hold for a moment and return.

7. *Bird's Nest—One Foot.* Do the bird's nest and remove one foot from the ring, extending that leg straight out behind.

8. *Bird's Nest—One Foot and One Hand.* Do the bird's nest and remove one foot and then release opposite hand and hold the position with only one hand and one foot.

9. *Skin the Cat.* Grasp the rings and bring the legs up between the arms and continue them over to an extended position with the toes reaching downward as far as possible toward the mat. Return to original position. Keep the knees close to the chest for better control of the movement.

10. *Single Leg Kip Up.* With the body in an inverted pike hang position, put the right leg across the right arm with the foot outside the ring. Rock forward, pulling with both hands and ending in a position with the head and shoulders above the rings with the right leg resting on the right arm. Return to pike hang.

11. *Single Leg Cut Off—Forward.* With the body in an inverted pike position, swing forward with both legs and at the same time spread them apart so as to cut one leg between a ring and a hand. Release the ring with the hand and allow

BIRD'S NEST

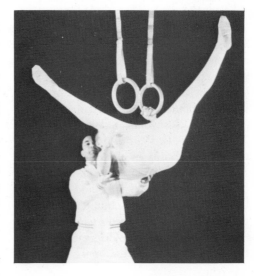

SINGLE LEG CUT OFF-FORWARD

DISLOCATE

the leg to pass between and then regrasp the ring. While doing the single leg cut off, the arms should be in a slightly flexed position as this will give added control to the stunt. The head and shoulders should be rolled up toward the rings before cutting off for a safer and easier execution of the stunt. This also may be done as a dismount by finishing in a standing position on the mats after the cut off.

12. *Double Leg Cut Off—Forward.* Same as single leg cut off except that both legs are swung between one ring and hand. Regrasp the ring after the legs pass between it and the hand. The spotter should stand behind the performer for this stunt.

13. *Dislocate.* With the body in an inverted pike position, extend the legs up and backward and at the same time push the arms out to the side and arch the body. With the arms completely out to the sides and the body in an arched position, dislocate the shoulders and swing the feet on toward the mat. Turn the

thumbs outward while dislocating. Allow the feet to continue toward the mat to a standing position or bend the legs and swing on through to the original pike position. Just as the dislocate is completed, pull up slightly with the arms as this will absorb the shock or strain at the completion of the stunt. This is done only at first while learning the stunt be-

SPOTTING A DISLOCATE

INLOCATE

cause when it is mastered the arms should be straight throughout. Assistance in this stunt is accomplished by the instructor lifting up on the shoulders and by holding the legs parallel to the mat until the dislocation of the shoulders is completed.

14. *Inlocate.* From an inverted pike position swing the legs forward, downward and backward. At the peak of the backward swing turn the arms inward, drop the head forward, pike the body, and inlocate to an inverted pike position. Assistance can be given by lifting up on the legs as the performer swings into the pike.

15. *Jump to Straight Arm Support.* Grasp the rings and jump upward into a straight arm support position above the rings. Keep the arms near the side of the body while in the straight arm support position. The rings in this particular stunt should be at shoulder height.

16. *Forward Roll.* From a straight arm support position above the rings roll

FORWARD ROLL

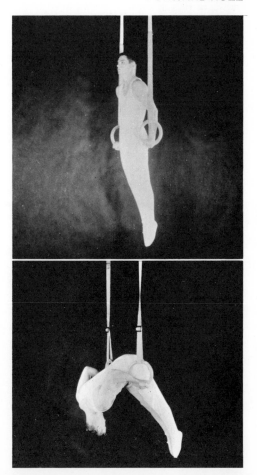

MUSCLE UP

forward slowly into a pike position be-low the rings. Be sure to elevate the hips as the head is dropped forward prior to the roll. Lower the body slowly by keep-ing the arms flexed as the roll is com-pleted.

17. *Muscle Up.* Grip the rings with the palms of the hands resting above the rings in a false grip or overgrip. Bring the legs between the arms in a pike position. Flex the arms as in chin-ning and roll forward slowly, trying to

get the head and shoulders above the rings, keeping the rings close to the body. When the head and shoulders reach a position above the rings, the arms are then straightened to finish with the legs either in an *L* position or low-ered to a straight position. The spotter may assist by placing one hand on the back and the other hand under the buttocks, lifting the performer as he does the muscle up.

18. *Kip to Straight Arm Support.* From a pike position under the rings, extend the legs upward and forward and pull with the arms. Continue the kip until the body is above the rings in a straight arm support position with the shoulders and arms resting against the straps. The spotter may assist by pushing upward under the hips.

19. *Back Uprise.* The rings should be elevated to the regulation height of about 8 feet while trying this stunt. Bring the legs up into a pike position and then extend them forward and downward. Continue the swing of the legs under the rings and as the legs swing backward pull with the arms and finish above the rings in a straight arm support position. A forceful downward

KIP TO STRAIGHT ARM SUPPORT

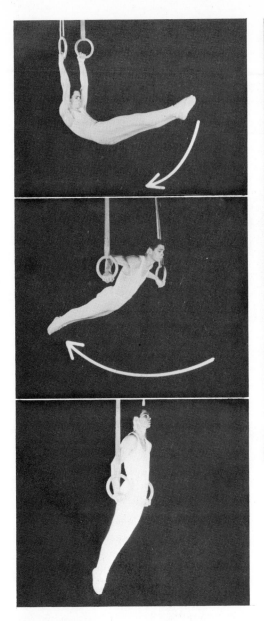

BACK UPRISE

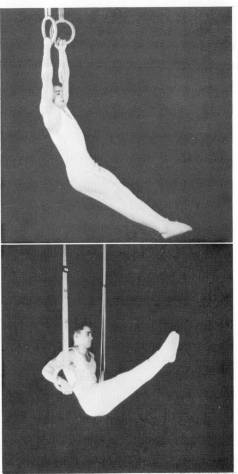

FRONT UPRISE

swing is of great importance in executing this stunt.

20. *Front Uprise*. This stunt can be first tried on the still rings at the regular elevated height of 8 feet. Swing the feet back and forth a few times and prior to the front end of the swing, pike slightly and start pulling with the arms. After a quick pike of the body, extend the body by thrusting the hips up toward the rings. Pull hard with the arms and on the way up to a position above the rings, shift the wrists from a hanging position to that of a support position. Straighten the arms and finish in a straight arm support position.

21. *Shoulder Balance*. From a straight arm support position bend forward, lifting the hips above the head and flexing the arms so that the shoulder balance position can be reached. Keep the head up and slowly lift the feet upward to a straight shoulder balance position. Hold an arch in the body and point the toes. The arms should be flexed enough so that the upper arms may apply pressure against the straps in order to maintain the balance. Spotter should be used in

SHOULDER BALANCE

REVERSE KIP

learning this stunt. Also, the feet may be placed along the ropes during the learning period.

22. *Reverse Kip.* Grasp the rings and swing the feet back and forth a few times. Finally, as the feet swing forward, continue them upward between the straps of the rings. Shoot the feet into the air and attempt to change the grip of the hands from a hanging position to a support position above the rings. In learning this stunt, it may be advisable to think of it as a high dislocate. Try to stop the dislocate half way through and catch the body above the rings in a support position. The spotter can assist by pushing upward under the performer's shoulders as he attempts the shoot into the reverse kip. Be sure to finish with the rings in front of the body and not behind the hips.

23. *Muscle Up into Forward Roll.* This is a combination of the muscle up (No. 17) and forward roll (No. 16). Try to make the action a slow and continuous motion so that the forward roll is at the same speed as the muscle up.

24. *Kip to Forward Roll.* This stunt is

BACKWARD STRADDLE DISMOUNT

similar to stunt No. 23 in that it is a combination of a kip and forward roll. Be sure that the kip is executed high enough so that the forward roll is commenced with the shoulders above the rings. The spotter should be sure to help the performer so that he does not drop too forcefully into the roll, causing strain on the shoulders and sometimes a loss of grip.

25. *Back Hip Circle.* From a front support position, swing the legs backward slightly and then forward into the back hip circle action. Keep the rings close to the hips, which simulates a back hip circle around the horizontal bar. Again the spotter should help the performer throughout the action to prevent him from dropping below the rings too far.

26. *Backward Straddle Dismount.* From a swing below the rings bring the legs upward above the hands and into a straddle position. Pull hard with the arms and continue the motion upward and backward, releasing the hands and passing the legs outside the rings to finish in a standing position on the mat. At the time of the releasing of the hands,

the head and shoulders should be lifted to assist the performer in completing the backward somersault movement to a standing position. After releasing the hands, the body may maintain a layout or pike position in dropping to the mats. As proficiency improves, the height may be increased to a point where the hips rise above the rings. This action is best learned by swinging forward below the rings and shooting upward into a handstand action, with the legs in straddle position, but without the release of the hands. Several of these swings upward to handstand position give the performer the feel of a truly high straddle dismount (See picture).

27. *Flyaway.* This is similar to a straddle dismount except the legs are between the rings and not straddling them. As the body reaches the position where the hands release the rings, pike at the hips sharply to bring the legs downward to the mat in a neat manner.

28. *Back Lever.* Start from a straight body inverted hang and slowly lower the body backward to a position parallel to the mats with the stomach facing

BACK LEVER

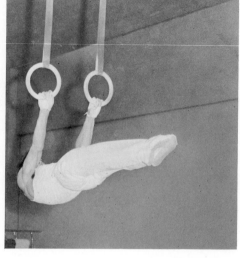

FRONT LEVER

downward. The spotter can assist by holding the legs in the desired position.

29. *Front Lever.* Start from a straight body inverted hang and slowly lower forward to a position parallel to the mats with the back facing downward. The spotter should assist by holding the hips in the desired position. For progression the performer may try this stunt with one leg straight and the other bent with the foot on top of the opposite knee.

HANDSTAND

Also this may be tried at first with the arms bent.

30. *Handstand.* From a straight arm support position lift the hips upward, bending the arms slightly. Continue the movement and when the hips are over the rings the legs are extended upward into the handstand position while the arms are straightened. Hold the handstand position with the arms straight and the hands turned sideward so that the palms face each other. In a top-flight performance, the gymnast does not touch the straps with his arms. If the performer overbalances, he should pike the body so as to control the roll into the hanging position. While first learning this stunt, the legs as well as the arms may be bent as the performer moves upward into the handstand position.

31. *Straight Body Bent Arm Press to Handstand.* From a support position lean forward, bending the arms but keeping the body straight; move upward into a handstand position. This stunt requires considerable strength and can be practiced on the parallel bars and floor.

32. *Reverse Kip Back Hip Circle.* This stunt is a combination of a reverse kip and a backward hip circle. Care should be taken that the rings are under control as the reverse kip is completed and the back hip circle begins. This can be done by keeping the rings close to the hips and trying to maintain a constant speed of movement.

33. *Shoot to Shoulder Balance.* From a swing below the rings, pass the legs forward and upward as if performing a reverse kip. As the legs reach a position near the straps, they should extend upward between the straps and at the same time the arms pull and the hands shift from the hang position to a support position as the body moves into the shoulder balance position. The head is lifted upward to control the balance.

34. *Shoot to Handstand.* Similar to No. 32 except the shoot upward is more forceful, the pull of the arms is stronger, and the final position is a handstand.

35. *Kip to L Support.* This stunt is a regular kip ending with the body in an *L* support position with the legs parallel to the floor. A high forceful kipping action along with a powerful arm pull is necessary to execute this stunt. The spotter may assist by pushing upward on the hips.

36. *Crosses*

a. *Straight Body Cross.* From a support position, lower slowly downward, spreading the arms to the side until the arms are straight out from the shoulders. Hold this position at this point. To come out of this stunt, the usual procedure is to lower the body into a hanging position below the rings, although some stronger gymnasts will push upward into a straight body support position above the rings. The spotter may assist by standing in front of the performer and holding the feet with his

STRAIGHT BODY PRESS
TO HANDSTAND

KIP TO L SUPPORT

STRAIGHT BODY CROSS

LEARNING CROSS WITH INNER TUBE

OLYMPIC CROSS

L CROSS

hands, thus taking some of the weight off the performer's shoulders and arms. Another method is to use an old bicycle inner tube that has been cut into one length. Place one end through each ring. Jump to a support position with the hands holding each end of the tube and then place the feet on the hanging part of the inner tube. This will give support

as the body is lowered into the cross position.

b. *Olympic Cross.* From a support position, turn the shoulders so the head is facing one strap. Then lower the body downward into the Olympic cross position.

c. *L Cross.* From a support position, lower downward into a regular straight body cross. While in this position lift the legs upward to an *L* position and hold.

d. *Inverted Cross.* From a handstand position, lower downward, spreading the arms until they are straight out to the sides in an inverted cross position. Hold this position.

37. *Planche.* From a support position on the rings, lift the legs backward to a point parallel to the mats. This places the body in a planche position above the rings. Upon first learning, the performer may place his feet slightly higher than his head for ease of learning. He may also do it at first with his legs in a straddle position for a slightly easier approach to the move. Another learning method is to lower himself downward from a handstand to the parallel or planche position. Many performers practice the movement on the floor with the legs in straddle position.

38. *Maltese.* This stunt is similar to the planche except the body is down in a position between the rings with the arms to the side. Considerably more difficult than the planche.

39. *Backward Giant Swing.* From a handstand position, lower slowly toward the inverted cross position with the arms outward to the sides. As the chest nears the level of the rings, allow the body to swing downward and through the bottom of the swing and upward into a shoot to handstand movement. Be sure the arms are pushed to sides and kept straight and not forward during the downward swing of the body. This stunt should first be tried in an overhead safety belt. Then try with two spotters under the rings with one arm placed behind the performer's back as he reaches the bottom of the swing.

40. *Forward Giant Swing.* From a handstand position, lower downward, ducking the head and shoulders to activate the forward giant swing action. As the shoulders pass below the rings, allow

INVERTED CROSS

PLANCHE

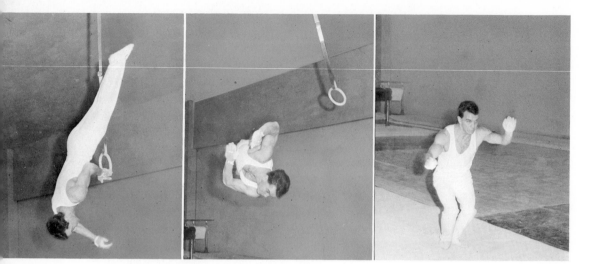

FULL TWISTING FLYAWAY

the legs to swing downward forcefully so as to whip the body back upward into a back uprise action to a handstand. This completes the forward giant swing. Again, spotters should place themselves under the rings to assist and prevent the performer from slipping off the rings.

41. *Flyaway with Half Twist.* The performer starts to do a regular flyaway and just as the hands are released, the shoulders and head are turned to the left. The body then executes a sharp half turn and lands on the mat facing in the opposite direction. The spotter should position himself so that he can grasp the hips as the twist is executed.

42. *Flyaway with Full Twist.* The performer starts to do a regular flyaway and as the hands are released, the shoulders and head are turned to the left. The right arm is thrust across the chest to cause the body to complete a full twist and then the performer lands on the mat in a standing position. This stunt is best learned on the trampoline with a twisting belt and also on the rings with an overhead rigging.

43. *Double Flyaway.* The performer

swings forward and upward from below the rings. As soon as the legs start the upward swing, the knees are bent and the double flyaway action is started. The knees are brought up close to the chest and the head is pushed backward. The hands, upon releasing the rings, grasp the shins to form a tight tuck. After completion of the second somersault, the performer opens smartly to a landing position on his feet on the mat. The mechanics of the double somersault should be tried on the trampoline in an overhead rigging and also should be attempted in the rings with an overhead safety rigging about the performer.

ROUTINES

Creativity, imagination, and resourcefulness can be developed in the sport of gymnastics by the individual's construction and performance of his own sequence of stunts. The following are suggestions of combinations that can be enlarged upon within the pupil's ability:

1. On low rings (rings at shoulder height) pull up to an inverted hand

layout position, slowly lower legs into a pike position and then continue on backward to a skin the cat. Bring the legs back to the pike position and execute a single leg cut and catch with the right leg. Return to pike hang and do a single leg cut (left leg), dismount to a stand, grasping rings with the hands.

2. On low rings (rings at shoulder height) pull up to an inverted hang layout position, lower legs to a pike hang position, and then place the feet into the rings and execute bird's nest (an additional challenge would be to have performer do a bird's nest with two hands and one foot with the other foot free of the ring). Return to pike position and then a single leg cut off dismount.

3. Jump to support (rings at shoulder height) above the rings and then do a forward roll to a pike hang position; do a single leg kip-up and then drop back to a skin the cat and then back to a single leg cut and catch and then a skin-the-cat dismount.

4. On higher rings, muscle up to above the rings into a forward roll to a pike hang and then execute a dislocate into a straddle dismount.

5. With a false grip on the rings, kip up into a support position and then press to a shoulder balance. Roll forward and swing legs backward into an inlocate to to a pike hang. Lower the legs to a back lever position and hold momentarily. Bring legs back to a pike hang position and then do a dislocate pike flyaway.

6. Bring legs slowly upward to a straight body hang and then execute a dislocate to a reverse kip to an L position above the rings. Press to a handstand and then lower the legs down to a support position above the rings and from here lower to a straight body cross. Hold momentarily and then drop below the rings into a pike hang position and then do a dislocate high straddle dismount.

7. Dislocate to a shoot to a handstand and then lower body to a regular cross. Drop below the rings and do a dislocate to a reverse kip to a backward roll to L position above the rings. Press to a handstand; lower legs and bring the feet forward to forward cast to an inlocate to a back uprise to a backward roll and then drop below the rings to a dislocate flyaway with a twist.

CHAPTER TEN / *women's floor exercise*

In the floor exercise for women the performer works on the floor or on a thin pad within a square area, the dimensions of which are 12 meters (39′ 4″). The duration of the exercise is from one minute to a minute and 30 seconds. The total space of the square should be used in the composition of the routine. Exercises should make use of the entire body and contain artistic movements, leaps, poses, and balances. These are done with a change of pace and with expression. The routine should be performed with musical accompaniment using a single instrument. The nature of the music should conform to the type of movements being done. A great amount of inventiveness and artistic thinking can be displayed throughout the floor exercise routine. It is one of the most creative events in women's competition.

values

The specific values of working floor exercise are:

1. Floor exercise develops an appreciation for rhythm and timing.

2. The event will develop coordination and balance to a high degree.

3. An ability to create will be developed through repeated attempts at composing a fine artistic exercise.

4. Strength and endurance is developed through the hard workouts necessary for the accomplishment of the final routine.

organization

Many of the stunts done in floor exercise for women should be tried first on a tumbling mat. Later they may be transferred to the floor. It is also highly recommended that a spotter be used while learning some of the more difficult stunts such as valdez, walkovers, backbends, yogi handstands, and so on.

In composing a routine, it is suggested that some of the individual stunts or movements be learned thoroughly first and then molded into a neat fundamental exercise. This may be done in the form of a problem to be solved by the performer, using creativity within the limits set by the instructor and the knowledge and ability of the performer. This will give the performer a feeling for the event, and later, as more difficult stunts are learned, they may be inserted at the performer's discretion. Routines should make use of the entire body and include movements and jumps that are full of expression, elegance, individuality, and originality. Remember that an effort should be made to make the connecting moves harmonious when changing rhythm, style, or pace.

It is further suggested that many of the stunts be done before a mirror or a reflecting surface so that grace and fine performance can be cultivated early.

program of instruction

The stunts or movements that can be done in the women's event will be placed into four groups: ballet, flexibility, balance, and agility. They appear within these groups in recommended order of learning.

BALLET MOVEMENTS

As previously mentioned, the women's floor exercise routine contains several

TOE STAND

ballet movements, and with this in mind the following are a few that may be used:

1. *Toe Stand.* Start from a standing position and then raise up on the toes, extending the arms to the side, palms down. Then drop down to a full standing position with the arms at sides.

2. *Body Wave.* From a standing position with the hands at the side, bend slightly forward and bring the arms

BODY WAVE

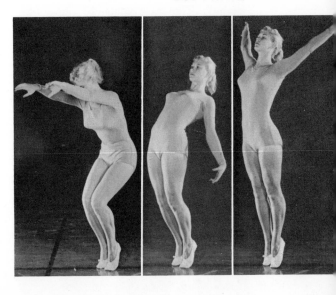

BALLET TOUCH

BODY SWEEP

STAG LEAP

backward and upward in a graceful manner. The body executes a facsimile of a waving motion and then returns to the starting position again.

3. *Ballet Touch.* With one foot ahead of the other, the performer from a standing position gracefully leans forward to touch the forward foot with one hand. This is often used as a transitional movement from one stunt to another.

4. *Spiral.* From a trunk bending position with flexed knees, little steps are taken to turn in place while arms and body move to one side in a winding motion to toe stand and stretched body. Usually a full turn.

5. *Body Sweep.* This is another ballet movement and is done as pictured. A graceful sweep of the body is executed by swinging one arm forward with the weight on the other arm and knee, keeping the other leg extended backward.

6. *Grand Jeté.* Run across area and leap into the air, spreading the legs in a split position, and then land on leading foot.

7. *Stag Leap.* Same as grand jeté except while in the air in an extended split position, bring the lead foot back quickly to the back knee in a stag position and then land on the lead foot.

8. *Cabriole.* Jump into the air and lift legs forward and place one on top of the other for a split second and then drop to the back, or under, foot. This can also be done by extending the legs backward instead of forward.

9. *Tour Jeté.* Step forward on left foot, swing the right leg forward and upward and while in the air turn body a half turn and land on right foot with the left leg extended straight.

10. *Soada Bas.* Like the tour jeté except a full turn is executed, with the performer landing on the foot that is kicked upward, and during the turn, the

other leg is flexed with the foot placed near the shin of the straight leg.

11. *Fouetté*. This is like the tour jeté except that the leg kicked into the air is held aloft, and landing is done on the same foot that the performer leaps from.

12. *Arabesque Movement*. The performer turns and then leaps forward, assuming an arabesque position while in the air.

13. *Pirouette à la seconde*. Start with the left foot forward slightly and right foot back, with the right arm flexed across the front of the chest. Left arm is extended straight out sideward from the shoulder. Right arm is then extended backward behind the shoulder and the left arm is pulled in toward the chest and the body executes a full turn to the right on the left foot, with the right leg extended outward in a straight position during the turn.

14. *Tour en l'air*. Consists of a full turn (pirouette) in the air. Start with the feet close together with the right arm flexed across the chest and the left arm straight out sideward from the shoulder. From this starting position, the performer jumps into the air, executing a full turn (pirouette) of the body and then landing back on the feet. Variations of this are that the legs may be straight while turning or one leg may be extended out to the side or one leg flexed with the foot near the other knee. Also, some performers execute the turn with the arms pulled into the chest or extended outward from the shoulders.

FLEXIBILITY STUNTS

Just a few of the many stunts that belong in the flexibility group are as follows:

1. *Splits*. This, as implied, simply means the performer drops downward

STRADDLE LEAN

from a standing position into a neat split. The hands may be raised outward from the shoulders and held in a graceful position. For description of the varieties of splits refer to Chapter 4.

2. *Straddle Lean*. This consists in doing a straddle stand and dropping downward into a wide front split and then leaning forward until the chest touches the floor.

3. *Needle Scale*. The position of the body when the legs are straight and the forehead is touching the shins is called the needle scale. It may be done in various ways: (1) From a standing position bend forward and touch the fore-

NEEDLE SCALE

SUPINE ARCH UP

BACK WALKOVER

touch the floor and then kick one leg up and over, followed by the other, to finish in a standing position again. Be sure to have a spotter during the learning stages of this stunt to lift under the hips while the weight is being shifted from the feet to the hands.

6. *One Leg Balance.* From a standing position, raise one leg to the side as high as you can, grasp its instep with one hand while you gracefully sweep the other arm straight up, palm facing in.

7. *Front Walkover.* Start from a standing position and lean forward, placing the hands on the mat or floor ahead of the feet as if going into a handstand. Continue the feet on over to the floor again and land on one foot; then lift the hands off the floor and bring the other foot to the floor. Again a spotter is essential while first learning this stunt to lift under the hips while shifting the weight from the hands to the feet.

BALANCE MOVEMENTS

This division indicates the stunts that mainly require a balancing technique. Many of the balancing stunts described

head to the shins while keeping the legs straight. (2) Same as (1) except one leg is elevated straight overhead. This is a good combination from a front scale. (3) From a sitting position, bend forward and touch the shins with the head while keeping the legs straight.

4. *Supine Arch Up.* From a supine position on the floor, simply elevate the back upward from the floor, sliding the hands from a position near the hips backward to a support position. This can also be done from a sitting position.

5. *Back Walkover.* From a standing position, bend backward until the hands

ONE LEG BALANCE

in Chapter 3 may be used. Additional ones are included here. The balance positions in floor exercise are mainly transitional moves rather than held positions. A momentary holding position is called a pose and may take many forms.

1. *Arabesque.* From a standing position, raise one arm upward and lift one foot off the floor. Hold this position in a graceful manner.

2. *Front Scale.* This stunt consists in standing on one foot with the other leg raised to a height parallel to the floor or higher, with the forward part of the body lowered to a position parallel to the floor. The arms may be held outward from the shoulders in a graceful manner or one arm may be raised straight ahead with the other along the body. The head is up with the back arched and the leg fairly straight with the toes pointed.

3. *V Sit.* This stunt consists in simply sitting on the floor with the legs together, elevated to make a V with the body. The hands may be either on the floor behind the performer or raised outward from the shoulders.

4. *Hand Balance.* The techniques of a hand balance are thoroughly covered

FRONT WALKOVER

A POSE

FRONT SCALE

ARABESQUE

V SIT

in Chapter 3. Many different methods of moving into the hand balance position can be left to the imagination of the performer. A straight kick up, back bend, or cartwheel into hand balance are some suggested methods.

5. *Yogi Hand Balance.* As pictured, this consists in holding a hand balance in an unusual position of the body. The hips are forward, with the legs back, and the head is lifted so that the entire stunt looks fascinating and challenging. One of the easiest methods of moving into the yogi position is to jump into it with the hands on the floor. Push off both feet

YOGI HAND BALANCE

and immediately execute the yogi hand balance.

AGILITY STUNTS

Many tumbling stunts such as those described in Chapter 2 may be used in floor exercise. Additional moves requiring agility are included here.

1. *Shoot Through.* From a front leaning rest position with the arms straight, arch the back slightly and then lift the hips to shoot the legs between the arms and finish in a sitting position. The shoot through can be continued into a back arched position.

2. *Swedish Fall.* From a standing position, fall forward, landing on the hands with the arms straight at first, and with a flexing of the arms, continue downward to the chest. Lift one leg as the fall is executed so that in the finish position one leg is lifted gracefully and one leg remains on the floor; the upper part of the body is almost resting on the floor, with the weight supported by the arms.

3. *Valdez.* The performer sits on the floor with one hand behind the hip and the other arm elevated straight out from the shoulder. One leg is straight and the other is flexed, with the foot near the seat. This is as pictured. From this position the elevated arm is thrown overhead and backward, and the straight leg is lifted upward. The performer executes a fast back-bend motion and finishes either in a handstand position or continues the movement to a standing position on the feet.

In learning this stunt, the performer can turn in the direction of the hand on the floor and execute a cartwheel. A further variation is to do the cartwheel action into the handstand position and then lower into a forward roll.

4. *Knee Turn and Spiral Up.* From a kneeling position on the left knee with the right leg extended to the side, bring the right knee alongside the left knee, turning the body to the left, with the right arm coming across the chest and the left arm behind the left shoulder. After completing a full turn on the knees, step forward on the left foot and do a spiral up to a standing position.

VALDEZ

SHOOT THROUGH

SWEDISH FALL

In women's vaulting the vaults are performed over the side of the horse with the pommels removed. After a running approach, the performer takes off from a springboard and placing the hands on the middle of the horse, vaults over the horse. For competition, each vault has a predetermined difficulty rating and the performer is allowed two trials. In judging, two phases of the vault are considered: (1) the flight, which includes arriving on the horse, and (2) the pushing off and afterflight of the vault.

The approximate measurements of the horse are: 5' 3" long and 14" wide, and the height of the horse from the mat to the top of the horse during the vaulting competition is 3' 7".

APPROACH FOR TAKE-OFF

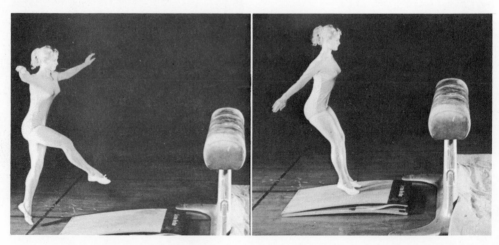

SQUAT STAND

SQUAT VAULT

values

The specific values of vaulting are:
1. Develops coordination, timing, and agility.
2. Develops strength and power in the large muscle-groups of the entire body.
3. Develops courage and confidence.

organization

To avoid duplication of words it is suggested that reference be made to the lengthy discussion on vaulting in Chapter 6. The same general principles apply for women in learning the correct techniques of springing from the beat board and over the horse.

It is suggested that the horse be set at a comfortable height for beginners. It is further suggested that a considerable amount of time be spent on practicing the correct fundamentals of taking off from the beat board. Be sure to post a spotter on the far side of the horse while practicing the vaults and if available, have two spotters, with one in front and the other in back of the horse.

program of instruction

The following series of vaults is suggested for learning in the order given.
1. *Squat Stand—Jump Off Dismount.* After the approach and take-off, place the hands on the horse and bring the legs up between the arms and stop in a squat stand position. From this position leap forward to the mat.
2. *Squat Vault.* Take off from the beat board, place the hands on the horse, and bring the knees up between the arms. Push hard with the arms and pass over the horse in a squat position and land on the mat on the other side.
3. *Straddle Stand—Forward Jump Off.* Jump to a straddle stand on the horse, with the legs outside the arms. From this position, straighten up and jump forward to the mat.

STRADDLE STAND—
FORWARD JUMP OFF

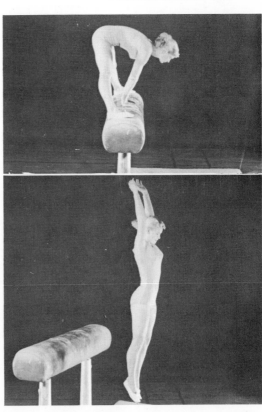

4. *Straddle Vault.* After the approach, place the hands on the horse and push downward with the arms, and at the same time straddle the legs in order to pass over the horse in a straddle vault position. Keep the head and chest up and try to sail over the horse in a neat straight position rather than in a low forward leaning position.

5. *Flank Vault.* This stunt consists in passing over the horse with the side of the body closest to the horse. Lean on the supporting arm and keep the body fairly straight while passing over the top of the horse.

6. *Front Vault.* This is done somewhat like the flank vault only the front part of the body is turned toward the top of the horse while it is passing over it. Allow the feet and legs to lift into the air so that a graceful arch of the body is obtained. Land on the mat with the inside hand resting on the horse for support.

7. *Rear Vault.* This vault entails passing over the horse in a sitting position with the seat of the performer closest to the horse. Upon taking off, lift the legs

to the side and pass them over the horse in a pike position. Continue on over, change the hands and land on the mat facing the direction of the turn, with the inside hand resting on the horse.

8. *Thief Vault.* This consists in taking off from one foot and then lifting the other leg upward toward the take-off foot and sailing over the horse in a sitting position. The hands drop to the horse and push strongly as the body continues on over to the mat. The feet are elevated as the hands touch the horse and a neat shoot forward is executed.

9. *Stoop Vault—Bent Hips Ascent.* This vault is similar to the squat vault only the legs are kept straight instead of bent as they are brought through the arms. Also, the ascent to the vault itself is done with the body in pike position.

10. *Stoop Vault—Straight Body Ascent.* This is done like the stoop vault above except that the body is extended straight upward at the beginning of the vault into a partial handstand before the legs are cut through the arms into the stoop vault.

STRADDLE VAULT

FLANK VAULT

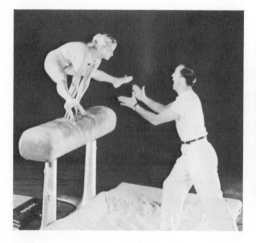

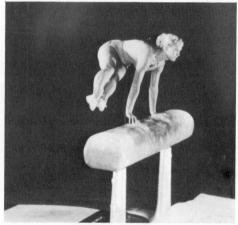

11. *Handspring.* This consists in springing from the board and upward into a handstand position on the horse with the arms straight. From this position, bounce off the hands into a handspring or arch-over motion to the mat. It is advisable to use a spotter on this stunt, as pictured.

12. *Handstand Pivot Cartwheel.* This vault starts by springing into a momentary handstand with the arms straight. As the legs pass over the hands, do a quarter turn, placing the right hand by the left hand, and execute a cartwheel to the mats. A good lift of the

legs will provide the momentum necessary to carry the body over the horse straight.

13. *Giant Cartwheel.* This is similar to the handstand pivot cartwheel except that a quarter turn is performed in flight while leaping to the handstand.

competitive vaulting

The following series of figure drawings (courtesy of the *AAU Gymnastic Handbook*) illustrate the competitive vaults with their degrees of difficulty.

1. STOOP VAULT,
   BENT HIPS ASCENT   6-5 POINTS

5. SQUAT VAULT,
   STRAIGHT BODY ASCENT   8-5 POINTS

2. THIEF OR WINDOW VAULT WITH
   HANDS TOUCHING HORSE AFTER
   BODY AND LEGS ARE OVER   7-0 POINTS

6. FLANK VAULT,
   REARWARD 3/4 TURN   9-0 POINTS

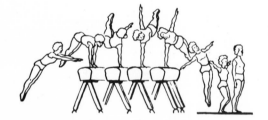

3. FLANK VAULT   7-0 POINTS

7. STRADDLE VAULT,
   STRAIGHT BODY ASCENT   10-0 POINTS

4. STRADDLE VAULT,
   BENT HIPS WITH 1/2 TURN   8-0 POINTS

8. STOOP VAULT,
   STRAIGHT BODY ASCENT   10-0 POINTS

9. SWAN VAULT (LEGS TOGETHER)   10-0 POINTS

10. SWAN VAULT, LEGS SPREAD   10-0 POINTS

11. HANDSTAND, STRAIGHT BODY   10-0 POINTS
    ASCENT, 1/4 TURN

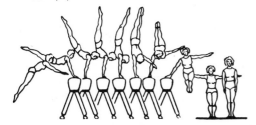

12. HANDSTAND, STRAIGHT BODY   10-0 POINTS
    ASCENT, STRAIGHT ARMS HAND
    SPRING

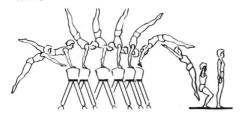

13. HANDSTAND, STRAIGHT BODY   10-0 POINTS
    ASCENT, 1/4 TURN PIVOT CARTWHEEL

14. HANDSTAND SQUAT VAULT,   10-0 POINTS
    STRAIGHT BODY ASCENT

15. HANDSTAND STRADDLE VAULT,   10-0 POINTS
    STRAIGHT BODY ASCENT

16. HANDSTAND STOOP VAULT,   10-0 POINTS
    STRAIGHT BODY ASCENT

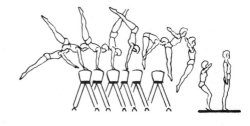

17. GIANT CARTWHEEL,   10-0 POINTS
    STRAIGHT BODY

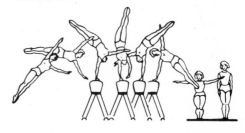

CHAPTER TWELVE / *women's balance beam*

Balancing is an important part of gymnastic activities so that the use of a beam for balance work provides an interesting challenge to the gymnast. Basically, balance beam work consists in performing on a beam approximately 4″ wide, 16′ 4″ long, and held off the floor by supports at each end. Competitive rules allow the beam to be at a height of 2′ 6″ to 3′ 9″. A beat board or "take-off" board may be used in mounting. On the beam, gymnasts perform basic locomotor movements including steps, runs, jumps, and turns, along with rolls and balances. This activity presents an exciting challenge to the performer because much control, balance, and courage must be used to maneuver the body through the intricacies of a routine.

Each competitive routine consists of a mount, combinations of stunts and movements on the beam, and a dismount, done within a time limit of 1′ 20″ and 1′ 45″. The exercise must be lively and continuous, avoiding monotony of rhythm. Not more than three held positions should be used, and the movements should show different levels including sitting and lying positions. The routine should present a picture of confidence and control as well as elegance and grace.

values

The specific values of working the balance beam are:
1. An accurate sense of balance is gained.
2. A feeling of confidence at heights and in a narrow and restricted area is developed.
3. Control and coordination of bodily movements is also developed.
4. Strength is developed throughout the entire body.

organization

AREA AND EQUIPMENT

As can be seen from the dimensions of the balance beam, a long and narrow area is required. Several feet on both sides of the beam should be cleared for dismounts and possible falls. However, the full length of the beam is not needed for individual stunts.

For teaching purposes, one need not have an official beam at the regulation height. A line on the floor may be used to introduce many movements. A beam with the top edge about 18″ off the floor is advantageous for use with beginners. Although commercially made beams are superior, inexpensive training models can be constructed by someone with a little skill in carpentry.

TEACHING METHODS

It is advisable to practice all the stunts on a straight line on the gymnasium floor first. The line could be painted on the floor or put on temporarily with tape. Not only is this a good practice method for individuals, but it lends itself readily to the mass method of instruction. This could be handled much like mass calisthenics.

The next step in learning stunts on the balance beam is to try them on a low beam about 18″ off the floor. Some schools find it feasible to construct several of these low beams and thus enable more students to work at one time. When confidence has been established, try the stunts on the high balance beam with an assist from the instructor. Because of the equipment needed, instruction here would be suited best to squads or individuals. Perhaps a system of rotating squads from a line on the floor to the low beam to the high beam would be good to use in a class.

safety

A few safety rules to be followed in working the balance beam are:

1. Mats should be used on the floor under and at the sides of the high balance beam to provide a soft landing place.

2. The finish on the top of the beam should be a natural lacquer so that it is smooth but not slippery.

3. Progression in the use of equipment as mentioned above.

4. Learn the stunts in a progressive order so that the proper lead-up activities will be included.

5. Use spotters, particularly on the high beam. One spotter on each side of the beam is preferable.

program of instruction

Instruction on the balance beam involves three basic steps:

1. Individual Stunts.

2. Combinations. As a person learns a new stunt, she should be challenged to combine it with another stunt as smoothly as possible. Because a stunt must be learned well in order to combine it with another, the use of combinations in the teaching progression stresses proper execution and increases the safety of performance. In addition, the smaller combinations serve as building blocks for longer routines. Combinations can be suggested by the instructor or coach or can be created by the performer.

3. Routines. Ultimately, a pupil

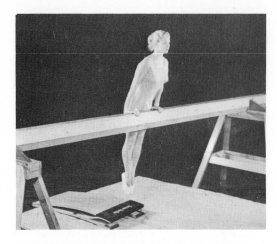

STRAIGHT ARM SUPPORT MOUNT

STRADDLE SEAT MOUNT

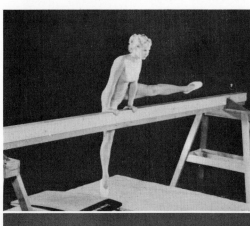

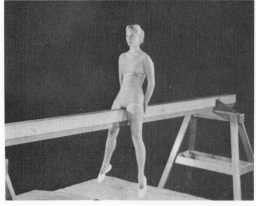

should strive to combine stunts into a routine. Competition is based on routines, required or optional. The approach to optional routines is one of problem solving. Certain requirements involving the types of movements and a time limit are presented as a problem for the performer to solve creatively within his own capabilities. The instructor, coach, and pupil can coordinate their thoughts on the development of a particular routine. For sample routines refer to the end of the chapter.

MOUNTS

1. *Straight Arm Support Mount.* Start from a stand or take two or three running steps forward and after a double foot take-off, place the hands on the top of the beam, shoulder width apart, and jump up to a straight arm support position, with the arms straight and the thighs resting on the beam. Hold the head up and arch the body, pointing the toes.

2. *Straddle Seat Mount.* Jump to a straight arm support position and then swing the left leg over the beam with a quarter turn right of the body. The right leg remains on the approach side of the beam and the left leg then swings down and the performer assumes a straddle seat position with the hands on the beam in back of the body.

3. *Knee Mount.* Jump to a straight arm support position, placing one knee on the beam and assuming a kneeling position with the hands supporting the body on the outside of the knee with the other leg stretched backward.

4. *Squat Mount.* Similar to wolf mount execpt that both legs are pulled up between the arms and the feet are placed on the beam between the hands.

KNEE MOUNT

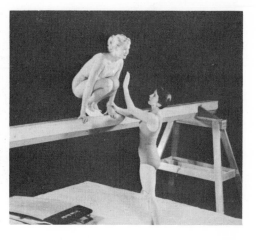

SQUAT MOUNT

5. *Wolf Mount.* Jump into a straight arm support position, bringing one leg in a squat position between the arms and the other leg in a straight extended position to the side and outside of the arms.

6. *Straddle Mount.* Jump to a straight arm support position and at the same time spread the legs and place the feet on the beam on the outside of the hands to a straddle support position. Be sure to have a spotter on the opposite side of the beam while trying this stunt for the first few times.

7. *Fence Mount.* Approaching from an oblique angle with the beat board placed almost parallel to the beam, leap into a scissors movement, passing over the beam and landing in a side seat position.

8. *Scissors Mount to Stand.* Approaching from an oblique angle with the beam to the right, take off from the beat board by lifting the right leg above the beam. Then swing the left leg up beside it as the right foot drops to the beam. The continued momentum of the left leg will enable the performer to rise to a stand on the beam.

WOLF MOUNT

STRADDLE MOUNT

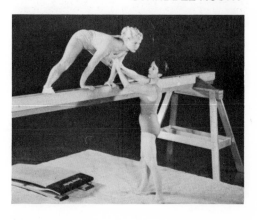

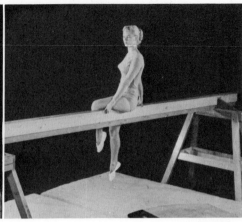

FENCE MOUNT

CHEST BALANCE MOUNT

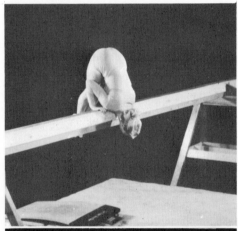

9. *Chest Balance Mount.* With the hands on the top side of the beam, jump upward into a pike position, bending the arms so that the chest barely touches the beam. Continue the lifting of the legs up and over the head and finally reach the chest balance position. Remember that the weight of the body is continuously on the hands and not the chest. Allow the feet to rise slowly and with sureness of grip, balance the body in a bent arm hand balance with the toes pointed, body arched, head up, and so on.

10. *Diving Forward Roll Mount.* Facing the end of the beam, run a few steps and execute a two-foot take-off from the beat board. Place the hands on top of the beam, lift the hips, duck the head, and perform a piked forward roll to a lying position with the legs pointing straight up. After the upper back touches the beam, both hands shift to the bottom of the beam for a strong pulling action.

MOVEMENTS ON BEAM

One of the basic requirements of a routine is the use of locomotor movements. They are used to combine the stunts in a fluid manner and to give grace and elegance to the routine. This section will deal with the various steps, jumps, and turns that are used on the beam.

1. *Steps on Beam.* Walking on the beam should be practiced until it becomes almost as natural as on the ground. The arms are always swung gracefully and freely as the performer moves along the beam. The body should be kept straight with good posture at all times. Begin by simply walking forward and backward and then progress to the following variations:

a. *Dip (Plié).* Take a small dip of the knee with each step and allow the free foot to drop slightly below the top edge of the beam on each dip.

b. *Duck Walk.* This is simply walking forward with the body remaining in a squat position.

c. *Run.* This is the same as walking, except at a faster pace. Start by using exceedingly small steps. Later, as skill improves, the steps may be lengthened.

d. *Gallop.* A gallop step is a running step forward with an uneven rhythm. As the back foot comes forward, the leading foot pushes off the beam slightly so as to produce a hopping action before the back foot lands.

e. *Side Step.* This is moving sideways along the beam by sliding one foot to the side and then bringing the other foot beside it. A variation is to cross one foot in front of the other in the sliding action.

f. *Cat Walk.* In walking forward, jump off the left leg, bring both knees up toward the chest, extend the legs, and land on the right leg, closely followed by the left leg. The landing should be soft like a cat.

g. *Step-Tap-Hops.* In stepping forward

DUCK WALK

on the left foot, bend the right knee and touch the right foot to the left knee. Then hop on the left foot while extending the right leg forward. Land on the left foot, followed immediately by a step onto the right foot.

h. *Goose.* A goose step is a running step forward while keeping the legs stiff.

i. *Sissone.* Start with the right foot along the right edge of the beam and parallel to it and the left foot behind the right heel and diagonal to the beam. Bend both knees and jump slightly forward, landing on the right foot and placing the left foot just forward of the right foot. Now jump straight up and land with both feet in original position.

2. *Jumps.* Jumps have several different methods of execution. A performer can jump or leap from a run or from a dip position. The following variations may be done:

a. *Jump Change.* From a dip position with one foot in front of the other, the arms are swung upward and the legs are extended. At the end of the straightening process, a leap is executed with an interchange of position of the feet.

JUMPS ON BEAM

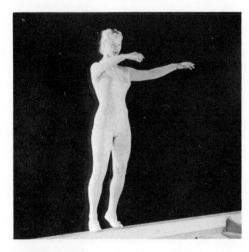

PIVOT TURN

PIROUETTE

b. *Stag Leap*. From a forward running step, bend the right knee as the left leg is extended to push up and forward into the leap. The right foot touches the left knee momentarily before landing on the right foot.

c. *Scissors*. Step forward on the left foot and swing the right leg forward and up to the level of the hips. Then swing the left leg up in the same way as the right leg drops down for a right foot landing on the beam. The legs pass each other in a scissors action.

d. *Tuck Jump*. From a squat position with one foot in front of the other, swing the arms upward and jump up high. When in the air, bring the legs to the squat position again and land on the beam in the original position.

3. *Turns*. The following varieties of turns may be done on the beam:

a. *Pivot*. With one foot ahead of the other, raise up on the balls of the feet and turn the body 180° and then lower the feet to a walking or standing position.

b. *Pirouette*. This turn is done on one foot and may be a half turn or a complete turn. The arms are held overhead for balance, and the body rotates around on the forward part of the supporting foot as the free leg swings backward. Upon the completion of the turn, the free leg drops immediately to the beam to assure balance.

c. *Reverse Pirouette*. This is similar to the pirouette except that the turn is made in the opposite direction as the free leg swings forward.

d. *Squat*. While in a squat position, execute a pivot turn.

e. *Pivot in Wolf Position*. While in a wolf position, with the left leg straight, release the left hand and swing the left leg forward, circling it outside the beam as the body rotates on the right foot.

Release the right hand and place it behind the right heel. Place the left arm in front of the left leg in putting the hand on the beam as the half turn is completed. This may be continued to a full turn if desired.

f. *Straddle Reverse.* From a straddle seat position on the beam with the hands in front of the thighs, swing the legs backward hard enough to lift the legs and hips above the beam. With the weight forward on the hands, twist the body a half turn in the air, scissoring the legs, and land straddling the beam facing in the opposite direction.

PIVOT IN WOLF POSITION

STUNTS ON BEAM

After reaching the top side of the beam by a mount, a routine consists in combinations of stunts and movements. Many of the stunts are described in this section.

1. *V Sit.* This stunt is the same as the one described in Chapter 10, except that the hands should remain on the under side of the beam behind the body. Start by pulling the knees into the chest with head forward and then straighten head and back and extend legs upward. Hold this V sit.

2. *Front Scale.* This stunt consists in standing on one leg with the other leg elevated to a position at least parallel to the beam and the upper body bent forward to a similar position parallel to the beam.

The body should have an elegant arch and the raised leg should be straight with the toes pointed. The arms should be extended from the side in a graceful manner, with the head up and eyes looking toward the end of the beam. Side scales are variations of this, done to the side instead of forward.

V SIT

FRONT SCALE

SWAN SCALE

KNEE SCALE

SWEDISH FALL

ONE LEG SQUAT

3. *Swan Scale.* Place the right shin along the beam with both hands forward on the beam. Slide the left leg on the beam behind the right foot until the leg is straight. Lift the hands and straighten the upper body until the head and shoulders are directly above the hips. Place the arms gracefully out to the sides.

4. *Knee Scale.* Start from a kneeling position with one knee behind the other. Lean forward, lifting the back leg into the air and with arms straight, place the hands on the beam in front of body.

5. *Swedish Fall.* This is similar to the one done in floor exercise. From a standing position, fall forward landing on the hands. Flex the arms as the fall continues toward the chest and lift one leg gracefully until it is pointing straight up.

6. *One Leg Squat.* From a standing position, lower into a full squat position on one leg with the other leg lifted parallel to the beam. This may start in the squat position and go to a stand.

7. *Body Wave.* The techniques are the same as described in Chapter 10.

8. *Pose.* A pose is a momentary hold of a position and may take many forms. For example, it may be holding a slightly flexed leg in front or back while sup-

STRADDLE HOLD

SPLITS

ported on one foot and the hands gracefully out to the side. It may also be done while in a kneeling position. A great variety of poses can be developed by the gymnast.

9. *Straddle Hold.* From a straddle stand, balance the weight on the hands between the legs, and lower your feet forward, supporting yourself with straight arms. For greater difficulty, try lowering to this position from a handstand.

10. *Needle Scale.* Start by leaning into a front scale and continue the lean until the forehead touches the shin of the supporting leg with the other leg elevated directly overhead. The performer may grasp the bottom of beam to aid in the balance.

11. *Splits.* Forward or side splits can be done on the balance beam. Be sure these are done successfully on the floor before attempting on the balance beam.

12. *Back Shoulder Roll.* From a lying position on the beam, move the head to one side of the beam. Place the hands beyond the head, with the hand on the same side of the beam as the head, holding the top of the beam and the other hand on the bottom of the beam. Pull

BACK SHOULDER ROLL

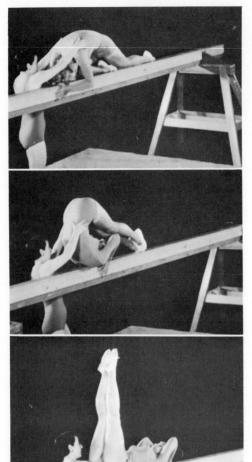

FORWARD ROLL

SHOULDER BALANCE (CANDLE-STICK)
OR EXTENDED SHOULDER PLANCHE

the knees up toward the chest, keeping the legs straight, and roll over the shoulder. The legs continue on over toward the beam and one knee is placed on the top of the beam on the completion of the backward shoulder roll. From this position the performer may continue on to the feet or go into a kneeling scale.

A variation would be to do a backward head roll in which the head stays on the beam. Place the hands on top of the beam under the neck and lift the legs harder to get more momentum. End with both knees side by side on the beam.

13. *Forward Roll.* Start this stunt from a kneeling position or standing position. Place the back of the head on the beam, with the hands gripping the beam so the fingers circle the sides of the beam. Slowly move the hips up and into the forward roll motion. Continue the roll so the body finishes in a full lying position on the beam. From this position, the performer may swing the legs downward on each side of the beam to a straddle seat or *V* sit or other such movements.

14. *Shoulder Balance (Candlestick).* Start this from a kneeling position. Place one shoulder on the beam. The hands grip the underside of the beam. Slowly lift the hips upward by pushing gently with the legs. Finally lift both legs up and over the head and assume a shoulder balance position. A spotter should assist the performer throughout this stunt.

A difficult variation of this stunt is an extended shoulder planche. Lower the body forward so that it is at a 45° angle with the beam. This requires a hard pull of the hands and a general tightening of the muscles of the body.

15. *Cartwheel to Hand Balance.* Basically this consists in simply doing a cartwheel into the hand balance position. This movement should be practiced

CARTWHEEL TO HAND BALANCE

SHOULDER BALANCE

many times on the floor before attempting it on the balance beam. Start with the legs in a straddle position with the body turned slightly, ready to lean into the cartwheel. Place one hand on the beam and at the same time kick the back leg upward toward the hand balance position. Then place the other hand on the beam into a good hand balance position and bring the other leg upward to join the first leg and move the entire body into a solid hand balance position. Be sure to work with a spotter or two at all times while first learning this stunt. This could be used as a dismount by arching over from the hand balance to a stand on the mat.

16. *Cartwheel.* This stunt consists of a cartwheel on the balance beam. Be sure to practice this on the floor and the low beam before trying it on the high beam. Spotters are essential in safe learning of this advanced stunt.

17. *English Hand Balance.* This is a hand balance facing the length of the beam with the hands close together on each side of the beam. Start from a standing position and then bend forward and place the hands on the beam with the fingers down the sides and the thumbs on top, almost touching each other. From this position the performer kicks into the English hand balance. Remember to keep the head up, body arched, toes pointed, legs together, and so on.

A variation would be to execute a scissors action of the legs as they are lifted and returned to the beam from the momentary hand balance. The landing is on the opposite foot from which the take-off is executed.

Another variation of the English Hand Balance would be to flex one leg and bring the foot in the direction of the other leg which is extended in a straight position overhead.

18. *Back Walkover*. This consists in doing a back bend on the beam, placing the hands behind the feet and then lifting the legs up and over the body to a standing position on the beam. A spotter assists the performer in lifting under the performer's hips as in helping a back walkover in floor exercise. This stunt should be first tried on the beam marked on the floor and also the low beam before attempting on the high beam. A mat draped over the beam may be used at the first attempt.

19. *Front Walkover*. This consists in doing a front walkover on the beam by placing the hands on the top side of the beam in front of the feet, lifting the legs up and over the head. Arch the body completely over, with the feet landing on the beam one foot ahead of the other and then bringing the hands up, lifting the shoulders upward to a standing position on the beam. This stunt should be tried on the floor and the low beam many times before attempting on the high beam. A spotter is essential in safe learning of this stunt and assists by lifting under the hips and shoulders as in spotting a front walkover in floor exercise. A mat draped over the beam may be used when first attempting.

20. *Valdez*. The performer starts by sitting on the beam, with one leg flexed, with the foot near the thigh, and the other leg extended straight ahead. One hand is placed on the beam behind the hips with the hands turned so that the thumb points away from the hips. The other hand is extended straight ahead from the shoulder, parallel to the beam. The performer then lifts the straight leg up and over and throws the forward arm over toward the beam and at the same time the foot on the beam provides a push into the valdez motion. The performer continues on over, the arm behind the hip, and the performer finishes in a handstand position on the beam. This may also be done to a dismount with the valdez providing the early part of the movement.

DISMOUNTS

There are several methods of dismounting neatly to the mat at the end of the routine:

1. *Half Pirouette*. From a stand facing one end of the beam, swing the arms above the head and jump off the left side. Execute a half turn to the left and land on the mats facing the opposite end and with the left hand on the beam.

2. *Straddle Touch Dismount*. From a stand on the beam, jump into the air and straddle the legs, touching the feet with the hands. Then bring the legs together for a landing on the feet on the mats. The performer may touch only the knees or shins at first while learning the dismount. As skill progresses, the hands may reach to the feet or even the toes.

3. *Side Seat Dismount*. From a side seat position in the middle of the beam, lean forward and place the right hand on the top side of the beam. Swing the outside leg backward and at the same time lift the body from the beam. Move the body slightly to the side and drop to the mat.

SIDE SEAT DISMOUNT

FRONT DISMOUNT

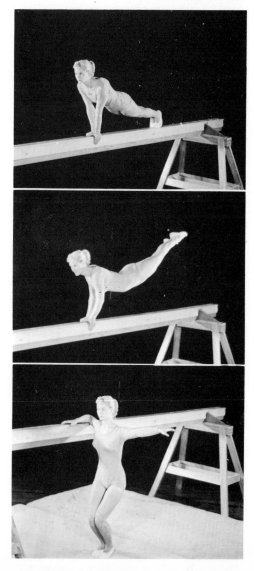

4. *Front Dismount.* From a front leaning rest position, resting on the toes and straight arms, kick one leg upward followed by the other and at the same time move body slightly to the side. Drop to the mats.

5. *Knee Scale Dismount.* From a knee scale supported on the right knee, swing the left leg down beside the beam and then up above the beam, pushing off with the right knee and joining the right leg with the left leg. With the legs elevated above the beam, push sideward and do a front dismount to the left side of the beam, landing on the mats with the right hand remaining on the beam for support.

6. *Shoulder Balance Side Dismount.* From a shoulder balance, dismount to the mat by executing a cartwheel movement sideward off the shoulder to the side opposite from the head. Keep the hand on the near side of the beam, constantly in contact with the beam to provide support and balance upon landing on the mat.

7. *English Hand Balance Dismount.* From a standing position, swing the arms down and place the hands on the beam in an English hand balance position.

ENGLISH HAND BALANCE DISMOUNT

Continue the feet upward into a partial hand balance. From this position, simply move the body slightly to one side and execute a front vault dismount to the mats.

8. *Cartwheel.* Near the end of the beam, lean sideward and execute a cartwheel on the end of the beam and continue off the end of the beam to the mat. Be sure to lengthen the cartwheel so the landing is done squarely to the feet and not too far over to the side of the body.

9. *Back Roll to Headstand Dismount.* The performer executes a backward roll, extending the legs upward over head so performer finishes in a head balance position. From this position, the gymnast may push off sideward and allow the body to continue over, parallel to the beam but to one side, to a standing position on the mat with the inside hand resting on the beam.

10. *Roundoff.* The performer stands on the beam near the end and places the hands on the beam and then lifts the legs up and over into a roundoff action to the mats. Be sure to try on the low beam prior to attempting on the high beam. A spotter stands on the mat facing the beam and catches the performer around the waist as she drops to the mats from the beam.

11. *Barani.* The performer stands near the end of the beam within a foot from the end and throws forward into a roundoff action without touching the hands to the beam. Instead, with ample whip of the leading leg and a good push with the remaining leg and a strong throw of the arms, the performer executes a barani, which is a roundoff in the air to a standing position on the mats. A spotter assists by lifting upward under the hips while the performer is learning this stunt on the low beam. A mat draped over the end will provide for safe learning of this dismount.

12. *Handstand Arch Over.* From a handstand position, execute an arch over to the mat. Have a spotter present to prevent falling backward toward the beam.

13. *Hand Balance Squat Through.* From a hand balance in the middle of the beam, execute a squat through to the mats.

14. *Front Aerial Dismount.* The performer stands on the beam a short distance from the end. By stepping forward, placing the lead foot at the end of the beam, the gymnast leans forward and whips the lead leg up and over while pushing with the remaining leg. The body executes an arch over in the air and completes a somersault movement to a standing position on the mats. Two

spotters assist during early learning stages by grasping the arms of the performer. A mat draped on the end of the beam will provide for safe learning of this dismount.

15. *Back Somersault.* The performer stands at the end of the beam facing the length of the beam. She then lifts up and backward into a backward somersault to a stand on the mats. This stunt first must be learned on the low beam with a hand belt and/or combination of two spotters. A mat is draped over the end for safe learning of this dismount.

ROUTINES

1. Jump to straight arm support in middle of beam.

2. Swing one leg over to straddle seat position.

3. Hands in front and swing both legs backward and elevate the feet to the beam with the body in a squat position.

4. Stand and execute a pose.

5. Four running steps and lift up on toes and execute a half turn.

6. Do a cat walk step.

7. Walk three steps and do a scissors jump.

8. Lean forward into a Swedish fall. Swing upper leg down beside beam and then swing both legs up to a fence dismount.

1. Jump to a straddle stand mount in middle of beam.

2. Turn to splits position.

3. Bring one leg around and do a V seat on beam with the legs straight and elevated.

4. Hands forward and swing the legs down and backward and do straddle reverse to another straddle seat.

5. Hands forward and swing the legs backward and up to a stand on the beam.

6. Four gallop steps and then do a tuck jump.

7. Stand and do a body wave.

8. Then step into a pose.

9. Then execute a forward roll.

10. One leg squat to stand.

11. Turn sidewards on the beam and execute a straddle touch dismount.

CHAPTER THIRTEEN / *women's even and*
uneven parallel bars

The even parallel bars is an event that has been in the women's gymnastic field for many years, while the uneven bars were first introduced to the competitive world in 1936 and have been used continuously since the Olympic Games in 1952. By that time the International Federation of Women's Gymnastics had realized the great possibilities of performing many more varied stunts on the uneven bars and also the preponderance of support work involved in the even parallel bars. The change to uneven parallel bars that they recommended has since been accepted in Olympic, international, and national competition.

Even though greater emphasis is now placed on the uneven bars in women's competition, there still exists a fine place for the even parallel bars in the women's physical education field. The dimensions of the parallel bars are similar to those of the men's, which have previously been covered. The measurements of the uneven bars are: Height of the high bar from the floor to the top of the bar is approximately 7′ 6″ and the height of the low bar is approximately 4′ 9″. The width of the inside measurements is between 16″ and 18″. As in the balance beam event, it is permissible to use a beat board for mounting purposes.

A competitive routine on the uneven parallel bars should consist predominantly of exercise of hanging and swinging. Support exercises should be used only as momentary positions, and balancing movements are permitted on condition that they are characteristic of the bars.

values

The specific values of working on the even and uneven parallel bars are:

1. Develops strength and endurance in the arms and the upper body.

2. Develops confidence in one's ability to control the body while maneuvering through stunts of moderate difficulty at substantial height.

3. Develops a sense of balance and timing while working from one bar to the other and while performing balancing stunts on one bar aided by the other.

organization

The organization of a class for instructional purposes in women's parallel bars is similar to that of men's parallel bars, which is treated in an earlier chapter. Reference should be made to that chapter for this information. It may be advisable to teach stunts on the even parallel bars before proceeding to the uneven. Not only will the stunts be a little easier but the performer will gain confidence, which will help her when starting the uneven bars.

Because some of the stunts on the uneven parallel bars are similar to horizontal bar stunts, a low horizontal bar may be helpful to supplement the instruction. The horizontal bar lowered at a comfortable height will provide for easier learning and safer spotting. The spotter should spot stunts done on the higher bar from a position underneath that bar, as is done on the horizontal bar. It is preferable that, while learning routines, two spotters be used in order to cover safely the variety of stunts. The even parallel bars should be lowered to their lowest height during the early learning phase. Be sure to progress slowly and surely so that the fundamental movements are mastered.

program of instruction

Instruction on the parallel bars involves three basic steps:

1. Individual Stunts.

2. Combinations. As a person learns a new stunt, she should be challenged to combine it with another stunt as smoothly as possible. Because a stunt must be learned well in order to combine it with another, the use of combinations in the teaching progression stresses proper execution and increases the safety of performance. In addition, the smaller combinations serve as building blocks for longer routines. Combinations can be suggested by the instructor or coach or can be created by the performer.

3. Routines. Ultimately, a pupil should strive to combine stunts into a routine. Competition is based on routines, required or optional. The approach to optional routines is one of problem solving. Certain requirements involving the types of movements are presented as a problem for the performer to solve creatively within his own capabilities. The instructor, coach, and pupil can coordinate their thoughts on the development of a particular routine. For sample routines refer to the end of the chapter.

Stunts will be presented here for both the even and uneven parallel bars. Only a few will be given for the former because more emphasis is now placed on the latter. For more stunts that can be done on even bars consult the chapter on men's parallel bars.

EVEN PARALLEL BARS

1. *Straight Arm Support.* This is a position for many of the stunts that are done on the parallel bars. It consists in jumping upward into a straight arm sup-

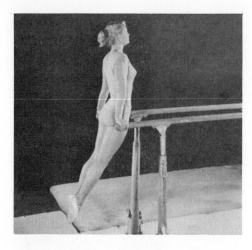

STRAIGHT ARM SUPPORT

STRADDLE SEAT

RIDING SEAT

port position, either on the ends of the bar or in the middle. Keep the arms straight, head up, back arched, and toes pointed. One may travel the length of the bars in this position by merely shifting the weight from hand to hand.

2. *Straddle Seat.* From a straight arm support position on the end of the bars, swing the legs forward and up above the bars. When the legs reach the height of the bars, separate them in a straddle position and place them on the bars and finish in a straddle seat position with the hands on the bars behind the back. One may also travel the length of the bars in a straddle seat travel by placing the hands on the bars in front of the legs, leaning forward, and swinging the legs backward and then forward between the bars to another straddle seat.

3. *Side Seat (Riding Seat).* From a straight arm support position swing forward and pass both legs up and over one of the bars. Finish in a neat side seat position with the hands behind the body on each of the bars.

4. *Forward Roll.* Start from a straddle seat position and then bend forward, placing the hands on the bars in front of the body, and start a forward roll motion. Roll over on the upper arms and when about half way over, place the hands behind the back with fingers almost touching and form a bridge on which the body continues to roll over into a straddle seat position again. Use a spotter on this stunt.

5. *Shoulder Balance (Upper Arm Balance).* Start from a straddle seat position with the hands on the bars in front of the body. Lean forward and place the upper arms on the bar and slowly lift the hips and legs up into the shoulder balance position. Keep the head up and slowly move into a neat shoulder balance with the back arched, legs straight, and toes pointed.

UPPER ARM BALANCE

FRONT LEG CUT ON
TO STRADDLE SEAT

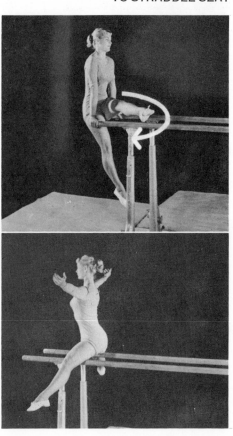

FORWARD ROLL

6. *Front Leg Cut On to Straddle Seat.*
From an approach stance, jump upward
to a straight arm support position. At
the same time swing the left leg over
the left bar and continue it over the
right bar, stopping it short of the right
hand. Pivot body backward to the right
and bring the right leg up and over the
left bar to finish in a straddle seat position facing out.

7. *Back Roll to Straddle Seat.* Start in
a rear stand approach facing away from
the bar. From this stance lift your legs
up into an inverted hang and then continue them over towards the bars, circling each around a bar to a position
of straddle hook. Continue the backward
roll movement, using the legs to elevate
the body up and on top of the bars into
a straddle seat.

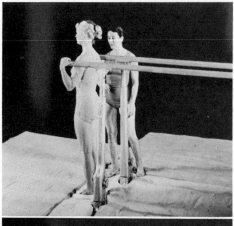

8. *Single Leg Cut Off Forward Dismount.* From a straight arm support position facing out away from the bars, swing back and forth a few times. On the back end of one of the swings, lift one leg up and over the bar. Release the grip on one hand and allow the leg to pass between it and the bar. Continue moving forward and land on the mat in a dismount fashion. Use a spotter on this stunt. For more difficulty, try a forward straddle dismount with the legs straddling the right and left bar respectively.

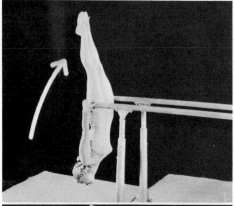

SINGLE LEG CUT OFF
FORWARD DISMOUNT

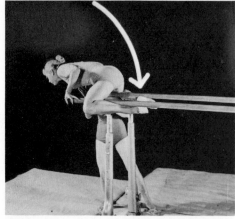

BACK ROLL TO STRADDLE SEAT

REAR DISMOUNT

SINGLE LEG FLANK DISMOUNT

9. *Rear Dismount.* Swing back and forth a few times in a straight arm support position, and on the forward end, swing both legs up and over the bar. Continue the movement to the side, passing over the right bar if the dismount is done to the right side and finish facing the same direction, with the right hand free and the left hand holding the bar for support.

10. *Front Dismount.* This is similar to a rear dismount except on the backward swing lift the legs over one bar and drop to a stand on the mats outside the bars.

11. *Single Leg Flank Dismount.* Start with body in a resting position sideways across the bars, with one leg over forward bar and the other leaning on rear bar. Swing back leg up and around the bars and push off the front bar and drop to the mat in a neat landing.

UNEVEN PARALLEL BARS

The stunts that can be done on the uneven parallel bars will be grouped into the following three divisions: mounts, stunts or combinations of movements, and dismounts.

MOUNTS

There are numerous methods of mounting to the uneven parallel bars and the following material covers a few of these:

1. *Mount to Straight Arm Support.* Stand facing the low bar with the hands grasping the bar with a regular grip (fingers over the top, with the thumbs underneath). The performer then jumps up toward the bar and finishes in a straight arm support position with the thighs resting on the bar, arms straight, chest and head up, legs straight, and toes pointed.

STRAIGHT ARM SUPPORT

SHOOT OVER LOW BAR FROM HANG ON HIGH BAR

2. *Jump to Hang on High Bar—Swing Legs Sidewards to Rest on Low Bar.* The performer stands beneath the high bar, facing the low bar, and jumps up, grasping the high bar with both hands, and promptly swings the legs sidewards over the low bar and then places them on the bar with the legs resting on the back of the thighs.

3. *Jump to Hang on High Bar—Swing One Leg Over Low Bar.* The performer stands beneath the high bar, facing the low bar, and jumps up, grasping the high bar with both hands, and then swings one leg up and over the low bar. Generally, from here the performer drops backward into a single knee circle, grasping the low bar with both hands.

4. *Shoot over Low Bar from Hang on High Bar.* Start behind the high bar facing the low bar, and after the approach and take-off, grasp the high bar, then swing both legs up and over the low bar and finish in a position with the back of the thighs resting on the low bar and the hands holding the high bar so the body is in a hanging lying position.

As a variation, the legs may pass over the bar in a straddle position.

5. *Cross Seat Mount.* Start by standing

CROSS SEAT MOUNT

between the bars, facing the length, with the right shoulder toward the low bar and the left toward the high bar. From this position, jump upward and grasp the high bar with the left hand and the low bar with the right hand and then swing both legs up and over the low bar to a cross seat position.

6. *Jump to Hang on High Bar—Place Feet on Low Bar—Push Kip to Support on High Bar.* Stand beneath the high bar, facing the low bar, and jump up to grasp the high bar with both hands. Then bring both legs up and place the feet firmly on the low bar and flex the knees slightly. Then straighten the legs and pull with the arms and shift the body from a hanging position to a support position above the high bar.

7. *Squat Stand Mount.* Start a few feet away from the low bar, after an approach and a double foot take-off, place both hands on the bar and lift the knees up toward the chest and place the feet on the bar in a squat position. Upon reaching the squat position, immediately rise upward to a straight standing position and grasp the high bar with both hands.

8. *Single Leg Swing-Up.* Start facing the low bar with the hands resting shoulder width apart on the top of the bar. Jump into the air and bring one leg into a tuck position between the arms and quickly circle the bar with this leg. Allow the body to swing down and under the bar, swinging on the hock of one leg, supporting part of the weight

JUMP TO HANG ON HIGH BAR—
PLACE FEET ON LOW BAR—
PUSH KIP TO SUPPORT ON HIGH BAR

SQUAT STAND MOUNT

SINGLE LEG SWING UP

with the two arms. On the return swing, whip the free leg downward forcefully and pull with the arms. Continue the circle so the body rides up to the top of the bar, with one leg in front and the other behind and the hands supporting the body.

9. *Single Leg Shoot on Low Bar to High Bar Grasp.* Stand under the high bar and face the low bar. Grasp the low bar and do a single leg swing up with one leg coming up between the arms and over the top of the low bar. As the leg passes up and over the low bar, release the grip on the low bar and quickly grasp the high bar.

10. *Back Pullover Mount.* Start facing the low bar with the hands grasping the bar in an overgrip. Pull in toward the bar with the arms and lift one leg up and over the top of the bar, following it immediately with the other. Continue to pull both legs over the bar. Keep pulling with the arms and complete the back hip circle so that the body finishes in a straight arm support position.

11. *Flank Mount (Low Bar).* Face the low bar, and after a few running steps toward it and a double foot take-off, place both hands on the low bar and execute a flank movement left over the low bar and then immediately release the left hand and grasp the high bar. Keep right hand on low bar. Finish in a side seat position on the low bar, facing toward the high bar.

SINGLE LEG SHOOT ON LOW BAR
TO HIGH BAR GRASP

BACK PULLOVER MOUNT

FLANK MOUNT (LOW BAR)

12. *Flank with Half Twist.* Start behind the high bar facing the low bar. After the run and double foot take-off, grasp the high bar and lift both legs up to the right and execute a flank movement over the low bar. When the legs pass over the low bar, then turn half way in toward the low bar and finish with the hips resting on the low bar and with both hands grasping the high bar.

13. *Jump to One Leg Stand on Low Bar to Half Turn.* The performer approaches toward the low bar side and jumps off the beat board, placing both hands on the low bar, and then pushes the body up, placing the right leg on the bar in a flexed position. At the same time, the left hand reaches upward toward the high bar. Then resting on the left foot and hanging on with the left hand on the high bar, the performer turns a half turn to the left, supporting the body with the left foot and the left hand. The right hand reaches beyond the left hand on the high bar and grasps it in a regular grip. The performer finishes the half turn with the left leg straight out from the bar and the body facing the approach direction.

14. *Jump to Squat Vault over Low Bar to Hang on High Bar.* The performer approaches toward the low bar side and jumps off the beat board, pushing downward with the hands on the low bar. The body then passes over the low bar in a squat vault position and the hands release the low bar and quickly regrasp the high bar, with the legs extending downward. The performer may then execute a half turn, and so on, to continue the routine.

15. *Jump to Forward Hip Circle on Low Bar to Immediate Stand on Bar.* The performer approaches toward the

CAST OFF LOW BAR WITH A
QUARTER TWIST

SINGLE LEG FLANK VAULT DISMOUNT

low bar side and jumps off the beat board, landing on the low bar on the abdomen, and immediately circles forward into a forward hip circle, with or without the hands, and upon nearing the finish, places the hands on the bar and then whips the legs up to a stand on the low bar.

DISMOUNTS

Because much of the elementary work on the uneven bars consists of mounting and immediately dismounting, it may be feasible to concentrate at this time on the various methods of dismounting from the bars.

1. *Cast off Low Bar with Quarter Twist.* This is done from a straight arm support position on the low bar facing the high bar. Allow the feet to swing under the bar slightly and then force them backward. As the legs lift off the bar, push with the arms, turn the body a quarter turn, and simply drop to the mat in a standing position a few inches away from the bar, with the left side closest to the bar and the left hand continuing to hold for support.

2. *Single Leg Flank Vault Dismount (Low Bar).* Start in a crotch seat position with the left leg in front and the right leg behind the low bar and the back toward the high bar. The left hand is in an undergrip on the low bar and the right hand is in an overgrip on the high bar. Swing the right leg up and over the right side of the bar. Support the body mostly with the left arm. As the right leg passes over the bar, the right hand releases its grip and the body is stretched toward the right and continues downward to the mats. Land on the mat with the left hand still on the bar and the left side of the body closest to the bar.

3. *L Position Shoot Off Dismount.* From a sitting position on the low bar, with the back toward the high bar, lift the feet into the air and cast the body away from the bar. Push with the hands and then land on the feet a few feet away from the low bar.

4. *Rear Vault with Quarter Turn Dismount.* Start between the bars, grasping the low bar and high bar as you lean forward. Swing your legs up and over the low bar. Push off high bar, turning your body to an *L* seat position over the low bar. Continue the motion into the dismount to the feet. This may also be done from a handstand on the high and low bars, bringing the legs down between the bars into the vault.

5. *Forward Roll Off High Bar.* Stand on the low bar, facing high bar. Lean into the high bar, placing the abdomen on the bar and the hands in reverse grip position. Continue to roll on over the top of the bar and down to a straight hang position. Then with a small whip of the legs snap outward to the mat.

6. *Flank Vault (Low Bar).* Start this in a straight arm support position on the low bar with the back toward the high bar. Bring the legs up and over the right side of the bar and execute a flank vault over this bar. Land on the mat with the back toward the low bar.

7. *Underswing Dismount (Low Bar).* Start in a straight arm support position on the low bar, with the back toward the high bar. Swing the legs slightly backward and then in toward the bar. Start a back hip circle movement, but at the bottom of the swing, shoot the feet up and away from the bar. Pull with the arms and continue the shoot to the mat so as to land in a standing position a few feet away from the low bar. A graceful arch of the body while shooting away

REAR VAULT WITH QUARTER
TURN DISMOUNT

from the bar makes this an easy, yet pleasant, dismount.

8. *Underswing Dismount from High Bar.* Stand on the low bar, facing the high bar and with the hands resting on top of the high bar. Jump into a partial pike position and swing the legs under and upward under the high bar. Continue the swing into an underswing dismount. This is similar to the underswing

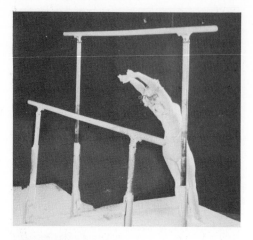

UNDERSWING DISMOUNT FROM
HIGH BAR

on the low bar, but with the added
height it becomes an attractive dismount.

9. *Squat Through Dismount.* Start
from a straight arm support position on
the low bar. Lift the legs upward and
immediately squat the legs through the
arms and pass the feet over the bar.
Continue the movement toward the mat
and land in a standing position on the
mats with the back toward the bar. This
same dismount can be done with the legs
straight and thus it becomes a stoop
vault dismount, or the legs can be in a
straddle position and thus it is a straddle
dismount.

10. *Front Vault from High Bar over
Low Bar.* From a front lying position on
the high bar, lean forward and downward toward the low bar. Grasp the low
bar with a mixed grip, with the left hand
in an undergrip and the right hand in
an overgrip. When the hands are securely grasping the low bar, with the
aid of the high bar whip the legs out
and over the low bar. Allow the body
to pass over the low bar in a front vault
position and land on the mat on the
other side of the low bar. Continue to
hold onto the low bar with the left hand.

11. *Squat Dismount—Low Bar.* Start
from a front support on the high bar,
facing the low bar. Lean forward and
place the hands on the low bar, allowing
the feet to continue upward into a handstand position. Then bring the legs
through the arms smartly to a squat dismount. This also may be done in a
straight leg stoop dismount or a straddle
dismount.

12. *Squat Dismount—High Bar.* Stand
on the low bar facing the high bar. Place
the hands on the high bar and spring up
into a handstand position. Then execute
a squat through dismount to the mats.
This may be done also with the legs
straight or in a straddle position.

13. *Hip Circle Dismount—Low Bar.*
Start from a support position on the
high bar, facing the low bar. Push off
the high bar and swing down and under
the high bar toward the low bar. Upon
striking the low bar with the abdomen,
execute a backward hip circle, and when
about two-thirds completed, extend the
body smartly and lean outward away
from the low bar. This should send the
body into an arched dismount to the
mat. A variation of this is to turn slightly
toward the low bar as the dismount is
executed, placing the right hand on the
bar if the turn is to be right, thus executing a half twist to a stand on the mat.

14. *Jump Backward Over the High
Bar to Cut-off Dismount.* The performer
stands on the low bar with the back to
the high bar and jumps backward over
the high bar, with the legs together and
the hands grasping the high bar on each
side of the legs. The body then swings
downward in a pike position, and on the
return swing upward, the legs are swung
to one side and cut between the bar and
the hand and continued down toward
the mats. The performer drops to a
standing position. This also may be done

by straddling the legs to a straddle cut dismount. The spotter stands behind the performer to grasp the hips if necessary.

STUNTS OR COMBINATIONS

1. *Right Leg over Bar.* This stunt is generally done after a single knee swing up to a support position. The left leg is in front and the right leg behind (scissors fashion). Lift the right leg up and over the right side of the bar. As the leg passes over the bar, lift the right hand and then grasp the high bar. Finish in a side seat position, with the left hand grasping the low bar and the right hand the high bar.

2. *Crotch Seat.* From a straight arm support position on the inside of the low bar, bring the right leg up and over the right side of the bar. Continue the leg over the bar and finish the stunt in a crotch seat position, with the left hand on the high bar and the right hand on the low bar.

3. *Seat Balance.* From a side seat position or a straddle seat position, bring the right leg up onto the bar, and extend the left leg as in the V seat position. Aid the balance by holding the high bar with the left hand and the low bar with the right hand behind the back.

4. *From Back Support Position, Half Turn to Front Support.* The performer rests in a lying position, with the backs of the legs resting on the low bar and the hands grasping the high bar. The body turns to the right, with the right hand reaching down and grasping the low bar. The body continues to turn to a front support position, as the left hand grasps the low bar with the body in an arched position, and rests on the front part of the thighs with arms straight and head up.

CROTCH SEAT

SEAT BALANCE

ONE LEG SQUAT

ONE LEG SQUAT TO SCALE

SQUAT STAND ON LOW BAR, SWING
UP TO FRONT SUPPORT ON HIGH BAR

5. *From High Bar, Underswing to Crotch Seat on Low Bar.* The performer starts in a front support position on the high bar, facing in the direction of the low bar. From here the performer circles the legs under the high bar toward the low bar and drops down, spreading the legs so that one leg goes over and one leg goes under the low bar. The performer ends in a crotch seat position and shifts the hands to the low bar for support.

6. *One Leg Squat.* Start with the right foot on the low bar with the body in a completely squat position with the left hand on the top bar and the right hand on the low bar in front of the foot. From here, raise upward into a scale position, with the left leg raised back in a scale position and the right hand lifted straight forward.

7. *Squat Stand on Low Bar, Swing up to Front Support on High Bar.* Start with the right foot on the low bar and the left hand on the high bar. Swing the left leg up and over the high bar. Bring the right leg over also and finish in a front support position with the hands on the high bar on each side of the body.

8. *Swan Support.* From a straight arm support position on high bar, hold the arms straight out at the sides and execute a swan arch position.

SWAN SUPPORT

9. *Kick Off Low Bar to High Bar Support.* Start from a hanging position on the high bar and then swing slightly forward and place one foot on the low bar. On the return swing, push the foot, whip the other leg down, and pull the body up and over the top bar. Continue the movement so that the body ends in a straight arm support position on the high bar. This can be done with both feet on the bar instead of just one.

KICK OFF LOW BAR TO HIGH
BAR SUPPORT

THIGH REST

10. *Hip Flexion, Swing to Push-off Low Bar to Front Support on High Bar.* The performer swings on the high bar, facing the low bar, and when the abdomen strikes the low bar, the hips are flexed a little. Then the legs are extended backward sharply and then forward again as the legs are lifted to place the feet on the bar. From this position, the legs are flexed and then extended, which pushes the performer from the hanging position to a support position on the high bar. The spotter stands below the performer and pushes on the back during the last part of the stunt.

11. *Thigh Rest.* From a front rest position on the high bar, drop downward and grasp the low bar with the hands, arms straight. Lift the legs so that the body is arched and resting on the hands and thighs.

DOUBLE LEG CIRCLE OVER LOW BAR

12. *Double Leg Circle over Low Bar*. Start from a hanging position on the high bar. Swing the legs up and over the low bar without touching it. Continue the swing back to the starting position.

13. *Double Leg Bounce to Back Pullover*. Start from a hanging position on the high bar. Lift both legs over the right side of the low bar and allow them to drop forcefully on the bar, and with an effect of a rebound bring the legs up and over the high bar. Pull hard with the arms and continue the movement into a back hip pullover on the high bar. Finish in a straight arm support position.

14. *Crotch Seat Circle*. With the performer in a crotch seat position, circle backward (or forward) by extending the body outward and fall backward (or forward) and circle the bar completely. The hands hold the bar with one on each side of the legs. A spotter is helpful in pushing the performer up on the last part of the circle.

15. *Crotch Circle Forward with Grasp of High Bar*. The performer, sitting on the low bar in a crotch seat position, circles forward. When near the finish of the circle, the hands are released from the low bar and grasp the high bar in a regular grip.

DOUBLE LEG BOUNCE TO BACK
PULLOVER

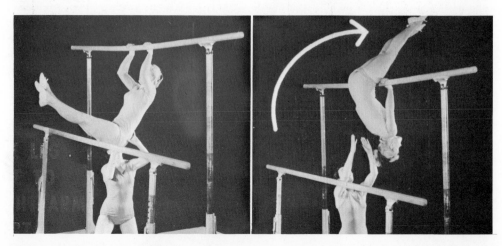

16. *Arch Back.* Hang on the knees on the high bar, facing low bar, and reach backward toward the low bar with the hands. Grasp the low bar and pull the body up and over the bar, continuing to hang on the high bar with the knees. Finish in an arched position with the arms straight from the low bar and the back of the legs resting on the high bar.

17. *Single Knee Circle Backward.* After executing a single knee swing up on the low bar, facing the high bar with the left leg in front and the right leg behind, shift the body backward and at the same time allow the hock of the left leg to hook onto the low bar. Swing the right leg downward and under the bar. Continue this back knee circle movement under the bar and over the other side of the bar. Pull with the arms near the completion of the stunt and finish in the original starting position, with the left leg forward and the right leg behind. The single knee circle may be done forward also.

18. *Straddle Seat.* From a single leg straddle position, bring the other leg up and over into a straddle seat, with the hands supporting the body between the legs.

19. *Back Hip Circle.* Start from a straight arm support position on the low

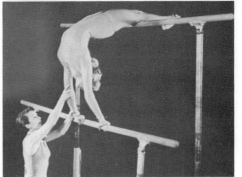

ARCH BACK

STRADDLE SEAT

BACK HIP CIRCLE

HALF TURN SWING ON HIGH BAR
TO BACK HIP CIRCLE ON LOW BAR

bar. Lift the legs up in back and then allow them to swing downward toward the bar. Just as they reach the bar, swing the hips downward and under the bar, pulling with the arms. Pike the body slightly as the backward hip circle continues around the bar. Be sure to shift the wrists so that at the end of the circle they are in a support position again. Continue the backward movement until the body finishes in a straight arm support position.

20. *Half Turn Swing on High Bar to Back Hip Circle on Low Bar.* Start by sitting on the low bar, facing the high bar. Grasp the high bar with the hands in a mixed grip, the left hand in an overgrip and the right hand in an undergrip. Swing the legs under the low bar slightly and then swing them forward away from the low bar. The body is then supported by the arms in a hanging position. At the peak of the forward swing, execute a half turn to the left and continue the body toward the low bar. Upon contacting the low bar, execute a backward hip circle, grasping the low bar with the hand.

BACK HIP PULLOVER ON HIGH BAR

HALF TURN JUMP FROM LOW BAR
TO HIGH BAR

21. *Back Hip Pullover on High Bar.* Start in a standing position on the low bar, with the hands in an overgrip on the high bar. Push off the feet and pull with the arms and pass the legs over and around the high bar in a back hip circle movement. Continue the hip circle until the body reaches the straight arm support position.

22. *Straddle Leg Swing-Up to a Hang Lying on Low Bar.* Start by standing underneath the high bar facing the low bar. Grasp the low bar and glide the legs under the bar on the forward part of the swing. On the return swing, quickly bring the legs up and on the outside of the arms, and shoot them over the bar. When the body reaches a position of half sitting on the low bar, then reach upward and grasp the high bar. Finish in a lying position across the low bar, with the hands grasping the high bar and the arms supporting the upper body.

23. *Half Turn Jump from Low Bar to High Bar.* From a front support position on the low bar, swing the legs underneath the bar slightly. Then whip them

backward and at the same time push with the hands, executing a half turn to the left. Finish by grasping the high bar with both hands in a hanging position. Be sure to use a spotter in learning this stunt.

24. *Double Knee Hang to a Side Hand Balance on Low Bar.* From a double knee hang on the high bar, facing the low bar, reach forward and grasp the low bar, with both hands in an overgrip. Pull the body over the low bar with the arms and place one foot on the high bar. Slowly lift the other leg off the bar and gently remove the foot off the bar so that a free hand balance on the low bar is held. Generally a drop down into a backward hip circle is executed from this position.

25. *Side Cross Hand Balance.* From a front lying position on the high bar, lean forward toward the low bar. The left hand is on the high bar in an undergrip and as the body is lowered downward, the right hand is placed in an overgrip on the low bar. Turn the body slightly to the left and slowly press the body away from the high bar so that a cross hand balance may be executed. Keep the right arm straight and the left arm bent. Keep the body close to the high

SIDE CROSS HAND BALANCE

bar throughout the learning phases of this stunt. Later, as proficiency develops, a flag handstand may be tried, which simply places the body away from the bars with the left arm straight as well as the right arm.

26. *Skin The Cat—Squat Turn On Low Bar.* Hang on the high bar with back toward the low bar. Bring both knees up between the arms and then place the insteps on the low bar. Release the right hand and turn left, with the weight on the left foot. Come to a stand on the low bar, circle the right foot outside the low bar and over the high bar, and finally stand on the low bar.

27. *Back Foot Circle on Low Bar to Swing to High Bar.* The performer starts with the legs in a straddle stand position on the low bar, facing the high bar, and the hands between the feet. Then the body circles backward in a sole circle movement, and as the body passes the uprights at the bottom of the swing, the legs are released from the bar and extended upward toward the high bar, and the entire body is pushed in this direction. The hands release the low bar and quickly regrasp the high bar, with the legs passing on beyond the high bar into an arched position. The spotter stands below the high bar and assists the performer on the release by placing the hands under the hips as the performer reaches for the high bar.

28. *Back Hip Circle on Low Bar to Eagle Hang on High Bar.* After the performer completes a back hip circle on the low bar, with the back toward the high bar, the body snaps from the low bar and shoots backward, with the hands reaching backward over the shoulders in an eagle position (hands turned outward with the fingers toward the bar). The hands grasp the high bar in this manner and hold the body in a hanging

position. The spotter places himself behind the performer and grasps the hips and holds the body upward while the hands are reaching for the high bar.

29. *Straddle Leap Over Top Bar to Back Hip Circle on Low Bar to Eagle Grip on High Bar.* The performer stands on the low bar, with the back toward the high bar. One hand may be back on the high bar to steady the balance. With a lift into the air, the performer then straddles backward over the high bar, grasping the bar with both hands between the legs as the body passes over the bar. From here the performer extends the legs back and together, allowing the body to swing backward and down under the high bar. Continue the swing until the abdomen strikes the low bar and then promptly execute a back hip circle on this bar. Upon the completion of the circle, extend the body backward toward the high bar. Grasp the bar by the hands with the hands twisted in an *L* position, with the fingers pointed away from the body. A spotter may assist by standing under the high bar to catch the performer as she passes over the high bar and also to grasp the hips as she flings backward into the eagle grip on the high bar after the hip circle on the low bar.

30. *From High Bar, Swing Legs over Low Bar and Drop to Back Hip Circle.* The performer starts in a front support position, with the back toward the low bar. After a slight flexion of the hips, the legs are extended backward over the low bar, either straddle or in a straddle manner, and then the arms are extended so the body drops to the low bar with the abdomen touching the bar. When the stomach hits the low bar, a backward hip circle is executed.

31. *Glide Kip.* From a standing position face outward, with hands on the

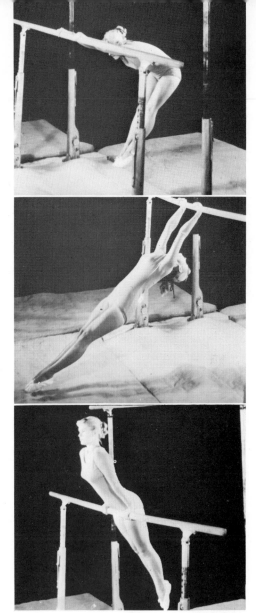

GLIDE KIP

low bar, and jump backward slightly. With the legs straight, glide forward with the feet just inches off the mat. Upon reaching the full extension position, pike the body sharply and bring the feet up toward the bar. Kick upward and outward, with the legs pulling strongly with the arms, and finish in a front support position.

32. *Drop from High Bar to Glide Kip on Low Bar.* The performer hangs on

the high bar, facing the low bar. After a slight swing forward, the hands release the high bar and drop to an overgrip on the low bar. The body assumes a pike position in dropping. When the hands reach the low bar, the body extends into a glide kip action on the low bar. The spotter stands under the performer and holds the hips and holds the performer while she is dropping to the low bar.

routines

1. Jump to straight arm support on low bar from under the high bar.

2. Bring one leg around and do a straddle seat.

3. Execute a forward crotch circle and grasp high bar.

4. Bring one leg over low bar and do push kip.

5. Assume a straight arm support position.

6. Circle backward under the high bar to crotch seat on low bar.

7. Bring back leg over bar and turn to front support position on low bar.

8. Flex hips and then push dismount to stand on the mats.

1. Grasp the high bar facing the low bar.

2. Swing both legs sidewards over the low bar.

3. Execute a thigh bounce to a backward hip circle on high bar.

4. To front support.

5. Do a backward underswing to crotch seat on low bar.

6. Forward crotch circle to grasp of high bar.

7. One foot on low bar and do push kip to top bar.

8. Forward roll to thigh bounce on low bar into full circle of legs around low bar to thigh bounce into . . .

9. Back hip circle on high bar and continue on.

10. Backward and under the high bar into a shoot over low bar dismount to a stand on mats beyond the low bar.

CHAPTER FOURTEEN / *rope activities*

Rope activities include such activities as rope skipping, jumping, and climbing.

Rope skipping employs a single light leap to each swing of the rope, with the rope being swung by the individual doing the skipping. Rope jumping refers to the more erratic, jolting movement over a longer rope swung by two helpers. The term may also refer to jumping over a static rope at various levels or as it wiggles on the ground. Rope climbing refers to the actual climbing of a suspended rope or the stunts done while on such a rope.

values

1. Children of all ages can have a great deal of fun in skipping and jumping because it is such a natural play activity. One can witness this enjoyment among a group of children indulging in normal play on a summer afternoon. It definitely serves as a release for pent-up muscular energy.

2. Rope skipping is fundamentally simple, but it can be advanced to a high degree of skill and achievement and is interesting enough to carry over into post-school life. Because one can skip rope in a small space and during any free time, it promotes self-enjoyment, thus providing a good medium for recreation and sport expression, regardless of age or sex.

3. The physical benefits derived from rope activities are numerous as can be seen by their heavy use in conditioning programs of boxers and other athletes. Rope skipping exercises, such as those boxers perform, develop agility, motor coordination, and a sense of rhythm and balance. Rope activities also build endurance and stamina and strengthen the skeletal muscles. Rope climbing is especially good for building up the arms,

shoulder and chest muscles, and for developing explosive power. For this reason it is of particular value in training pole vaulters, wrestlers, and gymnasts.

organization

The rope activities of skipping, jumping, and climbing can be easily added to the physical education program. First, they are very inexpensive to incorporate into existing facilities. Only the climbing ropes require a structure, and any substantial beam or ceiling can be used as a point of suspension. The ropes seldom need replacing because of their durability. Rope activities are also economical in space requirements in that a small storage space is required for the skipping or jumping ropes, and the climbing ropes may be pulled out of the way easily.

program of instruction

ROPE SKIPPING

Sneakers or moccasins are recommended for skipping rope. Shoes may be used, but the rope is apt to catch on the heel. If allowance is made for the heel, the jump is too high for good skipping form. For exhibition skipping, pliable dress shoes with the heel removed and a patch of rubber sole to prevent slipping is recommended. These shoes are light and flexible yet give good support.

A number 8 or number 9 sash cord is recommended for use in rope skipping, although any rope can be used with varying degrees of success. It should be long enough to extend from armpit to armpit as the skipper stands on the center of the rope, or from hip to hip as the skipper stands in a stride position on the rope. For speed skipping, one or two knots in each end will shorten it enough for maximum performance. Some skipping ropes are adjustable through a device within the handles.

Any available space with sufficient headroom can be adapted for skipping rope. However, some surfaces have preference over others. All surfaces should be free of loose dirt and dust.

1. A smooth, hard-packed dirt surface is fair. The people at the rear of the skipper should be cautioned about the stones and dirt picked up and thrown by the rope. Dust will be stirred up and inhaled if the earth is too dry.

2. A hard wooden surface is good if not too slippery and hazardous. Care should be taken to see that the skippers do not overdo so that the muscle attachments become irritated in the legs.

3. A semihard wooden surface is good because of the "give" that it has. It helps performance and reduces fatigue.

4. Cement, asphalt tile, or marble floors can be used and are more efficient for speed skipping, but they are fatiguing and may be injurious to the metatarsal arch and may cause shin-splints. If the surface is rough, it retards performance and causes undue wear on the rope.

Rope skipping lends itself to mass instruction. A comfortable distance must be provided between jumpers. The instructor may find it advisable to teach from a small platform, two or three feet high. It is also imperative that the instruction start from the simple and progress to the more difficult. The following are some suggestions in handling the entire class:

1. Demonstration of rope skipping can be done by the instructor or by other students during the class period.

2. Class may be divided into squads and instructed by squad leaders.

3. Rope skipping competition in the fundamental skills can be held with emphasis on quality rather than on quantity.

4. The use of films on rope skipping will help the teacher instruct students in the fundamental and advanced skills.

5. Current articles on rope activities should be made available for added motivation.

The following suggestions may be used to introduce and teach the activity of rope skipping:

1. *Mimetic games.* These involve jumping, hopping, and skipping. This serves as a warm-up for the activity of skipping rope.

2. *Jumping in response to commands.* The instructor asks the class to hop to a cadence that is called out; it should be varied by the instructor to maintain alertness.

3. *Jumping in response to music.* To develop a sense of timing, the instructor may play several records of different rhythms, or a piano may be played and the students asked to hop to the beat of the music.

4. *Jumping with an imaginary rope.* Using no rope but allowing the hands to respond as if a rope was present, try skipping this imaginary rope and keeping the following techniques in mind:

a. Feet, ankles, and knees together.

b. Head erect, back straight, chest out, and eyes up.

c. Jump off the floor about one inch.

d. Each landing must be on the balls of the feet, with the knees bent slightly to break the shock of the landing.

e. The upper arms are close to the sides, with the hands 8 to 10 inches from the thighs.

f. The hands describe a circle of about 5 inches in diameter while skipping.

5. *Introduce the rope to the students.* Have all of them try skipping the rope independently of each other. Allow the students a sufficient amount of free time to practice on their own.

6. *Mass skipping.* Have all the students start with the rope behind them and do 5 to 10 forward consecutive skips. They should start on a given command, and a cadence should be kept while the entire class executes the specified number of skips. Progress to series of 20 skips or more.

7. *Skip rope backward.* Have the entire class first try skipping backward with an imaginary rope and after the "feel" has been accomplished then at-

ROPE SKIPPING CLASS

tempt 2 or 3 skips with the rope. Start with the rope in front and lift it over the head into the backward spin. Start this on a given command and execute a specified number of backward skips.

8. *Skip forward or backward at a faster pace than in first learning the skill.* This improves confidence and results in skilled performers.

9. *Skip the rope forward while hopping on one leg.* Try alternating the foot after so many hops on one foot with the same number on the other foot.

10. *Alternating spreads.* Spread the legs sideward on every other jump. The legs are spread apart on one jump and brought together on the second.

11. *Consecutive spreads.* This is done as in (10) except the legs are brought together on each downward swing of the rope and spread apart to land.

12. *Leg flings.* One leg is flung sideward or forward alternately as the rope passes under the feet and brought together as it descends for the next jump.

13. *Sideward and forward jumps.* Both legs are lifted sideward or forward as the rope passes under the feet.

14. *Alternate to the sides.* Jump rope forward, and on every other circle of the rope, allow it to pass by the side of the body instead of under the feet. Thus it will pass first under the feet, then to the right side of the body, then under the feet, then to the left side of the body, and so on.

15. *Crisscross—forward and backward.* As the rope descends, the arms are crossed at the elbows, forming a loop with the rope large enough for the performer to skip through. The arms are uncrossed on the second skip.

16. *Double jump—forward and backward.* As the rope descends, an extra snap of the wrist gives the rope more speed, and it passes under the feet twice with one jump.

17. *Partner skipping.* Two students skipping in the same rope, with one of them turning the rope.

18. *Combinations.* Any of the above suggested stunts in rope skipping can be combined into clever and stimulating routines. It is important to start with the simple routines and progress to the more difficult.

Competition. Rope skipping competition may be held to determine the champion of each room, grade, sex, or school. Some suggested items to be used for testing or competition are as follows:

1. A set number of consecutive forward skips.

2. A set number of consecutive backward skips.

3. A set number of consecutive forward alternate to the sides (front, left side, front, right side, etc.).

4. Same as (3) except backward.

5. A set number of consecutive forward skips on one foot.

6. A set number of consecutive backward skips on one foot.

7. A set number of consecutive forward crisscrosses.

8. Same as (7) except backward.

9. A set number of consecutive forward double jumps.

10. Same as (9) except backward.

11. Highest number of consecutive skips in 30 seconds (may use any of the above mentioned stunts for this).

12. Time required for 50 skips.

13. Relay contests may be used with individuals running in a skipping rope.

ROPE JUMPING

For variety and additional stimulation, the class may divide into small groups and attempt some rope jumping. Rope jumping consists of two persons swinging the rope while a third person jumps it. The rope should be approximately 10′ long and heavy enough to describe the circle without losing its tautness. The rope should be swung at a clean, brisk pace. Some suggested rope jumping skills include:

Entering a turning rope. The student should place himself near one of the twirlers and on the side where the rope circles downward toward the floor. As soon as the rope passes him and strikes the floor, the student jumps into the area of the skipping. The rope in the meantime continues on up and over into another circle, and on the down swing, the student proceeds to jump and continues thereon.

Exit from turning rope. The exit is done from the opposite side that the entrance is made. After the rope passes across the floor and proceeds to lift up into the arch, the student leaps out with the flow of the rope and "exits" to the side.

1. *The twirlers swing the rope back and forth across the floor* without describing an arch and the jumper jumps over the rope each time that it passes under his feet.

2. Same as (1) except that after a couple of half swings, the twirlers should send the rope into a complete circle and the jumper jumps it.

3. During (1) and (2) the jumper should face one of the twirlers, but now he should face outward with his side to the twirlers and execute the jumps with the rope describing complete circles.

4. *One leg jump combinations.* The jumper may try jumping the rope by hopping on both feet, then on one foot, and then alternating from one foot to the other. The jumper may also try spreading his legs, and so on.

5. *Doubles jumping.* Two students jump the rope at the same time.

6. *Complicated maneuvers.* Many complicated maneuvers may be attempted, such as having a doubles team enter and exit a turning rope, or having a student simply run through the rope with a fast entrance and exit, or do the same except with a jump or two prior to exiting. A doubles team can work in tandem fashion: the first person enters the rope and executes a skip or two and then exits, with the second person entering just as the first person exits. Two persons may try entering, jumping, and exiting at the same time.

7. *Skipping along with jumping.* The student may try to skip an individual rope while jumping in the larger jumping rope. All the variations suggested for both single skipping and long rope jumping may be tried together in this phase of the activity.

8. *Circling rope.* One person in the center swings the rope along the floor in a wide circle. Any number of persons standing within the range of this circling rope must jump over the rope as it approaches them.

ROPE CLIMBING

The activity of rope climbing can be interesting and challenging in a modern physical education program. It is basically the activity of climbing up and down a vertical rope suspended from a support overhead. The rope should be 1½″ Manila; secure it safely from beams overhead and place a mat under it. Knot the rope at the bottom to prevent fraying.

In climbing for the first few times it is suggested not to climb too high. Just a few feet at a time will accustom the climber to the rope and the techniques involved. Be sure to learn to climb downward as well as upward. Never

ROPE CLIMBING

slide down the rope as this will burn the hands and legs severely.

Because of the tiring effect of this activity, it is advisable to limit the amount of time devoted to it. When first introducing the activity to the students, a full period may be devoted to it for demonstration and presentation of safety hints. Thereafter it is best when undertaken at the end of the period. Rope climbing at this time can serve to bring the group together and to motivate them to an all-out effort. Contests of various sorts can also be planned, which will keep interest and enjoyment high.

The following list represents a progressive order of learning the art of rope climbing, finishing with the intricate skill of climbing the rope with the hands alone for speed. This latter method is specified for official competition.

1. *The activity of chinning,* with legs either vertical or horizontal to floor.

2. *Start from a standing position,* climb two pulls (strokes) upward and lower slowly to a standing position. In-

crease the number of strokes upward with each try.

3. *From standing position,* hold onto rope and lower down to the mat to a supine position.

4. *From supine position,* pull up to a standing position.

5. *From supine position,* grasp rope and do chin-ups by pulling with the arms.

6. *From standing position,* lower hand over hand to a sitting position, pull back up to a standing position (legs receive no support from floor although touching it).

7. *From standing position,* grasp rope, flex the arms, and raise legs to L position (parallel to floor) and hold for two or three seconds. Increase holding time with each try.

8. *From standing position,* grasp rope and raise legs to an inverted hang position, then lower slowly to standing position.

9. *Grasp rope and climb upward 3 to 4 strokes* and raise body to an inverted hang position.

10. *Climb upward, using the foot and leg lock method.* In this method the rope passes between the legs and around the back of the right leg and across the instep of the right foot. Step on the rope with the left foot. Pull with the arms and allow rope to slide through and then make fast with the foot. From this clamp or lock position straighten the legs and reach upward with the arms for new grip. Climb and descend with this lock.

11. *Climb upward, using the stirrup method.* In this method, allow the rope to pass along the side of the body down along the leg and under the near foot and over the other foot. Grasp rope and pull knees up, with the rope passing through this position. Clamp the feet to-

gether, hold body in position, straighten the legs while the hands reach upward for new grip.

12. *Climb upward, using the cross leg method.* In this method, allow the rope to pass down between the legs, over the instep of one foot, and against the back of the other foot; clamp the two feet together while reaching upward for new grip.

13. *Using feet and hands, climb upward for speed* 10 to 20 feet (start from a standing position).

14. *Using hands only, climb upward for speed* 10 to 20 feet (start from a standing position).

15. *Using hands and feet, climb upward from sitting position* 10 to 20 feet.

16. *Using hands only, climb upward from sitting position* 10 to 20 feet.

At times it may be desirable to hold a position on the rope in order to rest a few moments. Three hold or rest positions will be described here.

1. *Foot and Leg Lock Rest Position.* Climb rope, using foot and leg lock method. At rest position, hold the foot and leg lock on rope and pass right arm in front of rope so rope is along right side of body and back of right armpit. Circle both arms in back of body and grasp wrists. This position is held by applying foot and leg lock and squeezing right arm against rope.

2. *Inverted Hang Rest Position.* Climb upward to the rest position, spot and swing legs upward to an inverted hang position. Place one leg in front of rope and one in back. Reach behind head with right hand and grasp rope and pull it across the back and in front of chest, passing under left armpit. Squeeze with legs and arms, and the position is accomplished.

3. *Single or Double Leg Seat Position.* Climb upward a few feet and then stop and reach down with either hand and pull rope up to rope above. Grasp both ropes and hold seat rest position. The rope may pass between legs to make a single leg seat or may pass under both legs and make a double leg seat.

Two ropes close to each other can also be used in the climbing program (see photograph).

COMPETITIVE ROPE CLIMBING

Competitive rope climbing is truly an art and skill by itself. It does not involve all the intricacies and maneuvers of apparatus work, yet the art of climbing can be detailed and exacting in nature. A great deal of practice is involved to produce a champion rope climber. Because the record for climbing a rope 20 feet high with the hands alone is under 3 seconds, it is easily understood why considerable practice is necessary for top performance. With this in mind, the following paragraphs explain in detail the techniques of climbing the rope for speed:

Start standing on the floor, with the rope in front of the body about arms' length away. Grasp the rope with the arms straight out from the shoulders. The hands should grip the rope with the back of the hands facing the climber. Lower the body to a sitting position on the floor so just the back side of the thighs touch the floor. The rope should continue to be in a vertical position with the body leaning slightly backward with the elbows bent a little. The take-off is the most difficult part of the climb and with this in mind the two-hand pull should be very forceful and strong. After this initial pull of both arms, continue to lean back with your upper body and look up toward the tambourine during the climb. Pull one hand down on the rope and continue the pull until that hand is near the hips, and at the same time reach straight up with the other

INVERTED HANG ON TWO ROPES

hand for the next pull. Try to avoid sweeping across the chest to grasp the rope and always keep your palms away from your body. Avoid a straight *L* position of the body during the climb but instead strive for an open *L* or almost open horizontal position of the body.

The legs add power and speed by kicking down just before the pull with the hand. The leg action should not be wild or exaggerated but instead should be smooth and controlled.

The number of strokes taken by the best climbers for the 20 feet is usually seven or eight and the reach. The reach should be made with a straight up motion. When practicing, the reach should always be made with the same hand so strength and general timing is perfected to the finest detail. A good reach should be more than three feet and closer to four. Only the fingertips need to touch, and to pull beyond that height will add to the climber's time.

The best exercise for rope climbers is climbing itself. Each time the climber works out, he should be timed several times for speed.

TUG OF WAR

Another rope activity that involves some of the same action as rope climbing is a tug of war. Such contests are usually greeted with enthusiasm and interest from both participants and spectators. Teams may be composed of almost any number of members, and each one gets an equal amount of exercise. The only equipment that is needed is a rope that is the size of a climbing rope, or larger, and some marks on the floor or ground, past which the front man must be pulled for the victory. A little teamwork in pulling will make up for the lack of individual strength.

/ *springboard trampoline*

The springboard trampoline is a recently invented piece of gymnastic equipment that is meeting with unanimous approval throughout the country. Commercially manufactured under such names as "Trampolet," "Mini-Tramp," "Gym-Tramp," and "Takeoff-Tramp," its purpose is that of a springboard.

Mechanically speaking, it consists of a rigid steel tubular ring about 3' in diameter or a square frame about 3' wide supported by legs and cushioned with rubber traction shoes, which will grip smooth gym floors. The legs are adjustable so that the angle of the woven web bed may be changed to suit the performer. The woven web bed is suspended by rubber cables or springs. This provides a maximum bounce for the performer.

values

The specific values of working on the springboard trampoline are:

1. Supplements or assists instruction in such activities as tumbling, diving, trampolining, cheerleading, and vaulting.

2. Fulfills the natural desire to jump into the air and to execute various other expressive movements.

3. Develops agility, coordination, and balance as the performer learns to maneuver his body while in the air.

4. Because of its compactness and easy maneuverability, it is an excellent device in staging exhibitions.

organization

Before elaborating on the many stunts that can be done on the springboard "tramp," a few basic safety hints should be mentioned:

1. Progress slowly in learning the use of the apparatus. The first few attempts should merely consist of bouncing off to the feet. Practice the art of leaning

forward or backward, depending on the stunt in mind.

2. The springboard tramp may be padded with mats for safety. This is especially effective when first trying stunts with it. As skill is developed, the mats may be eliminated.

3. Use the safety belt in attempting somersaults for the first time.

4. Be sure the mechanical phases of the device are always in readiness: all shock cords securely fastened; rubber pads on the legs secure; adjusting screws tightened; and so on.

5. In spotting the activity, have two spotters standing one on each side of the tramp to assist the performer through the first few attempts at the particular stunt.

6. When used to assist in tumbling or as an activity by itself, the springboard tramp may be placed on mats so that the landings can be on mats.

program of instruction

The springboard trampoline may be employed in many ways: for tumbling, diving, cheerleading, vaulting, and so on. Before elaborating on these, a detailed program of instruction will be presented for activity with the device itself.

The art of simple bouncing off the springboard tramp is learned in much the same way as the approach and take-off on a diving board. The performer merely trots toward the apparatus and just prior to reaching it, lifts one leg up followed immediately with the other and leaps onto the bed of the tramp. This acts as the hurdle. Upon landing on the bed, the performer sinks downward, and the recoil of the tramp bed sends him into the air for the execution of the stunt.

At the time of the bounce, the arms are lifted into the air and the head and chest are also raised. Diligent practice is needed to master the basic technique of bouncing off the springboard tramp, for only then can the many fine and enjoyable stunts be performed.

1. *Ball-Up.* This stunt is a slight variation of simply bouncing forward off the tramp. Upon taking off, bring the knees up to the chest and momentarily grasp the shins. This ball-up or tuck position is assumed for a split second, then released, and the legs are extended downward in preparation for the landing on the mat.

2. *Straddle Touch.* The performer, upon leaving the tramp, leaps into the air and extends the legs forward and to the sides in a straddle position. The toes are touched lightly with the hands and then the legs are snapped downward to the mat. This takes practice, so it is suggested that the performer try touching the knees first, then the shins, and finally the ankles or toes. This also can be done with the arms down between the straddled legs.

3. *Half Twist.* Take off from the tramp in a forward bounce. While taking off, start a half turn to the right by pulling the right shoulder back. Look in the direction of the turn and execute the half twist. Land on the feet facing the tramp.

4. *Full Twist.* This is similar to the half twisting jump except that a complete full turn is executed before landing on the mat. Be sure to keep the body straight while twisting. Also do not twist too hard off the tramp as this will cause the body to tilt and an improper landing will result.

5. *Stag Leap.* This stunt consists in

BALL-UP   STRADDLE TOUCH

bouncing forward off the tramp and assuming a stag leap position while in the
air. See "Women's Floor Exercise" for
the stag leap.

6. *Half Turn on Tramp.* This stunt
involves bouncing straight up off the
tramp and executing a quick half twist,
landing back on the bed, and then
bouncing off to the feet in the direction
of the original run.

7. *Backward Bounce Stunts.* For the
most part, the stunts listed above, such
as straight forward leap, tuck bounce,
straddle touch, half twist, clap hands,
and so on, may also be tried going backward from the tramp. Be sure to get the
proper lean backward so that the feet
clear the frame upon landing.

8. *Leap to Feet into Forward Roll.*
Leap forward from the tramp and land
on the feet and then go into a neat forward roll. Be sure to emphasize to the
students that they must land squarely

on the mat with their feet before starting
the forward roll.

9. *Leap Backward to Feet into Backward Roll.* Bounce backward from the
tramp and land on the feet and then go
into a quick backward roll.

10. *Bounce Twice on Tramp into a
Backward Leap.* Bounce straight up on
the first rebound and then hit the bed
again with the feet and lean back slightly
to a backward bounce to the feet. Try
this stunt first from an extremely low
bounce. On second bounce, be sure to
anticipate the backward leap so that the
feet will clear the frame upon landing
on the mat.

After the fundamentals of bouncing
have been taught and the performer
feels at home on the springboard tramp,
it may be used effectively to assist in instruction in other areas or to use as a
performance in itself. Some of these
areas are as follows:

BACK SOMERSAULT (TUCK)

BACK SOMERSAULT WITH
HALF TWIST

BACK SOMERSAULT WITH
FULL TWIST

BACK SOMERSAULT (LAYOUT)

TUMBLING

This apparatus is a fine device with which to assist the tumbler in executing his somersaults, twisters, and so on. Some suggested stunts are:

Over the low or back end:

1. Back somersault—tuck, pike, or layout position.

2. Hand balance on high end, kickdown, back somersault.

3. Back somersault with half twist.

4. Back somersault with full twist.

Over the high or front end:

1. Front somersault—tuck, pike, and layout.

A method of hand spotting the front somersault is as follows:

The performer stands between two spotters all facing the springboard tramp. The inside hands of the two spotters grasp the wrists of the performer.

FRONT SOMERSAULT (TUCK)

ASSISTED FRONT SOMERSAULT
OFF MINI-TRAMP

Have the other hand ready to grasp the upper arm of the performer as he commences the front somersault. All three run toward the small tramp, and just as the performer leaps to the bed, the spotters turn in toward him and grasp his upper arm. With a hold on the wrist with the inside hand and on the upper arm with their outside hand, the spotters then assist the performer through the forward somersault movement. Retain the grip on the wrist and upper arm upon completion of the forward somersault as this allows for a safe and softer landing by the performer.

2. Barani.
3. Gainer.
4. Front somersault with full twist.
5. Front somersault with one-and-a-half twist.

Although these tumbling stunts are generally executed in a gym onto mats, they are also fun on a sandy beach. This type of apparatus has been used a great deal at the famous Santa Monica Beach in California.

CHEERLEADING

This apparatus has become widely used by cheerleading squads throughout the country. It is beneficial to the squad in practicing their leaps, endings, and so on. It has become a clever means of counting the score, by having each cheerleader jump off for a count of the team's running score. Somersaults may also be executed by the advanced tumbling cheer squad to count the score. Be sure to have a spotter next to the tramp while the girls and/or boys are performing their somersaults, and so on, because the grass can become slippery and thus somewhat hazardous. Because of its compactness, the springboard trampoline can be transported easily from game to game.

DIVING

The diving can be used effectively for diving practice. By using the overhead safety belt, many "dry-land" dives can be tried with comparative ease. It can also be used as a substitute for a diving board alongside a swimming pool or on a pier.

TRAMPOLINE MOUNTING

Trampoline performers can use the device as a means of mounting onto the trampoline. In exhibition, this method of mounting is particularly effective. Some of these mounts are:

1. Swan dive to a front drop.
2. Swan dive over a back drop.
3. High bounce to a feet bouncing position—with half, full twist.
4. High bounce to a seat drop.
5. High bounce with a half twist to a back drop.
6. Back pullover out of (5).
7. Front somersault.
8. Barani.
9. Front one-and-a-quarter somersault to a front drop.
10. Front one-and-a-quarter somersault with a half twist to back drop into back pullover.
11. Front one-and-three-quarters somersault to a back drop.

STUNTS FOR TWO PERFORMERS

Two people can use the apparatus effectively in staging exhibitions of tumbling and balancing skills. Some of these stunts are:

1. Bounce to a swan position overhead.
2. Bounce to shoulder mounts.
3. Bounce to high arm-to-arm balance.
4. Bounce to hand-to-hand balances.

MOUNTING TO THE SHOULDERS

VAULTING

The device can be used for vaults over such apparatus as long horse, buck, side horse, and parallel bars (covered with mats). A few of the vaults that can be done are flank vaults, front vault, rear vault, squat vault, straddle vault, headspring, and handspring.

CHAPTER SIXTEEN / *gymnastic exhibitions*

A gymnastic exhibition is a display of the imagination and the productivity of the students and teachers, limited somewhat by what is available at the particular school in terms of equipment, talent, space, time, and various other determining factors. Some schools with unlimited facilities can stage large productions, while others with limited facilities must be content with smaller productions calling for greater ingenuity. It is the plan of this chapter to present some general ideas that may be helpful in planning any exhibition.

values

Some of the values of gymnastic exhibitions are:

1. Offers the opportunity to demonstrate to the community some of the activities that are included within the physical education program.

2. Provides recognition for the boys and girls who are not participating in varsity sports.

3. Provides a school project in which many students are involved. This may bring greater unity to the school in that several departments and teachers of the school can cooperate in the staging of the entire production.

4. Provides a fine means of gaining some money for worthwhile school projects.

5. Provides an entertaining show for the community to witness.

Gymnastic exhibitions can be of several types, depending on their purposes. They may be simply to provide a short period of entertainment for the half-time at a basketball game. Occasionally entertainment is requested for a social engagement, and this too will be a limited performance of gymnastics skills. Often gymnastics performances will occupy a large portion of physical education demonstrations or community recreation programs. In many cases, gymnastics will provide the entire program of entertainment in itself. Following are some suggestions for preparing a full length show.

PLANNING

Planning is definitely the key to a successful gymnastic exhibition. Extensive planning must be done early and involves considerable thought and direction by the teacher-director and his or her committee.

COMMITTEE ASSIGNMENTS

The initial work on any production is to divide the staff, class leaders, and students into various committees. People placed on these committees should be those who have indicated a keen interest in the show and are willing to work diligently on it. The director should appoint an assistant as this will save him the burdensome task of making all the decisions. To avoid further confusion, it is suggested that each committee chairman be given a copy of the tentative program with a detailed list of instructions to be followed. The successful show depends on each committee's fulfilling its obligations on time. A series of time deadlines for each committee should be worked out in order to keep things moving at a regulated pace.

THEME

One of the first decisions to be made is the theme. Pick out a particular theme for each show and build the entire production around it. Some themes that have been used successfully by schools include: Physical Panorama; Sight See-

GYMNASTIC EXHIBITION IN PROGRESS

OUTSIDE SHOW FOR THE COMMUNITY

ing Tour to Foreign Lands; Daze in Tulip Land; Fantasy Land; Toyland Capers; Playland, USA; and Out of This World.

LENGTH OF SHOW

The duration of the show should be approximately 1½ hours; it should not exceed 2 hours. It may be wise for the production committee to consider including a 15 minute intermission to break up the program.

PUBLICITY

With the publicity committee rests the major responsibility of stimulating interest in attending the big show. Some means of creating this interest and enthusiasm are as follows:

1. Mimeographed flyers may be made and distributed to all the students and to members of the community.

2. Posters advertising the show may be made and placed in convenient or strategic places.

3. News articles covering all the details of the show along with photographs of some of the acts may be distributed to the local newspapers.

4. Spot announcements on radio and television are possible in some areas.

TICKETS

The ticket committee has a very important position in the production of the show. Through consultation with the director, this committee proceeds to set the price of the tickets and arranges for the printing and distribution of them at the various purchasing sites. This should all be done two or three weeks prior to the show.

COSTUMES

The costume committee has a very difficult task to perform in that each costume should be attractive and in theme and yet kept to a minimum of expense. Whenever regular physical education activities are demonstrated, it is suggested that the regular gym outfit be used. The specialty numbers generally call for a different outfit. These may be made by the student involved, his or her mother, or perhaps by the home economics department of the school. All costumes should be approved by the committee chairman and the director of the show. None should be designed or cut so as to receive criticism from the parents or patrons.

POSTER ADVERTISING FORTHCOMING EXHIBITION

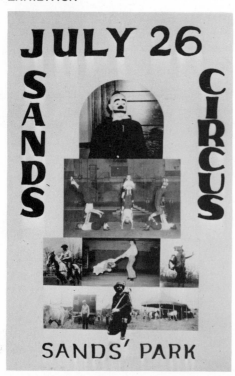

JULY 26

SANDS CIRCUS

SANDS' PARK

DECORATIONS

Decorations create the atmosphere for any type of performance and are an essential factor in a successful production. Gymnasiums are rather difficult to decorate, but any change of scenery will be an added attraction for the audience.

PROPERTY

Because numerous pieces of equipment and props must be moved about throughout the show, it is imperative that a good property manager and crew be obtained. Many times this committee can make or break a show.

CONCESSIONS

Another source of revenue in addition to tickets is the concession stand. Items such as popcorn, candy, soft drinks, and so on can be sold by the refreshment committee. Small extra revenue can also be obtained by posting a clown or two in the lobby of the building to sell canes, flags, pennants, or other souvenirs. It is suggested that balloons or other noise-making items not be sold.

PRINTED PROGRAM

When the schedule of acts has been decided on, a committee should begin working on a well-designed printed program. This program may or may not carry advertisements, depending on the policies of the school. The program should list the entire agenda along with the names of the participants and committee members. For public relations purposes, some of the administrative staff of the school and outstanding towns-

THE STAGE IS SET

AN OUTDOOR EXHIBITION AT MANISTEE, MICH.

people may be given special invitations and then listed as honored guests.

PROGRAM SCHEDULE

Although the program is variable and flexible, some principles to follow

253

in planning and arranging acts are presented here:

1. A parade, which should include all participants, is effective to use as the opening event.

2. Use the smaller children early in the program.

3. Acts involving beginners should be at the early part of the program so that a climax of advanced skills may be reached at the end of the show.

4. For variety, acts involving groups of performers should be mixed with acts involving individuals or small groups of two or three.

5. For variety, mix up the types of numbers. For example, a fast, snappy mass tumbling act would be good following a slow, precise doubles balancing routine. Also, if the program includes more than gymnastic acts, these activities should be intertwined with each other.

6. Interspersed throughout the program, short comedy skits can be included. These may be simple clown acts or comedy gymnastic routines.

7. Any lengthy delay between acts should be avoided. If a delay is necessary for reasons such as moving equipment, comedy skits could be used to fill in the time.

8. An intermission of about 15 minutes is advisable if the program is of considerable length. This allows for the moving of heavy equipment and props as well as concession-stand sales.

9. An act including the entire cast should be used as the finale.

program of instruction

Most of the gymnastic acts will involve stunts learned as part of the regular classroom instruction, just as described in the other chapters of the book.

Because it is important that comedy be included in some of the gymnastic acts, the following routines and stunts are suggested for the various pieces of apparatus. They represent those that have been either used or seen by the authors. Perhaps they will stimulate ideas in the development of more stunts of this type.

Not everyone is suited to be a comedian so be careful in casting these roles. Although it is essential that the clown wears a uniform that is different and funny, he must also have a personality that is suited for clowning. The comedian should also be a good performer because many of the funny stunts require special skill.

TIGER LEAPING

This involves long horse vaulting with the use of a springboard. The group should be comprised of 6 to 10 vaulters including the comedian. The general pattern is for the vaulters to follow one another in close order, with the comedian bringing up the rear. The vaulters should start with the easier stunts, such as straddle vaults or squat vaults, and gradually work up to the more difficult vaults such as cartwheels, headsprings, and handsprings. The comedian's routines may be as follows, keeping in mind that he is last in each series of vaults:

1. Hesitate as if bewildered and afraid to do the stunt but finally be persuaded to start the run. Immediately prior to reaching the springboard, veer off to one side and run past the equipment and circle back to the starting position.

2. Run toward the springboard, take a high hurdle but miss the end of the board, and land between the board and the horse with the end of the horse touching the abdomen.

DOUBLES BALANCING ACT

3. Run up the springboard onto the horse and off the front end.

4. Follow the last two vaulters, attempting to imitate their headspring off the neck. Instead, do a forward roll into a lying position on the neck with the arms and legs circling the horse. As soon as this position is reached, the other vaulters should straddle vault over the clown. When the last vaulter has completed his vault, slide off the horse and run back to the starting place.

5. A proficient tumbler may do a complete front somersault over the long horse. Emphasize poor form and clutch hat to head while sailing through the air.

6. Finish the tiger-leaping act by stacking several men on the neck of the horse. Build this up gradually, one man at a time, and when four or five or more men are piled up, do a straddle vault over all of them.

TUMBLING AND BALANCING STUNTS

This group could comprise 6 to 10 tumblers including the comedian. The general pattern of action on the tumbling mats is for the tumblers to follow one another down the mat. They should start with the easier stunts such as forward rolls and cartwheels and gradually work up to the more difficult stunts such as handsprings, somersaults, and twisters.

1. *Routine*. In this, as in tiger leaping, the comedian should be the last one for each trip down the mat. The routines for the comedian might be as follows:

a. Follow the last tumbler by simply running straight down the mat as if a difficult stunt is to be done, but never do it.

b. Do a series of cartwheels and tinsicas and then walk off the mat as if extremely dizzy.

c. After all the tumblers have executed successful dives and rolls over each other in a kneeling position, prepare to dive over the entire group. Audience participation may be obtained by asking for volunteers to kneel in between the tumblers. This is especially successful if children are in the crowd. After much preparation run up to first man but instead of diving over, run across the buttocks of all the kneeling persons.

d. Follow a tumbler who does a forward roll into a somersault or some such forward stunt and do a similar routine, but instead of completing the somersault out of the forward roll go only three-fourths of the way and land squarely on the buttocks, with the legs extended straight ahead. Jump up and run off holding the "injured" portion.

e. Have two tumblers and comedian straddle-jump over and forward roll under each other (see triple rolls in tumbling chapter). The comedian jumps higher and faster than the other two.

f. Log rolls (see tumbling chapter).

g. If comedian is a proficient tumbler, finish your performance with a good "straight" series of back handsprings, somersaults, twisters, and so on.

2. *Newspaper Dive and Roll.* A person is sitting on a low stool reading a newspaper. Another person does a high dive over the first person, grabbing the newspaper as he goes over, and then executes a roll with the paper in his hands. He may either end up sitting on the mat or continue rolling to a standing position. In either case he ends up reading the paper nonchalantly.

3. *Broom Swing Flip.* During an argument between two people, the one person swings a broom at the other one. The broom should be swung low at the legs. As the broom approaches the legs, the nonswinger does a back flip, thus

allowing the broom to pass under him without touching him.

4. *Wobbly Low Hand to Hand.* Comedy can be worked into a doubles hand balancing stunt, such as a low hand to hand. It involves the bottom man presenting a shaky support as the top man attempts to kick up into a balance position. The bottom man should be very relaxed and loose when the top man attempts to get into position. After some maneuvering to get the bottom man's arms solid, perform the stunt in the regular manner.

5. *Hand-Clap Routine.* One person is lying in a supine position with the other standing near his head as if to proceed into a low hand-to-hand balance. The top person claps his hands as if to motion "well, here we go" and promptly after he does this, the bottom man claps his hands with the same type of rubbing motion that would indicate "okay, here we go." Then the top man claps his hands again followed by the bottom man clapping his hands. This is repeated several times and each time the two performers' handclaps occur closer together until they both are clapping at the same time, which they continue to do briskly and at the same time turning to the audience as if applauding for themselves.

6. *Stiff Arm, Stiff Leg.* One person in a supine position with the other standing near his head as if about to proceed into a low hand-to-hand balance. Suddenly, one leg of the bottom person lifts up straight. The top man walks over to the leg and pushes it down and immediately one arm of the bottom man is elevated stiffly. The top person then walks around and pushes this arm down, at which time the other arm is lifted stiffly into an elevated position. The top person walks around to this arm and pushes it down, and the other leg of the bottom person is

lifted upward. The top person walks over to this leg and pushes it down and immediately the bottom person sits up right to a straight back sitting position. The top person then walks over the bottom person to a position straddling his waist facing the bottom person's shoulders and face. He then pushes the shoulders back as if to get him into the original supine position and then promptly the bottom person's legs are elevated swiftly, and they strike the top person in the buttocks. Supposedly the blow is hard enough to cause the top person to topple over the bottom person's head into a dive and roll.

HORIZONTAL BAR STUNTS

Not many stunts of the comedy nature can be done on the horizontal bar. A few will be described here. In addition to these, synchronized work done in opposite directions by two performers can be entertaining. Simple routines, not involving stunts causing the performer to move along the bar, will be suitable. Such a routine is: back uprise, back hip circle, underbar swing, single knee swing up, single knee circle backward, kip, underbar swing, hock dismount.

1. *Barber Pole.* Jump up and grasp one of the vertical standards with one hand. The jump should be with a slight forward motion so that the performer will rotate around the bar in a circular direction. By slowly releasing the grip, the performer will gradually descend as he rotates. One or two complete revolutions is usually sufficient to produce laughs.

2. *Double Hip Circles.* This stunt requires two performers. The first man does a belly grind mount. The second man grasps the bar inside of his partner's hands and pulls his legs up as if doing

the same stunt. However, he spreads his legs and hooks them behind his partner's back. The second man is now upside down. After a little rocking motion, they start into a backward hip circle. Halfway through the hip circle, the second man is upright and on top while the first man is underneath and upside down. The performers may pause here and then continue the action for a few more circles or do several circles in rapid succession. One person may hit the other's seat while he is in the top position.

3. *Straddle Stoop Gag.* While one man swings on the high bar, another man walks beneath the bar and stoops as if picking up a piece of chalk or some such object. Timing should be such that the man stoops as the high bar performer swings through, straddling his legs to avoid hitting him. This provides for a quick and exciting comedy gag.

PARALLEL BAR STUNTS

Many comedy stunts are possible on the parallel bars. Several involve falling, which requires careful attention and much practice to avoid injuries.

1. *Scratching Leg.* When holding a hand balance (or shoulder balance) casually scratch the calf of one leg with the toes of the other. It is best to scratch with the leg nearest the audience.

2. *Lazy Man's Kip.* This stunt is described in the parallel bar chapter as a lead-up stunt to the ordinary kip on the end of the bars. However, it can be used as a comedy stunt if the clown does it immediately following a performance of an ordinary kip by a fellow gymnast.

3. *Walking into the Bars.* This stunt may be used by the clown in pretending that he does not see the bars while walking along. Just before he supposedly hits his chin or head on the bar, he kicks one

foot up in front of him, and places his hands by the buttocks to brace himself when he falls on his back beneath the bars. Sound effects would be effective if carefully timed.

4. *Hock Swing Fall.* A hock swing dismount may be done from the parallel bars by lifting the legs between the bars and hooking them over one bar. From this position, perform the stunt as on the horizontal bar. The comedy part occurs in releasing the legs too soon and landing on the stomach between the bars. Most of the weight of the body is absorbed by the hands and arms as they hit the mats first. This may be more effective if preceded by a straight performer actually completing the stunt.

5. *Collapse.* From a straddle seat position relax completely and fall backward, releasing the grasp as you fall. The legs remain hooked over the bars as long as possible in order to lessen the force of the fall. If the body is kept straight, it will swing as in the hock swing dismount, and the ending can be a fall on the chest.

6. *Stoop-Kick.* This stunt involves two performers. One has just finished a stunt at the end of the bars and is slow leaving, because he stoops to pick up an object or to look at the mat closely. The second performer may either jump to an upper arm support or do a backward giant roll. With proper spacing and timing, the second performer's feet swing forward and kick the buttocks of the stooping first performer, thus causing him to lunge forward and fall.

7. *Arm Slide.* This is done by a performer wearing a long-sleeved shirt. The performer either takes a running jump to an upper arm support or does a fast backward giant roll. In either case he releases his grasp and allows the momentum to slide him on his arms along

the bars. The slide may even continue to the end and off from the bars, where the performer could land on his buttocks on the mats.

8. *Tickle Gag.* A gymnast maneuvers himself into a bird's nest position below the bars, holding on to the rails with his feet and hands. Maintaining that he is stuck, he calls for help from his fellow gymnasts. One or two proceed to push, pull, and shove him off the bars. Nothing seems to work, though, until one person holds up his hand as if to say "Ah, I've got the solution." Then he moves in close to the gymnast and "tickles" his stomach with his fingers, which causes him to drop to a prone position on the mats below.

TRAMPOLINE STUNTS

The trampoline is suited to comedy stunts. A little imagination can produce many funny routines because of the various ways a person may fall and bounce without getting injured. No attempt will be made to present all of the known comedy stunts. Instead, a few will be described as representative of the various types possible.

1. *Step Through Springs.* When attempting to mount the trampoline, the performer steps through the springs. This is best done by running toward one corner where the most clear area for stepping is available. A good gag to accompany this is to pretend to mash the face against the tramp bed after stepping through. By carrying a few beans in your mouth, one can spit them out as if they were teeth that had been knocked out.

2. *Rope Pull from End.* From a position of sitting on the end frame bar with the legs braced under the springs and tramp bed, the comedian falls backward

so that his body is parallel to the tramp bed. He pretends that someone from the other end has thrown him a rope and is pulling him up. He raises his body slowly by applying pressure on the tramp bed with the feet and occasionally slips back before coming to an upright position and mounting the trampoline.

3. *Suicide Dive.* From a high bounce, straighten the body and dive head first for the bed. Duck the head before landing and land on your shoulders and back. A screaming noise will add to the excitement of this stunt.

4. *One Leg Dive.* At the top of the bounce, the performer bends over and grabs one leg, allowing the other leg to swing backward, parallel to the tramp bed. As he nears the bed, he releases his grasp and straightens out his body, landing in a front drop.

5. *Waving Turntables.* While doing a series of turntables, look and wave at the audience each time around.

6. *Low Back Drops.* Do a series of back drops and get lower on each one. Then you can pretend you are pulling on a rope and gradually raise the height of each back drop until you end in a standing position.

7. *Back Walk Over.* Do a backward three-quarters somersault to a front drop. As you are doing the flip, move your feet as though walking.

8. *Highest Back Flip.* Start bouncing and work up to as high a bounce as you can. Then kill the bounce and immediately do a low back flip. Prepare for this stunt by announcing that you are going to do the highest back flip in the world. While bouncing, encourage the audience to shout "Higher!" with each bounce. Then the very low flip comes as a complete surprise.

9. *Basketball Bounce.* This stunt is done by two performers. The first per-

former does a back drop in a tuck position and remains in that position after the bounce. The second performer pushes the first performer into another back drop as though bouncing a basketball. Repeat the stunt several times.

10. *Straddle Over.* This stunt is done by two performers. The first performer bounces high with his legs in a straddle position. The second performer walks underneath while the first performer bounces. When walking underneath, he looks at the audience and waves at someone. Repeat this sequence a second time. On the third time, the man walking underneath only walks through halfway, pretending to be interested in something in the audience. Suddenly he looks up and sees his partner coming down on top of him. He lets out a shriek and does a back drop while the bouncer straddles him. The audience thinks the bouncer has landed on him.

11. *Wild Bouncing Routine.* An instructor or performer asks for a volunteer from the audience, and with the boy or girl on the tramp, the instructor suggests that the first thing to try to do is to learn the art of bouncing. The instructor then grasps the upper arm of the boy and tells him to bounce up and down. When the boy bounces, the instructor pulls the arm forward and backward with each ensuing bounce, which causes the boy to bounce forward and then backward. From the audience's viewpoint it looks like the boy is bouncing wildly and the instructor is just staying with the boy—hanging on to the arm.

12. *Girl's Seat Drop Routine.* Demonstrate the seat drop to the audience and at first show them a straight sit-down landing and then up to the feet. This, the performer states, is the way a man will do a seat drop. Now demonstrate the way a girl will do a seat drop and

after a few bounces the performer lifts his feet into the air and on the way down the performer wiggles his seat back and forth a few times prior to landing on the seat.

13. *Chewing Gum Routine*. If a volunteer from the audience is chewing gum, suggest to him that perhaps we should not chew gum while bouncing and so should find a place for it. The performer then takes the gum from the boy and looks about and finally places the gum on a spring. This is good for a small laugh but the climax is that when the boy is through, the performer retrieves the gum and gives it to the boy, who inadvertently will place it back in his mouth and commence chewing it after leaving the trampoline.

14. *Loose Pants*. A trampolinist bounces on the trampoline wearing a baggy pair of pants with extremely elastic suspenders and with hidden weights in the pockets to make the pants drop down below his knees on each bounce on the trampoline. A loud pair of swim trunks or underpants add to the humor of this stunt.

15. *Magic Rising Stunt*. Have a small person lie on his back on the bed with the instructor standing in a straddle position over him. On the count of one, two, and finally three, the instructor gives the bed a push with his feet, which sends the small individual up swiftly into the instructor's arms.

Selected List of Reference Materials and Visual Aids

Books

Babbitt, Diane and Werner Haas, *Gymnastic Apparatus Exercises for Girls.* New York: The Ronald Press Company, 1964.

Baley, James A., *Gymnastics in the Schools.* Boston: Allyn & Bacon, Inc., 1965.

Broten, G. A., *Gymnastics for Men.* Dubuque, Iowa: Wm. C. Brown Co., 1966.

DeCarlo, Thomas, *Handbook of Progressive Gymnastics.* West Nyack, N. Y.: Parker Publishing Co., 1963.

Drury, Blanche, and Andrea Bodo Molnar, *Gymnastics for Women.* Palo Alto, Calif.: National Press Publications, 1964.

Farkas, James, *Age-Group Gymnastics Workbook.* Tucson, Ariz.: United States Gymnastic Federation Press, 1964.

Frederick, A. Bruce, *Women's Gymnastics.* Dubuque, Iowa: Wm. C. Brown Co., 1966.

Frey, Harold, and Charles Keeney, *Elementary Gymnastic Apparatus Skills Illustrated.* New York: The Ronald Press Company, 1964.

Griswold, Larry, *Trampoline Tumbling.* Jefferson, Iowa: American Trampoline Co., 1948.

Hamada, Takemoto and Kono, *Horizontal Bar*. Los Angeles, Calif.: Frank Endo Supply Company, 12200 S. Berendo.

Harris, Rich, *Introducing Gymnastics*. Napa, Calif.: Physical Education Aids, 1963.

Hennessy, Jeff, *The Trampoline . . . As I See It*. Lafayette, Louisiana: Jeff Hennessy, Distributor, Box 672, University of S. W. Louisiana, 1966.

Hughes, Eric, *Gymnastics for Girls*. New York: The Ronald Press Company, 1966.

Johnson, Barry, *A Beginner's Book of Gymnastics*. New York: Appleton-Century-Crofts, 1965.

Keeney, Charles, *Trampolining Illustrated*. New York: The Ronald Press Company, 1961.

Kunzle, George C., and B. W. Thomas, *Olympic Gymnastic Series*. Toronto, Ontario: Ambassador Books Ltd., distributor, 1957.
    Vol. I *Free Standing* (Floor Exercise)   Vol. III *Pommel Horse*
    Vol. II *Horizontal Bar*   Vol. IV *Parallel Bars*

Ladue, Frank, and James Norman, *This is Trampolining* (Two Seconds of Freedom). Cedar Rapids, Iowa: Nissen Corporation, 1960.

Lienert, Walter J., *The Modern Girl Gymnast on the Uneven Parallel Bars*. Indianapolis, Ind.: 233 N. Parkview Ave., 1957.

Loken, Newt, *Trampolining* (rev.). Ann Arbor: University of Michigan, 1960.

Loken, Newt, "How To Improve" series. Chicago: The Athletic Institute.
    1. *Beginning Tumbling and Balancing*, 1951.
    2. *Advanced Tumbling and Balancing*, 1958.
    3. *Trampolining*, 1958.
    4. *Gymnastics for Girls and Women*, 1958.
    5. *Apparatus Activities for Boys and Men*, 1958.

Norman, Randi, *Gymnastics for Girls and Women*. Dubuque, Iowa: Wm. C. Brown Co., 1965.

Pond, Charles, *Tumbling for Total Gymnastics*. Champaign, Ill.: Stipes Publishing Co., 1965.

Prestidge, Jim and Pauline, *Your Book of Gymnastics*. London: Faber & Faber, Ltd., 1964.

Ruff, Wesley K., *Gymnastics—Beginner to Competitor*. Dubuque, Iowa: Wm. C. Brown Co., 1959.

Ryser, Otto, *A Teacher's Manual for Tumbling and Apparatus Stunts* (4th ed.). Dubuque, Iowa: Wm. C. Brown Co., 1961.

Sjursen, Helen Schifano, *Booklets on Girl's Gymnastics*. Fanwood, N.J.: 46 Poplar Place.

1. *Balance Beam*, 1964.
2. *Uneven Parallel Bars*, 1965.
3. *Even Parallel Bars*, 1965.
4. *Floor Exercise*, 1965.
5. *Side Horse Vaulting*, 1965.

Stewart, Nik, *Competitive Gymnastics*. London: Stanley Paul & Co., Ltd., 1964. Distributed by Sportshelf, P. O. Box 634, New Rochelle, N. Y., 10802.

Szypula, George, *Tumbling and Balancing for All*. Dubuque, Iowa: Wm. C. Brown Co., 1957.

Takemoto, Maseo, *Gymnastics Illustrated*. Los Angeles, Calif.: Frank Endo, distributor, 12200 S. Berendo, 1957.

Takemoto, Maseo, *Illustrated Women's Gymnastics*, Los Angeles, Calif.: Frank Endo, distributor, 12200 S. Berendo, 1958.

Takemoto, Maseo, *Japanese Gymnastic Pamphlets*. Los Angeles, Calif.: Frank Endo, distributor, 12200 S. Berendo, 1960.

U. S. Naval Institute, *Gymnastics and Tumbling* (2nd ed.). New York: The Ronald Press Company, 1959.

Periodicals

The Modern Gymnast
P.O. Box 611, Santa Monica, California

United States Gymnastic Federation Newsletter
Box 4699, Tucson, Arizona 85717

Athletic Journal
1719 Howard Street, Evanston, Illinois

Journal of Health, Physical Education, and Recreation
1201 Sixteenth St. N.W., Washington, D.C. 20036

The American Gymnast Magazine
P.O. Box 52, Iowa City, Iowa

The Physical Educator
3747 N. Linwood Avenue, Indianapolis, Indiana 46218

Scholastic Coach
902 Sylvan Ave., Englewood Cliffs, N.J. 07632

Gymnastics rule books

International Gymnastic Federation (FIG) Code of Points
c/o A. A. U., 231 West 58th Street, New York, New York

N. C. A. A. Official Gymnastic Rules
Box 757 Grand Central Station, New York, New York

N. A. I. A. Gymnastics Rules and Regulations
106 West 12th Street, Kansas City, Missouri 64105

United States Gymnastic Federation Guide
Box 4699, Tucson, Arizona 85717

D. G. W. S. Gymnastics Guide
1201 Sixteenth St. N. W., Washington, D. C. 20036

National High School Gymnastic Coaches Association Handbook
Nissen Corporation, Cedar Rapids, Iowa 52406

Teaching aids for gymnastics

American Athletic Equipment Co.
Jefferson, Iowa

Trampoline Wall Charts (set of 5)
　　Basic; Intermediate; Advanced;
　　Competitive; Spotting Techniques
Trampoline Lesson Plans

Burgess Publishing Company
426 South 6th Street
Minneapolis, Minn. 55415

Gymnastic Action Cards
　　by A. Bruce Frederick

Gym Master
3200 South Zuni St.
Englewood, Colorado

Chart of Basic Trampoline Skills

Gymnastic Supply Co.
247 West Sixth Street
San Pedro, California 90733

Men's Gymnastic Kit
Book; 17 Wall Charts; 100 Progress
Cards

Women's Gymnastic Kit

Marvin Johnson
Eastern Michigan University
Ypsilanti, Michigan 48197

Illustrated Graded Gymnastic Routines
by Marv Johnson and Newt Loken.
Includes four levels each in Tumbling; Trampoline; Parallel Bars;
Low Horizontal Bar; Side Horse;
Vaulting.

National Sports Company
360–370 North Marquette St.
Fond du Lac, Wisconsin 54936

Basic Tumbling Chart
Tumbling Chart
Sequence Gymnastics Chart

Newton Loken
University of Michigan
Ann Arbor, Michigan 48104

Sequence Gymnastics
by Newt Loken and Ed Gagnier.
Drawings of selected stunts in vaulting, horizontal bar, parallel bars,
and side horse.
Illustrated Graded Gymnastic Routines.

Nissen Corporation
930 27th Ave., S. W.
Cedar Rapids, Iowa 52406

Introducing Gymnastics Kit
Textbook
Wall Charts (10
Tumbling; Balancing; Doubles;
Trampoline; Vaulting; Balance
Beam; Parallel Bars; Rings; Bar-
Trapeze; Climbing Rope-Pole.
100 Score Cards

Gymnastic Skill Charts
by Dick Zuber
Men—Parallel Bars; Side Horse;
Horizontal Bar; Long Horse; Still
Rings; Floor Exercise.
Women—Side Horse Vaulting; Uneven Parallel Bars; Balance Beam;
Floor Exercise (2).

Charts on Basic Trampoline Skills

Porter Corporation   Wall Chart Set
9555 Irving Park Road
Schiller Park, Illinois

Audiovisual aids for gymnastics

Filmstrips

The Athletic Institute   1. *Beginning Tumbling and Balancing*
805 Merchandise Mart   2. *Advanced Tumbling and Balancing*
Chicago, Illinois 60654   3. *Apparatus Activities* (for boys and
   (Consultant: Newt Loken)   men)
                                  4. *Trampolining*
                                  5. *Gymnastics* (for girls and women)

Loopfilms

The Athletic Institute   Boys and Men
805 Merchandise Mart   1. *Parallel Bars* (14 loops)
Chicago, Illinois 60654   2. *Vaulting* (5 loops)
   (Consultant: Newt Loken)   3. *Tumbling* (8 loops)
                                     4. *Trampolining* (16 loops)
                                     5. *Side Horse* (8 loops)
                                     6. *Floor Exercise* (8 loops)
                                     7. *Rings* (12 loops)
                                     8. *High Bar* (9 loops)

                                  Girls and Women
                                     1. *Free Calisthenics* (6 loops)
                                     2. *Balance Beam* (6 loops)
                                     3. *High-Low Bar* (6 loops)
                                     4. *Side Horse* (6 loops)

Champions on Film   1. *Basic Trampolining* (18 loops)
745 State Circle   2. *Advance Trampolining* (18 loops)
Ann Arbor, Michigan 48104
   (Consultant: Newt Loken)

Motion Pictures

AAU Film Library   *Official AAU Gymnastic Championship*
Kennedy Airport   *Meets*
Jamaica, New York 11430

American Athletic Equipment Co.
Jefferson, Iowa

Basic Trampoline Skills 400 ft., sound, b & w

Encyclopedia Britannica
1150 Wilmette Avenue
Wilmette, Illinois

Headsprings in the Gym 10 min., sound, b & w

Federation International
Trampoline
c/o Jeff T. Hennessy
Univ. of Southwestern Louisiana
Lafayette, Louisiana

U.S. Trampoline Champions in Action 400 ft., b & w
1966 World Trampoline Championships 700 ft., b & w

Nissen Trampoline Co.
Cedar Rapids, Iowa

Up In The Air
12 min., b & w

N.C.A.A. Film Service
Box 757 Grand Central Station
New York, N.Y.

Official N.C.A.A. Meet Films

Educational Film Library
Syracuse University
Syracuse, N.Y. 13210
    Consultant: Paul Romeo

Tumbling and Floor Exercise
23 min., b & w
Side Horse Vaults & Support Exercises 17 min., b & w

National Collegiate Film
Service, Inc.
1030 W. Chicago Avenue
Chicago, Ill. 60622

N.C.A.A. Films available for rental

index

A.A.U. Gymnastic Handbook, 193
Agility stunts, 52
Alternate leg circles, 105
Amores, Francis, 166
Ankle pick-up, 26
Arabesque, 185, 187
Arch back, 229
Arched roll to hand balance or head balance, 51
Assisted back flip over arm, 24, 25
Assisted front somersault, 26, 27, 247

Back (ward):
  back to back toss, 22
  bounce stunts, 245
  dismount, 119
  double somersault, 80
  drop, 67, 68
  drop ball out to the feet, 79
  drop to front drop, 68
  extension, 10
  extension to low arm to arm, 42
  flip off partner's feet, 25
  flip toe pitch, 23, 24
  foot circle on low bar to swing on high bar, 232
  full fliffis, 82, 83
  giant roll, 152
  giant swing, 179
  handspring, 17, 18
  handspring to hand balance, 57
  hip circle, 122, 175, 177, 229, 230
  hip circle on low bar to eagle hang on high bar, 232
  hip pullover, 121, 148, 220, 231
  leap, 245
  lever, 175, 176
  one and one-quarter somersault:
    to a back pullover, 77
    to a seat drop, 77

one and three-quarter somersault to front drop to double cody, 84, 85
overbar somersault:
  to catch, 161
  dismount, 162
  to handstand, 162, 163
pullover, 72
pullover mount, 220
roll, 9, 54, 55, 245
roll off both bars dismount, 147
roll to head balance, 32, 210
roll to straddle seat, 215, 216
shoulder roll, 152, 205
somersault, 18, 74, 75, 211, 246
somersault with double twist, 79
somersault with full twist, 20, 78, 246
somersault with half twist, 20, 246
straddle:
  dismount, 175
  shoulder roll, 147
swan on feet, 37
uprise, 126, 129, 149, 160, 172, 173
uprise to a cut and catch, 158
walkover, 186, 208
Balance seat, 48
Balancing:
  double balancing, 34
  organization, 29
  program of instruction, 29
  pyramids, 43
  singles balancing, 29
  values, 28
Ballet touch, 184
Ball through arms to hand balance, 51
Ball-Up, 244, 245
Barani, 75, 76, 77, 210
Barani in full twist out double somersault, 86
Barani out fliffis, 82
Basedow, Johann, 1

Belly grind, 122
Bent arm press to hand balance, 50
Bent arm straight leg press to hand balance, 50, 51
Bent arm straight leg press to head balance, 50
Bird's nest, 169
Bird's nest—one foot, 169
Bird's nest—one foot and one hand, 169
Body sweep, 184
Body wave, 183, 204

Cabriole, 184
Candlestick, 206
Carbonate of magnesium, 118, 167
Cartwheel, 10, 11, 207, 210
Cartwheel to hand balance, 206, 207
Cartwheel vault, 96, 98, 193
Cast, 153, 154
Cast cross over to back uprise, 129
Cast off low bar with quarter twist, 221, 222
Cat walk, 201
Chest balance, 35
Chest balance mount, 200
Chin-ups, 168
Circus kip, 125
Cody, 78
Cody, double twisting, 84, 85
Cradle, 72
Cradle with one-half twist, 57, 58
Cross:
    inverted, 179
    L, 178
    olympic, 178
    straight body, 177
Crotch seat, 225, 226
Croup, side horse, 96
Czech, 113

Dip half turn, 154
Dips, 143, 201
Direct tromlet, 113
Dislocate, 134, 135, 170
Dislocate half twist, 136
Diving forward roll mount, 200
Double (s):
    around to L seat, 56, 57
    back somersault, 80
    backward roll, 21
    balancing, 34, 255
    cartwheel, 24
    elbow lever, 34, 48
    flyaway, 180
    forward roll, 21
    full fliffis, 85
    in, 111
    knee hang to a side hand balance on low bar, 232
    leg bounce to back pullover, 228
    leg circle backward, 122, 123
    leg circle over low bar, 228

Double (s): (Continued)
    leg cut off—forward, 170
    leg cut on, 146
    leg half circle, 106, 107
    out, 111
    rear dismount, 108, 109, 152
    tap handstand into forward roll, 55
    tumbling, 21
    twisting back somersault, 79
    twisting cody, 84, 85
Drop kip, 126
Duck walk, 201
Du Trampoline, 62

Eagle giants, 135
Early fliffis, 81
Early full twist fliffis, 82
Early one and one-half twisting front fliffis, 82, 83
Eastern National Clinic, 3
End kip, 152
English hand balance, 207, 209, 210
Exhibitions:
    committee assignments, 251
    concessions, 253
    costumes, 252
    decorations, 253
    horizontal bar comedy stunts, 257
    length of show, 252
    long horse vaulting comedy stunts, 254
    parallel bars comedy stunts, 257
    planning, 251
    printed program, 253
    program of instruction, 254
    program schedule, 253
    property, 253
    publicity, 252
    theme, 251
    tickets, 252
    tiger leaping, 254
    trampoline comedy stunts, 258
    tumbling and balancing comedy stunts, 255
    values, 250

Fence mount, 199, 200
FIG, 3
Flank circle, 110, 111
Flank vault, 90, 91, 192, 220, 221, 223
Flank with half twist, 221
Flexibility stunts, 59
Fliffis:
    back full fliffis, 82, 83
    barani out fliffis, 82
    double full fliffis, 85
    early, 81
    early full twist, 82
    early one and one-half twisting front, 82, 83
    front early, 81
    front late, 81, 82
    half in—half out, 82, 83
    late, 81, 82

Fliffis: *(Continued)*
   late one and one-half twisting front, 82, 83
Floor exercise:
   agility stunts, 52
   area and equipment, 45
   balancing stunts, 47
   flexibility stunts, 59
   organization, 46
   program of instruction, 46
   strength balance moves, 50
   values, 45
Flyaway, 131, 132, 175, 180
Flyaway with full twist, 180
Flyaway with half twist, 180
Flying leap, 53
Foot to hand balance, 37, 38
Forearm balance, 32
Forward:
   double somersault with barani in and full
      twist out, 85, 86
   giant swing, 179
   roll, 8, 54, 55, 171, 214, 245
   roll into back uprise straddle cut to support,
      158
   roll mount, 200
   roll off high bar, 223
   roll to head balance, 31
   roll to straddle seat, 146, 147
   somersault, 16
Fouetté, 185
Frey, Hal, 3
Front:
   aerial dismount, 210
   dive to back drop, 71
   drop, 67, 68
   drop to back drop, 70
   fliffis:
      with early twist, 81
      with late twist, 81, 82
   flip pitch, 22, 23
   handspring, 14, 15
   hip circle, 123, 124
   leg cut on to straddle seat, 215
   lever, 176
   one and one-quarter somersault to front drop,
      76, 77
   one and three-quarter somersault to back
      drop into front one and one-quarter
      somersault to feet, 79
   overbar somersault, 156, 157
   overbar somersault with half twist, 157
   scale, 47, 187, 203
   somersault, 72, 73, 247
   support mount, 119
   support turn, 144
   support with full turn, 55
   swan on feet, 37
   uprise, 149, 173
   vault, 90, 91, 192
   vault dismount, 144, 209, 217, 224
   walkover, 186, 187, 208
Full pirouette, 66

Full twist, 244
Full twisting backward somersault, 20, 78
Full twisting stutz, 164

Gallop, 201
Geier, Jake, 3
German giant swing, 137, 138
Giant cartwheel, 98, 193
Giant swing:
   backward, 179
   eagle, 135
   forward, 179
   German, 137, 138
   inverted, 136
   regular, 130
   reverse, 130, 131
Greeks, 1
Gulick, Luther, 3
Guts Muths, Hohann, 1
Gym Tramp, 243

Half:
   giant swing, 129
   in-half out fliffis, 82, 83
   pirouette, 66, 208
   turn jump from low bar to high bar, 231
   turn on tramp, 245
   turn swing on high bar to back hip circle on
      low bar, 230
   turntable, 71
   turn to front support, 225
   twist, 244
   twist change, 144
   twist to back drop, 68, 69
   twist to front drop, 68, 69
   twisting back dive to roll, 56, 57
   twisting backward somersault, 20
Hand balance, 32, 33, 48, 50, 51, 57, 154, 155,
      176, 187, 206
Hand balance, English, 207, 209, 210
Hand balance, one arm, 34, 49, 51, 52, 155
Hand balance–one bar dismounts, 157
Hand balance, squat through, 210
Hand balance, wide arm, 49
Hand balance, Yogi, 49, 188
Hand guards, 118
Handspring, 14, 17, 18, 94, 96, 98, 193
Handstand arch over, 210
Handstand pivot cartwheel, 96, 97, 98, 193
Head and forearm balance, 31, 32
Head balance, 30, 31, 50, 51
Head balance, arms folded, 31
Head to knees, 59
Headspring, 13, 14, 94
Headspring to straddle seat on floor, 56
Hecht, 96, 138, 139
Heineman, Gustav, 3
Helms Hall of Fame, 3
High arm to arm balance, 41, 43
Hip circle dismount–low bar, 224
Hip flexion, swing to push-off low bar to front
      support on high bar, 227

Hip pullover, 122, 148
History, 1
Hock swing dismount, 122
Hock swing with half twist, 123
Hold out facing in, 35, 36
Hold out facing out, 35, 36
Horizontal bar:
   area and equipment, 116, 117
   grips, 118, 119
   high bar stunts, 123
   low bar stunts, 119
   organization, 117
   program of instruction, 118
   routines, 139
   safety, 117
   teaching methods, 117
   values, 116
Hurdle, 16, 90, 95

Inlocate, 171
International Federation of Gymnastics, 3
Inverted:
   cross, 179
   giant swing, 136
   layout hang, 168
   pike hang, 168

Jahn, Friedrich, 2, 87, 116, 140
Judd, Leslie, 3
Jump backward over the high bar to cut-off
   dismount, 224
Jump change, 201
Jumps on beam, 201, 202
Jump to forward hip circle on low bar to
   immediate stand on bar, 221
Jump to hand on high bar:
   place feet on low bar–push kip to support on
     high bar, 219
   swing legs sidewards to rest on low bar, 218
   swing one leg over low bar, 218
Jump to one leg stand on low bar to half turn,
   221
Jump to squat vault over low bar to hang on
   high bar, 221
Jump to straight arm support, 171

Kaboom, 77
Keeney, Charles, 3
Kern, Gus, 3
Kick off low bar to high bar support, 227
Kip, 12, 124, 125, 172, 177
   circus, 125
   drop, 126
   end, 152
   glide, 152, 233
   reverse, 127, 128, 174, 177
   top, 150, 151
Kip to forward roll, 174
Knee and shoulder balance, 36, 37
Knee and shoulder spring, 21, 22
Knee barani, 75, 76
Knee drop, 68, 69

Knee front somersault, 73
Knee hang, 120
Knee mount, 198, 199
Knee scale, 48, 204, 209
Knee turn and spiral up, 189

Late fliffis, 81, 82
Late one and one-half twisting front fliffis, 82,
   83
Lazy man's kip, 147
L cross, 178
Leap to feet, 245
Ling, Pehr, 2
Log rolls, 21
Loken, Newt, 3
Long Horse:
   area and equipment, 87, 95
   competitive vaulting, 95
   take-off, 95
   values, 87
Loop dismount, 113, 114
Low arm to arm balance, 40, 42
Low balance beam, 197
Low bar kip, 125
Low hand to hand balance, 41, 43
Low, low hand to hand balance, 40, 42
Low parallel bars, 141
L position shoot off dismount, 223
L seat on hands, 49, 56

Maloney, Tom, 3
Maltese, 179
Mang, Louis H., 3
Meade, Bill, 3
Men's vaulting, 99–103
Mini-Tramp, 243, 247
Monkey shines, 21
Moore, 112, 113, 155, 156
Mounting to the shoulders, 249
Mount to straight arm support, 217
Muscle up, 172
Muscle up into forward roll, 174

Nachtegall, Franz, 2
National Association of College Gymnastic
   Coaches, 3
National Summer Clinic, 3
Neck, long horse, 96
Neckspring, 12, 13, 94
Neckspring from knee stand, 93
Neckspring with half twist, 57
Needle scale, 47, 48, 185, 205
Nip up, 12
Nissen Trampoline, 62
Normal College of American Gymnastics, 2
Northern California Clinic, 3
Northwestern Clinic, 3

Olympic cross, 178
One arm cartwheel, 11
One arm hand balance, 34, 49, 51, 52, 155
One half turn fall, 53

One leg balance, 186
One leg squat, 204, 226
Overhead back arch, 41
Overhead swan, 41, 42

Parallel bars:
  area and equipment, 139
  program of instruction, 141
  routines, 164
  safety, 141
  swing, 143
  teaching methods, 141
  values, 139
Peach basket, 160, 161
Phillips, Chet, 3
Pike bounce, 66, 67
Pinwheel, 122
Piper, Ralph, 3
Pirouette, 52, 66, 156, 202
Pirouette à la seconde, 185
Pivot, 202
Pivot in wolf position, 202, 203
Planche, 48, 49, 179
Plié, 201
Pommels, side horse, 87
Pond, Charles, 3
Pose, 187, 204
Price, Hartley, 3
Pyramids, 43, 44

Randolph, 80
Rear dismount, 107, 108, 109, 144, 145, 216, 217
Rear straddle (scissors), 97
Rear vault, 90, 91, 192, 217
Rear vault with half twist, 92, 150
Rear vault with quarter turn dismount, 223
Regular flyaway, 131, 132
Regular giant cross over to reverse giant swings, 134
Regular giant swing, 130
Regular grip, 119
Regular scissors, 108
Regular splits, 59
Reuther system beatboard, 95
Reverse flyaway, 132
Reverse giant swing, 130, 131
Reverse giant swing pirouette to regular giant, 134
Reverse grip, 119
Reverse half giant swing, 130
Reverse kip, 127, 128, 174, 177
Reverse pirouette, 202
Reverse scissors, 108
Reverse stockli, 113
Reverse stutz, 160
Riding seat, 214
Right feint, 106, 107
Right leg over bar, 225
Rings:
  area and equipment, 166, 167
  organization, 167

Rings: (Continued)
  program of instruction, 167
  routines, 180
  safety, 167
  teaching methods, 167
  values, 166
Roly Poly, 10
Romans, 1
Rope activities:
  competition, 238
  organization, 236
  program of instruction, 236
  rope climbing, 239
  rope jumping, 238
  rope skipping, 236
  teaching methods, 237
  values, 235
Rope climbing:
  competitive, 241
  cross leg, 241
  double leg seat, 241
  foot and leg lock, 241
  inverted hand, 241
  single leg seat, 241
  stirrup, 240
  use of two ropes, 242
Roundoff, 11, 12, 210
Roundoff–back handspring, 19
Roundoff–back handspring–back somersault, 19
Roundoff–back somersault, 19
Routines, 20, 60, 70, 86, 114, 139, 164, 180, 211, 234, 255, 256, 259, 260
Rudolph, 80, 81
Rudolph fliffis, 83
Run on beam, 201
Russian, 16, 112, 113

Sarasota Clinic, 3
Safety, 7, 64, 89, 117, 141, 167, 197
Scale:
  front, 47, 187, 197
  knee, 48, 204, 209
  needle, 47, 48, 185, 205
  side, 47
  swan, 204
Scissors from a straight arm support, 144
Scissors mount to stand, 199
Scissors with half turn, 96, 97
Seat balance, 225
Seat drop, 67
Seat full twist to seat, 70, 71
Seat rise, 126
Shoot over low bar from hang on high bar, 218
Shoot through, 188, 189
Shoot through to L seat, 56
Shoot to handstand, 177
Shoot to shoulder balance, 177
Shoulder balance, 148, 151, 173, 206, 207, 214, 215
Shoulder balance on feet, 39
Shoulder balance-side dismount, 148, 209
Shoulder roll, 9, 10

Side (ward):
  cross hand balance, 232
  horse:
    approach and take-off, 90
    area and equipment, 87, 88
    organization, 88
    program of instruction, 89
    safety, 89
    support work, 104
    routines, 114
    teaching methods, 88
    values, 87
    vaulting work, 90
  leg back flip pitch, 23
  roll, 9
  scale, 47
  seat, 208, 209, 214
  seat half turn to straddle seat, 145
  step, 201
  travel, 110, 111
Single:
  elbow lever, 34, 48
  knee circle backward, 121, 229
  knee circle forward, 121
  knee hang, 120
  knee swing up, 120, 121
  leg circle, 53, 106, 148
  leg circle to elbow lever, 55
  leg cut off–forward, 146, 169, 216
  leg cut on, 146, 215
  leg flank dismount, 217, 222
  leg half circle, 104, 105
  leg half circle travel, 105
  leg kip up, 169
  leg reverse circle, 106
  leg shoot on low bar to high bar grasp, 220
  leg swing up, 219
  rear dismount, 107
Singles balancing, 29
Sissone, 201
Sitting assisted back flip, 26, 27
Skin the cat, 120, 169, 232
Smidl, Henry, 3
Snap-up, 12
Soada bas, 184
Sole circle backward, 126, 127
Sole circle forward, 127
Spiess, Adolf, 2
Spiral, 184
Splits, 59, 185, 205
Spotting, 7, 14, 17, 29, 31, 74, 77, 89, 170, 191, 247
Springboard trampoline:
  cheerleading use, 248
  diving use, 248
  organization, 243
  program of instruction, 244
  trampoline mounting, 248
  tumbling use, 247
  two performers, 248
  values, 243

Springboard trampoline: (Continued)
  vaulting use, 249
Squat:
  hand balance, 29, 30
  head balance, 29, 30
  mount, 198, 199
  press to head balance, 50
  stand leap, 91
  stand–jump off dismount, 191
  stand mount, 219
  stand on low bar, swing up to front support on high bar, 226
  turn, 202
  vault, 91, 96, 97, 131, 157, 191, 224
Stag leap, 184, 202, 244
Steps on beam, 201
Step-tap-hops, 201
Stockli, 112
Stoop vault, 93, 96, 97, 157, 192
Straddle:
  cut and catch, 134
  dismount from kip, 131
  forward dismount, 150, 157
  hold, 205
  lean, 185
  leap, 52, 53
  leap over top bar to back hip circle on low bar to eagle grip on high bar, 233
  leg cut on, 151
  leg swing-up to a hang lying on low bar, 231
  mount, 199
  reverse, 203
  seat, 50, 142, 214, 229
  seat mount, 198
  seat travel, 145
  splits, 59
  stand–jump dismount, 92, 191
  touch, 208, 244, 245
  vault, 92, 96, 192
Straight arm support, 142, 213, 214
Straight arm support mount, 171, 198, 217
Straight arm walk, 144
Straight body bent arm press to handstand, 176
Straight body cross, 177
Straight fall, 52, 53
Straight leg roll, 55
Streilli, 162, 163
Strength balance moves, 50
Stutz, 158, 159
Stutz, full twisting, 164
Stutz, reverse, 160
Supine arch up, 186
Swan scale, 204
Swan support, 226
Swedish apparatus, 2
Swedish fall, 188, 189, 204
Swing and dismount, 123
Swinging dips, 143
Swinging dip travel, 143
Swing legs over low bar and drop to back hip circle, 233
Swing to a hand balance, 154

Swing to shoulder balance, 151
Swivel hips, 70
Szypula, George, 3

Takeoff-tramp, 243
Thief vault, 92, 93, 192
Thigh rest, 227
Thigh stand, 35
Three-quarter back somersault to front drop, 76
Tiger leaping, 254
Tiger press, 51
Tigna, 17
Tinsica, 15
Toe stand, 183
Toe kip, 150, 151
Tour en l'air, 185
Tour jeté, 184
Trampolet, 243
Trampoline:
    area and equipment, 62, 63
    organization, 63
    program of instruction, 65
    routines, 70, 86
    safety, 64
    teaching methods, 63
    values, 63
Triple rear dismount, 109
Triple rolls, 21
Tromlet, 111
Tuck bounce, 66, 67
Tuck jump, 202
Tug of war, 242
Tumbling:
    area and equipment, 5, 6
    doubles tumbling, 21
    organization, 6
    program of instruction, 8
    routines, 20
    safety, 7
    teaching methods, 6
    twisting tumbling, 20
    values, 5
Turns on beam, 202
Turntable, 71
Turnverein, 2
Twisting belt, 20, 79
Twisting handstand into forward roll, 55
Twisting tumbling, 20
Twisting trampoline, 78
Two high stand, 37, 38

Underbar somersault, 161
Underswing dismount, 119, 120, 223, 224
Underswing to crotch seat, 226
Uneven parallel bars:
    description, 212
    dismounts, 222
    mounts, 217
    stunts or combinations, 225
Upper arm balance, 148, 214, 215

Upper arm support, 142

Valdez, 57, 58, 188, 189, 208
Values, 4, 5, 28, 45, 63, 87, 116, 139, 166, 182, 191, 196, 212, 235, 243, 250
V seat, 48, 187, 188, 203

Walk on hands, 34
Welser, Lyle, 3
Western National Clinic, 3
Wettstone, Gene, 3
Wheelbarrow pitch to forward somersault, 25, 26
Wide arm forward roll, 54, 55
Wide arm hand balance, 49
Wolf Vault, 92, 199
Women's balance beam:
    area and equipment, 196, 197
    dismounts, 208
    movements on beam, 200
    mounts, 198
    organization, 197
    program of instruction, 197
    routines, 211
    safety, 197
    stunts, 203
    teaching methods, 197
    values, 196
Women's floor exercise:
    agility stunts, 188
    area and equipment, 182
    balance movements, 186
    ballet movements, 183
    description, 182
    flexibility, stunts, 185
    organization, 182
    program of instruction, 183
    values, 182
Women's parallel bars:
    area and equipment, 212
    dismounts, 222
    even parallel bars, 213
    organization, 213
    program of instruction, 213
    routines, 234
    stunts or combinations, 225
    uneven parallel bars, 217
    values, 212
Women's vaulting:
    competitive, 193–95
    equipment, 190
    organization, 191
    program of instruction, 191
    values, 191

Y.M.C.A., 3
Yogi hand balance, 49, 188
Younger, Max, 3

Zwarg, Leopold, 3